OUTSIDE MONEY IN SCHOOL BOARD ELECTIONS

OUTSIDE MONEY
IN SCHOOL BOARD ELECTIONS

The Nationalization of Education Politics

JEFFREY R. HENIG

REBECCA JACOBSEN

SARAH RECKHOW

HARVARD EDUCATION PRESS
Cambridge, Massachusetts

33

KH

Library of Congress Cataloging-in-Publication Data is on file.
Paperback ISBN 978-1-68253-282-9
Library Edition ISBN 978-1-168253-283-6

Published by Harvard Education Press,
an imprint of the Harvard Education Publishing Group

Harvard Education Press
8 Story Street
Cambridge, MA 02138

Cover Design: Ciano Design

The typefaces used in this book are ITC Legacy Serif and Rogliano.

10/3/19

CONTENTS

CHAPTER 1

·······················

The Puzzle of
Outside Money

SOMETHING PUZZLING is going on in America's school board elections. On the one hand, increased state and federal oversight of education policy has reduced the power and autonomy of local school boards. On the other hand, national reform donors and competing national interest groups are transforming dozens of local school board elections into major electoral battlegrounds, with millions of dollars in campaign funding and professional campaign consultants. These elements seem, at least on first glance, to be inconsistent. Are school boards increasingly antiquated and marginalized governing institutions in a system driven by encroaching state and federal oversight? Or are they recognized by national actors as strategic fronts in education policy debates and as essential venues for developing and translating policy into practice?

This puzzle reflects important changes in the landscape of American education politics. School boards are intensely local, often celebrated as "the crucible of democracy," but more recently portrayed as old-fashioned and dysfunctional, so much so that some school reform leaders have advocated for eliminating them altogether.[1] Traditionally, school board elections have been sleepy affairs where most candidates spend less than $1,000. In 2010, for example, less than 3 percent of candidates reported spending more than $25,000.[2]

Of the more than 13,500 school districts in the United States, the vast majority are independent governments, separate from cities and counties, and overseen by elected school boards. Most school board elections still fit the model of low-interest and low-spending local politics. But in a handful of recent electoral cycles, some school board contests have received the hot glare of national attention and efforts at outside influence. "The money keeps flowing into local school board races and education ballot initiatives from outsiders with deep pockets," wrote Valerie Strauss in the *Washington Post* in 2012.[3] The next year, a local radio station in Los Angeles reported that an "unprecedented $1 million donation" from Michael Bloomberg to influence Los Angeles school board elections "ups the ante in a school board race that is on its way to breaking fundraising records."[4] Four years later, unions squared off against education reformers supporting charter schools, combining to spend nearly $15 million and making the 2017 Los Angeles Board of Education race "the most expensive school board election in U.S. history."[5] An *Indianapolis Star* op-ed noted in 2015 that "big money donors" (such as Bloomberg and Sheryl Sandberg) have "put being on the school board out of the reach of ordinary Indy citizens."[6] The November 2017 San Diego County School Board election, "an obscure race that few even know exists," nonetheless attracted nonlocal donors like Michael Bloomberg, Alice Walton (of the Walton family, which founded Walmart), Reed Hastings (owner of Netflix), and Doris Fisher (Gap Inc.), and according to one account "is likely to run into the millions of dollars this season, while in the past, those costs were unlikely to pass a few thousand dollars."[7]

Outside money is not specific to education politics; it has become a widespread feature of Congressional elections and is beginning to show up more often in local elections. "The out-of-state money is crazy," declared US Secretary of Health and Human Services Tom Price, about a high-profile June 2017 special election to fill his vacated congressional seat in Georgia.[8] Even local races for district attorneys are targets for outside money; an organization funded by billionaire George Soros, for instance, has funneled more than $18 million into state and local races, including funds to help candidates for prosecutor support massive television advertising.[9] As an extreme case of localized politics, school board elections can provide insights into the power, universality, and outer limits of the outside money in local politics.

This book takes on the challenge of outlining and beginning to solve the puzzles of how and why some once-sleepy local school board contests have become flashpoints of national donor interest. We argue that the involvement of wealthy individuals and national organizations in local school board elections is a sign of a new stage in the evolution of the United States' multilevel system of setting and implementing education policy. We characterize this new stage as "the nationalization of local education politics." Nationalization is not to be confused with centralization within our federal system. Unlike centralization, which involves the shifting of power and authority up and out of local arenas, nationalization reflects a growing realization on the part of national political actors that local arenas continue to be important as sites for agenda setting and political engagement over educational issues. With nationalization, the formal boundaries of local districts operate less as walls demarcating the separation of the local from metropolitan, state, and national politics than as the meeting place where national and local actors form alliances around competing visions of what schools should be.

A key mechanism for the development of nationalization in education politics is the role of donors. Funding from out-of-state individual donors and organizations could enable a new pathway for elite influence in local school district governance, and crowd out or overshadow some local voices. Political scientists have started to closely examine the relationship between wealth and American politics in the context of growing socioeconomic inequality, often focusing on the behavior, attitudes, and political influence of the affluent.[10] In an era of growing wealth inequality in the United States, a small class of extremely wealthy individuals is well positioned to play an outsized role in funding political campaigns. Based on research on federal elections, we know that the role of very wealthy contributors is growing; for example, the percentage of campaign contributions from the top 0.01 percent of the voting age population grew from under 20 percent in the 1980s to 40 percent by the 2012 election cycle.[11]

Major donor interest in federal elections for the presidency and Congress is a widely reported aspect of American politics, and political parties and political action committees (PACs) invest heavily in raising donor funds and maintaining donor connections.[12] Yet the mobilization of a billionaire donor living in California to contribute to a school board candidate in Indianapolis is more puzzling. A donor in New York City might feel a direct stake in the election of a Congress member in Idaho because that member will be voting on legislation that affects the whole country, but the direct impacts of local school board decisions rarely travel beyond district borders. Local school board elections are not usually in the sights of major political party fundraising, and school board candidates are hardly household names, even in their own hometowns.

The connection becomes less puzzling when we consider the role of major donors in education policy more generally, including the role of living philanthropists, such as Bill and Melinda Gates, Eli and Edythe Broad, and more recently, Mark Zuckerberg and Priscilla Chan. These individuals have given millions (or in the case of the Gateses, billions) to fund education reform initiatives in local school districts. Philanthropic funding to influence educational policy, and public policy more generally, has been growing since the 1990s.[13] While not every philanthropist is also a major political donor, some donors do appear to coordinate their philanthropic and political contributing. Eli Broad is a prominent example of this; as David Callahan writes in his book on mega-philanthropy, *The Givers,* "Broad's political donations in California have worked in tandem with his philanthropy . . . Broad has pulled multiple levers of power to reshape education in LA—levers only available to the super-rich."[14] Furthermore, these donors often aspire to more than local change; they hope that local education reform efforts in places like Newark and New Orleans will become national models for other school districts to follow. Thus, major donors can be agents of nationalization through their ambition to support favored policies on a broader scale.

In this book, we examine both the mechanisms and consequences of nationalization. Our empirical evidence begins with individual donors—tracing the flow of money from outside donors, investigating the mobilization of money through organizations, and exploring the possible motivations of both individual and organizational donors. We zero in on the relatively small cluster of wealthy donors who give large donations in elections outside the states in which they live. These donors are generally aligned with a particular set of strategies to improve education—including charter schools, alternative modes to teacher preparation, and test-based accountability—and they have managed to capture the label "reformer," broadly implying that those who resist them and their agenda are simply protecting the *status quo*. They are new actors in a landscape that has often been portrayed as dominated by teacher unions, and as we will demonstrate, they and the organizations they work with often lock horns with teacher unions and others who see them as destabilizing, ineffective, or a basic threat to public education itself.

The high-profile elections where national forces collide often occur in districts with high rates of poverty and where the majority of students are nonwhite—indicating a wide demographic gulf between the wealthy outside donors and the students attending school in cities with big-money elections. But the local communities are not simply a backdrop: national reformers and teacher unions are competing for the attention and support of local donors, voters, and groups, making for a political brew that is more complicated and interesting than commonly understood.

Next, we examine the targets of outside money, including the candidates and their campaigns, and we situate these campaigns within the broader local political context. Candidates are not passive actors. Many are acutely aware of the changing landscape, offering insights to the myriad of ways they work with and/or respond to the arrival of outside funding. Finally, we consider the consequences of outside money for local education politics, including media coverage, voter turnout, and campaign strategy. We assess the possibility for positive consequences—that outside money could raise the quality of campaigns, improve the visibility of local elections and candidates, and increase voter turnout—as well as for negative consequences, such as growing negativity in campaigns or media coverage that focuses on donors and national issues at the expense of local-issue attention. Our findings are not uniformly positive or negative for outside money, but we do provide evidence that outside money has observable consequences for local education politics—consequences that can affect who runs for local office and the kinds of issues covered in a campaign. These findings show how a selective process of nationalization, facilitated by outside donor involvement, can alter the strategic opportunities of individuals and organizations at the local level. If outside donations are stones tossed into the pond of local electoral politics, our research is an attempt to describe the size and shape of the stones, the identities of the throwers, the locations where the stones land, the direction of the ripples on the pond's water, and the places where water sloshes onto the shore. There are thousands of local school district "ponds" in the United States, and we chose five—in these five, the tossed stones have recently become particularly large and numerous.

OUR CASES

To examine this new nationalization of local school board elections, we dive deeply into recent school-related elections in five cities: Bridgeport, Connecticut; Denver, Colorado; Indianapolis, Indiana; Los Angeles, California; and New Orleans, Louisiana. We selected these cities because each has had high-profile elections in at least one recent election cycle. As such, they are not representative of the thousands of school boards that continue to hold elections under the radar of national politics. But neither are they unique. Based on newspaper reports we identified forty-three localities with at least one school board election featuring outside money between 2009 and early November 2017 (see appendix A for a complete list). By examining our five cases intensely and with a variety of methods, we provide a window into the local contextual factors that attract national interests to a local election and the processes that are activated *when* the local arena comes to be regarded as having national significance. By examining multiple election cycles, we can observe variation in levels of outside money for candidates within the same urban area.

Five Urban Districts

A persistent challenge in studying urban politics has been finding the right balance between single case studies and cross-city research. Those who know individual cities well know that those cities have unique characteristics that evolved out of local culture, demography, economic strengths and weakness, influential leaders, and shared history.

But those steeped in knowledge about any one city might be less likely to spot patterns and tendencies that emerge when one looks across a range of cities as they tackle similar tasks. For various reasons, the field of urban politics "seems to have embraced complexity and richness in context at the expense of parsimony, a research strategy that has been instrumental in fostering a deep understanding of many key aspects of urban governance but that also has to some extent obstructed a systematic comparative analysis of urban governance."[15] We make an effort in this book to lean the other way—to use our cases to search out patterns and commonalities—but local context remains important and often particular, and when idiosyncrasies of place intervene, we try to make that apparent as well. In this section we offer an initial orientation to the cases, via short capsule summaries, and follow that with a discussion of how the cases compare to other large school districts and to one another.

Bridgeport, CT. Bridgeport school board elections were historically low-profile events that drew low turnouts and were rarely, if ever, featured in the national news. But events in 2011 and 2012 thrust the city onto the national stage. The result was a spurt of high-profile and big-dollar clashes featuring reformers who drew support from wealthy outside donors on one side, and the state teacher union and the Working Families Party, a progressive organization that draws on union support, on the other.

Interest in Bridgeport education politics peaked after the July 2011 state takeover of the Bridgeport district, in which the mayor, governor, state board of education, and a majority of the local board voted to have the state appoint a new school board to replace the locally elected one. This appointed board then hired as superintendent a nationally known education reformer, Paul Vallas, who had previously served in high-profile roles in Chicago, Philadelphia, and Louisiana. The state takeover was overridden by the Connecticut Supreme Court in February 2012, leading to a September 2012 special election to select a new elected board. Reformers responded by successfully pushing for a November 2012 referendum to end school board elections and place the mayor in charge. Wealthy donors from elsewhere in Connecticut, as well as out-of-state donors such as Michael Bloomberg, were drawn to the fracas by the perceived opportunity to cement an institutional change that would create a local regime more supportive of the reform initiatives they favored, such as teacher accountability and charter schools. Despite this support from the national reform community, the mayoral control referendum was defeated. In subsequent school board elections, outside money dropped precipitously. Thus, unlike our other cases where outside money can be found in multiple election cycles, Bridgeport's national attention was short lived. In addition to donations to school board elections during and immediately after the 2012 conflict, we also look at campaign contributions to groups for and against the referendum itself.

It should be noted that, unlike most school board elections, Bridgeport's are partisan. Even more unusual, school board candidates run on a party slate, and state law requires that at least one-third of the board's seats be held by the minority party. These aspects make Bridgeport's electoral structure somewhat unique and elevate the importance of political parties. The Bridgeport case provides a window into the resilient power of localism to generate a backlash against outside money.

Denver, CO. Although lacking the bitterness and polarization that has characterized urban school reform in a number of large cities, Denver has been on the national educational reform map for more than a decade. Its image as a hub of school reform began to come into focus after Michael Bennet—a rising star in the Democratic party who later would become a US Senator—became superintendent in July 2005. Even before Bennet, Denver had begun to attract attention for two reasons: for providing strong mayoral leadership without having adopted formal mayoral control of schools, and for instigating a teacher performance pay plan collaboratively designed between the district and the teacher union. As a further signal that Denver was a district known for urban school reform, the group Stand for Children, a national organization focused on school reform, opened a Colorado office in Denver in April 2009. Denver is also home to the Colorado chapter of the group Democrats for Education Reform.

With reformers holding a narrow edge on the elected school board, Denver became the focus of out-of-state campaign contributions in

2011 and 2013. An early sign of the growing contentiousness was a push, launched in January 2011, to recall Nathaniel Easley, who had been elected to the school board in 2009 with teacher union support but subsequently voted with reformers on a controversial strategy to aggressively intervene in failing schools. Reformers, supported by the governor and others, successfully resisted that recall effort. What followed in November 2011 was an election the *Nation* labeled "America's wildest school board race." Reporter John Nichols observed the involvement of national donors and organizations in Denver and posed the question: "[W]hat happens when all the pathologies of national politics—over-the-top spending by wealthy elites and corporate interests, partisan consultants jetting in to shape big-lie messaging, media outlets that cover spin rather than substance—are visited on a local school board contest?"[16] National money was an issue in Denver again in 2013; Michael Bloomberg was the largest single individual donor in an election in which the reform candidates solidified their hold on the school board. The Denver case illuminates the increased coordination of national donors, national reform organizations, local elites, and local reform organizations. While such coordination was high, it is also notable that it was not a guaranteed recipe for victory; reform candidates in Denver were not universally successful at winning their respective races.

Indianapolis, IN. Like Bridgeport, Indianapolis has been less visible on the national stage, yet it, too, was recently the site of significant outside funding for school board elections. Indianapolis differs from our other case study cities in that Republicans have governed it during the time period we examine; Mayor Greg Ballard (2008–2016) was a Republican, and both chambers of the state legislature were Republican controlled.

Indianapolis Public Schools (IPS) has long focused on providing educational alternatives for students, including magnet schools and charter schools. Some of these alternative schools performed well on Indiana state assessments, but many traditional public schools struggled. In 2011, a report from The Mind Trust, a local nonprofit based in Indianapolis focused on education issues, called for changes to district leadership and policies. The report seems to have prompted widespread interest in the 2012 school board election, including interest from large national donors.

Three new members were elected to the IPS board in that election, all of whom received contributions from Michael Bloomberg, and all of whom generally supported the vision of national school reformers, such as increasing the number of charter schools and supporting school choice. With the support of the recently appointed superintendent, Lewis Ferebee, the board enacted changes to IPS, including radically restructuring both leadership and curriculum at low performing schools, which were labeled priority schools. In 2014, IPS again held school board elections that attracted national donors such as Reid Hoffman, Michelle Yee, and Sheryl Sandberg.[17] The election marked the highest-spending campaign in IPS school board history. This level of spending has not been without local controversy; the role of Stand for Children was a central focus of a live radio interview with school board candidates. All three incumbents in 2014, each backed by the Indianapolis Education Association, lost their re-election bid. Three new members, all endorsed by Stand for Children, were elected to the board, continuing a pattern of electing reform-minded candidates.

Los Angeles, CA. California is often thought of as a national bellwether, a leading indicator of cultural, demographic, and political changes that subsequently appear elsewhere. Los Angeles, with more than one thousand schools and a budget of more than $7.5 billion, is the second largest school district in the nation. Governing the massive and sprawling Los Angeles Unified School District (LAUSD) can be a full-time job, and, as of 2017, school board members are paid an annual salary of $125,000 for their service. This salary makes the LA Board of Education distinctive as compared to the vast majority of school boards around the country; Hess and Meeks, in their national survey of school board members, found that only about 7.5 percent made more than $10,000 per year and a little over 62 percent were paid no salary at all.[18]

Compared to the other cities, Los Angeles has a longer history of big spending in local school board elections. In the late 1990s, Mayor Richard Riordan helped raise millions for school board candidates. More recently, Mayor Antonio Villaraigosa followed in Riordan's footsteps by stepping into school board electoral politics by mobilizing donor support for a PAC that backed his preferred candidates. In the 2007 election, Villaraigosa helped raise $3 million for the PAC, and mayoral-backed candidates won a majority on the school board.

Since then, PACs supporting competing slates of reform- and union-backed candidates have been a common feature in Los Angeles school politics, with candidates highlighting their differences on charter school expansion and union contract negotiations. Union involvement in LA school board elections is not the province of the teacher unions alone; more than seventy-five unions made campaign donations in the elections we cover, and intriguingly, other unions do not consistently support the same candidates as do unions representing teachers; sometimes they even compete head to head.

By 2017, Los Angeles gained notoriety for holding the most expensive school board election ever recorded in the United States, involving a bitter campaign between a union-backed incumbent, Steve Zimmer, and his reformer-backed challenger, Nick Melvoin. In previous elections, individual candidates with national reform backing had not always won, but the sustained efforts by reformers in Los Angeles contributed to the election of a reform-oriented majority in the 2017 election.

New Orleans, LA. The New Orleans education system has attracted national attention ever since the radical restructuring that occurred after Hurricane Katrina devastated the city in 2005. The complete disruption of the existing school system, coupled with decades of poor performance, created an opportunity for education reformers to build a new governance structure from the ground up. Starting in November 2005, the majority of New Orleans schools were placed in state control under the auspices of the Recovery School District (RSD), with only a handful of schools remaining under the control of the locally elected Orleans Parish School Board. The RSD began a process that led to the conversion of schools into charter schools operated by charter management organizations. Today, the vast majority of New Orleans public schools are charters, with only a few schools left that are still direct-run, making it distinct from other school districts.

In 2012, while most of the schools remained under state control, the local Orleans Parish School Board election was surprisingly high profile. The District 3 election garnered the most attention from major donors, while races for the other six seats remained relatively invisible. Sarah Newell Usdin, a District 3 candidate who was founder and former head of New Schools for New Orleans, a nonprofit founded shortly after Katrina to accelerate reform, received campaign contributions in excess of $110,000, nearly four times that of the incumbent. The 2012 race in District 3 showed that national influence can be injected into the race for one school board seat while other races in the same election unfold in a more traditional manner with far less spending and visibility. This is just one example of many we will present that underscore the strategic nature of national engagement.

By 2016, the Louisiana state legislature adopted legislation returning local control of the New Orleans schools that had been governed by the Recovery School District. The legislation specified that the Orleans Parish School Board would resume control of these schools by July 1, 2018, though their status as charter schools meant that the Orleans Parish school district will have much less control over schools than did the district that preceded Hurricane Katrina.

How Unusual Are Our Cases?

Any study that focuses on a small number of cases, as ours does, raises questions of generalizability. Table 1.1 presents descriptive information on an array of indicators of student characteristics, population characteristics, charter school penetration, school spending, and the racial and ethnic composition of the school board.[19] On some variables, our five cases uniformly differ from other large cities. All of our cases have lower white enrollment, larger proportions of students eligible for free lunch, higher poverty among young people, lower professional occupations among the general population, greater income inequality, more students in charters, and fewer white school board members. On other variables, our cases individually differ from other large cities, but with some being above and others being below the average. The Los Angeles Unified School District is, of course, dramatically larger than any of our other cases or of large districts generally; in the United States only New York City has a larger school enrollment. New Orleans, Indianapolis, and Bridgeport have higher-than-average proportions of black students. LA Unified and Denver have a

TABLE L1

Our cases as compared to other large school districts

	BRIDGEPORT	DENVER	INDIANAPOLIS	LOS ANGELES	NEW ORLEANS	OUR FIVE CASES	OTHER LARGE URBAN DISTRICTS*
Student population							
Total enrollment grades 3–8 (including charters): 2011–12	10,132	35,212	19,143	284,128	15,923	72,908	23,666
Percent white	7.9	21.4	24.5	9	6.3	13.8	38.8
Percent black	40.4	13.9	57.1	9.7	88.4	41.9	20.7
Percent Hispanic (white or black)	48.8	60.5	17.8	74.9	3.3	41.1	30.8
Percent Asian	2.7	3.5	0.3	6	17.8	2.9	6.2
Percent free lunch	95.2	66.9	67.4	61.3	80.9	74.4	46.4
Percent ELL	11.7	31.4	11.4	23.1	2.1	15.9	13.6
Percent special education	13.4	11^	18.9	12.4	9.6	13.6	11.7
General population							
Percent 5–17 year olds poor	27.6	25.2	39.1	26.1	36.4	30.9	17.2
Percent BA or higher	17.1	42.3	22	29.1	33.3	28.7	31.1
Percent profession occupation	5.5	15.1	5.8	11.2	12.1	10	18.9
Income ratio 90/10	13	11.8	13.3	10.5	15.6	12.9	9.4

(continued)

TABLE 1.1 (*continued*)

Our cases as compared to other large school districts

	BRIDGEPORT	DENVER	INDIANAPOLIS	LOS ANGELES	NEW ORLEANS	OUR FIVE CASES	OTHER LARGE URBAN DISTRICTS*
Education reform							
Percent 3–8th graders in charters	**9**	**14.9**	**21.6**	**14**	**94.4**	**14.9****	5.5
Percent white in charters	*1.6*	**10.5**	**21.2**	**25.4**	**98.8**	14.7**	6.1
Finance							
Per pupil expenditure	**$17,344.00**	**$14,064.00**	**$15,524.00**	**$13,979.00**	$10,594.00	$14,301.00	$11,018.00
Schoolboard racial and ethnic representativeness***							
School Board % Wht 2012 N=313 5/308	*55.6*	*42.9*	*42.9*	*57.1*	*57.1*	*51.1*	73.3
School Board % Black 2012 N=313 5/308	*44.4*	*28.6*	*57.1*	*14.3*	*42.9*	*37.5*	17.3
School Board % Hisp 2012 N=313 5/308	*0*	**28.6**	*0*	**28.6**	*0*	*11.4*	9.2

Italics–significantly lower than other large cities

Bold–significantly higher than other large cities

^ Colorado data on special education was missing in SEDA data; supplemented by other source

* Grade 3–8 enrollment >10,000

** Dropping New Orleans where nearly all students are in charters

***National School District Survey (K. Meier)

Source: Stanford Education Data Archive (http://purl.stanford.edu/db586ns4974)

below-average black student population but above-average percentages of Latinx students.

It is important to keep in mind that we are not suggesting that the five districts we are looking at are representative of the broad universe of districts with elected school boards. We do not claim that all, most, or even a high proportion of local board elections across the country are subject to outside money; indeed, we are confident in any given election cycle that most school board elections continue to fit the model of low-profile, low-turnout elections focused largely on individual candidates and parochial concerns. In the case of school board elections, nationalization occurs through a process of selective and strategic targeting by outside donors, with only some elections likely to be targeted at any point in time. To the extent that we will be drawing generalizations, we aim to draw lessons about this process of targeting and its consequences rather than about school boards in general. This approach should not suggest that we are disinterested in how our cases stack up against others. If our five cases were dramatically distinct from the average local school board election, this difference would raise questions about whether nationalization is so severely limited in its likely scope that it has any relevance at all to districts where localism still prevails. However, that is not the case; as we will show, these five cases are similar to many other districts and there are reasons to expect that nationalization will become a factor in additional places that so far have been sheltered from its reach. We are also interested in how our cases stack up against the typical school board election for more substantive reasons. Identifying clear markers that distinguish districts with outside involvement from those that remain parochial can help us get a handle on the motivations and calculations behind the targeting phenomenon.

We see the phenomenon of outside interest in school board elections as one important manifestation of a more general nationalization of American education politics. While a number of important books have highlighted a growing centralization of power, in which states and the federal government have become more assertive in holding local districts accountable and even telling them what to do, our book highlights something else entirely. While centralization implies that local arenas for democratic decision-making are being muscled aside, we show that national actors are realizing that these arenas are still quite important. Rather than being ignored, marginalized, and bypassed, local school politics is being penetrated by national politics in ways that rattle and reassemble traditional lines of coalition and cleavage, with important implications—some good, some bad—for both democracy and educational improvement.

DATA AND METHODS

Our investigation of nationalization—and its implications—required the collection and analysis of several types of data across our five cases. To identify and analyze school board election donors, as well as the recipients of donations, we assembled a unique dataset of campaign contributions covering multiple election cycles for each city (spanning the years 2008 to 2014). Our dataset comprises more than eighteen thousand campaign contributions from individual donors and organizations, including unions and major reform groups. Unlike campaign donations in national and state elections, donations for school board elections have no central repository, and the laws, regulations, and practices regarding reporting those donations vary considerably from place to place.[20] Table 1.2 summarizes the characteristics of all school board elections between 2008 and 2014 in each of our five sites. We include Bridgeport's September 2012 special election to replace the short-lived state-appointed board, as well as the November 2012 referendum that rejected a proposed shift to mayoral control. In Denver, we include a 2011 recall effort that failed.

For each site, we gathered data from the relevant state or local entity that collects campaign disclosures from candidates and organizations.[21] Campaign finance regulations and requirements for contribution disclosures vary from site to site. These varied regulations likely guide contributions toward divergent recipients. For example, Los Angeles has a $1,000 limit on contributions to candidates, while independent expenditure committees can raise unlimited funds. In Denver, PACs face contribution limits, but candidates do not.

We ended up with a database comprising 18,809 separate donations across the multiple cities and elections. We gathered two types of donations for each site. We collected primary donations—donations that do not go through an intermediary to travel to a recipient, including donations made directly to a committee for a candidate, ballot question, referendum, or recall. In addition, we collected secondary donations—donations that pass through an intermediary such as a PAC. Secondary donations include donations to political organizations that, in turn, make primary donations to candidate committees, ballot questions, recalls, or referendums. We included secondary donations only to political organizations that are local and education-focused, including various PACs and teacher unions. This approach allowed us to focus on secondary donations to organizations that are primarily involved in these local school board races, rather than groups that could be mobilizing for other elections as well. However, some of the donors to local education groups are state- and national-level organizations, including state and national unions.

Compiling this dataset took a fair amount of detective work. Both within and across the cities, we had to engage in multiple strategies to make sure we could link donations made by the same individual or organization at different times, even when variants existed in name entry. If an individual at a given address used a nickname or initial for first name in some cases but not in other cases, all entries for that individual were changed to the full first name. If an individual at a given address had more than one spelling for a name, we conducted a search using the individual's place of work or whitepages.com to determine the correct spelling of the name. Any obvious address discrepancies were changed, such as a misaligned city or state or a spelling error in a city or state abbreviation. All street addresses were written out so that *St* is *Street*, *Rd* is *Road*, and so on.

Discrepancies in names of political organizations (i.e., abbreviations in some cases but not others) were corrected by looking up the organization's statement of organization on the appropriate city website. Finally, in many instances, contributions had identical donor names (e.g., Joe Smith) but different donor addresses (e.g., Beverly Hills, California, and New Orleans, Louisiana). To determine whether Joe Smith from Beverly Hills was the same individual as Joe Smith from New Orleans, we first looked at occupations and employers. If this information was unavailable, we did an extensive Google search, which often involved looking at LinkedIn profiles or company

TABLE 1.2
Election sites and characteristics

	BRIDGEPORT	DENVER
School board name	Bridgeport Board of Education	Denver Board of Education
Frequency of elections	Every 2 years	Every 2 years
Timing of general elections (vs. national)	On-cycle	On-cycle
Available data	2009 General	2009 General
	2012 Special	2011 General
	2012 Referendum	2013 General
	2013 General	
Number of board members	9	7
Member terms	4 years	4 years
Partisan	Yes	No
District/at-large	At large	5 by district; 2 at large

(*continued*)

biographies. In the few cases where a Google search was not helpful, we used the following decision rules: (1) if contributions had identical donor names and donor addresses in the same metropolitan area or state, we assumed the contributions were made by one donor; and (2) if contributions had identical donor names but donor addresses in different states, we assumed the contributions were made by two different donors.

Just over three-quarters of the donations in our dataset were from individual donors; the rest were from organizations of various types. Although many more donations are made by individuals, the donations from organizations are much larger (averaging $4,055 compared to $675 for individuals), and in total account for almost twice as much in total funds as are provided by individuals. In chapter 3 we look closely at the individual donors, and in chapter 4 we look at organizations, with special attention to unions and reformers.

In addition to our data and analysis on the extent and patterns of campaign contributions, we gathered other information on large outside donors, compiled biographical information on more than one hundred candidates, interviewed twenty-six candidates, interviewed

TABLE 1.2 (*continued*)
Election sites and characteristics

INDIANAPOLIS	LOS ANGELES	NEW ORLEANS
Indianapolis Public School Board of Education	LAUSD Board of Education	Orleans Parish School Board
Every 2 years	Every 2 years	Every 4 years
On-cycle	Off-cycle	On-cycle
2010 General	2009 General	2008 General
2012 General	2011 General	2012 General
2014 General	2013 General	
7	7	7
4 years	4 years	4 years
No	No	Yes
5 by district; 2 at large	District	District

six local and national expert informants with special knowledge or ties to school board elections in our five cities, and performed a content analysis on 225 media reports. Candidate information was located through extensive internet searches and searches of public records databases. The sample we interviewed was representative of all five cities and reflected all three types of candidates—union-affiliated, reform-affiliated, and unaffiliated. Our expert informants, many of whom had been interviewed previously for other research projects, were chosen less systematically. They held specialized knowledge we deemed important to understanding the phenomenon of outside money in local school board elections, with diverse ties representing both union and reform groups. Some informants had specific local knowledge about one of our case cities, providing us with important contextual background information that helped us round out our understanding of relevant city-specific features that shaped how particular school board elections unfolded.

News articles about every school board election in our five cities from 2008 to 2014 were located using a defined set of search terms in Google, Google News, and LexisNexis. We included all forms of print media, including major newspapers, secondary newspapers, and personal and professional blogs (e.g., *Chalkbeat*). We coded and analyzed these data sources to examine whether and how outside money made a difference in campaign strategy, candidate visibility, voter turnout, and campaign issue coverage. We provide more information on these various sources of data and the way we analyze them, both in the book itself and in a more detailed methodological appendix that is available upon request.

CHAPTER OVERVIEW

Chapter 2 provides a historical overview of how local school governance has been viewed and treated over the years. We suggest three phases in the nation's relationship to localism in education decision-making; in our view, the phenomenon of outside money in school board elections represents the front edge of a new fourth phase. The first phase, in which localism was the dominant value and local decision-making was the dominant mode, was the longest, lasting from the beginning to the middle of the twentieth century. The second phase was marked by growing discontent with localism. Distinct constituencies representing different intellectual orientations and political interests took aim at different failures of school boards, some emphasizing amateurism, some bureaucratic rigidity, some indifference to the needs of growing proportions of students from racial and ethnic minorities. These waves of discontent helped set the stage for the third phase, which was marked by growing centralization within the federal system. As states and then the national government became more assertive, it appeared to some that local arenas were becoming less robust, a trend that some celebrated and others decried. But reports of the death of localism have proven to be premature. The injection of outside money into local school board elections reflects that local arenas continue to be important as sites for agenda setting and political engagement over national issues. As we explain in this chapter, we appear to be entering a fourth phase—the nationalization of education politics—in which outside actors selectively engage in local political skirmishes in pursuit of advantage in a battle being waged nationally. They do so not by an all-out assault to impose their interests on resistant locals, but by connecting with like-minded coalitional partners within the local districts to tip the balance in their favor.

Chapter 3 looks at the more than fourteen thousand donations made by individuals in our five case cities, with special attention to outside board donors, those who do not live in the district in which the school election is taking place. Some outside donors live within the metropolitan area, some live within the state, and others live in different states entirely. Although those who live outside the state make up less than 8.5 percent of the donations, they account for more than 22 percent of all dollars given by individuals. This chapter identifies the largest outside donors, describes what kinds of candidates they support, and begins to probe the relationships that connect donors to each other. Our analysis highlights the outsized role played by large national donors who contribute to multiple out-of-state school board elections. These thirty individuals, who are also highly involved contributors to federal elections and board members of many prominent education organizations, we call "strategic national donors." As a group, these donors tend to support the same candidates and organizations, making these few out-of-state individuals unusually influential in the financing of local school board elections.

While most donations come from individuals, organizational donors also are important; our data includes more than 4,500 donations by organizations, and these are the focus of chapter 4. Organizations serve as conduits for giving but also as guides to help individual donors decide whom to support, and as vehicles for recruiting candidates, mobilizing voters, and framing issues and themes. Much of the standard literature on this topic falls into one of two competing camps. One camp portrays a landscape dominated by powerful teacher unions that use their muscle to block reform ideas. The other argues that local districts are increasingly penetrated and controlled by national reform organizations promoting an agenda of market-oriented reforms including charter schools, contracts with private providers, and test-based accountability. Our analysis paints a different picture, one in which both teacher unions and reformers seek to gain tactical advantage, with neither reliably outmuscling the other, and in which other types of organizations, such as business organizations or nonteacher unions, sometimes emerge as important local allies in the national battles.

In chapter 5 we turn our attention to the candidates: those on the receiving end of outside money, and those who, either by choice or by necessity, rely on local funding only. We present data on the candidates' characteristics and backgrounds, their fundraising strategies and experiences, and their positions on contentious policies. Critics of outside money—whether they focus their attack on national reformers or on union leaders—tend to portray external funding as a corrupting force that selectively recruits sharply disparate candidates pledged to sharply disparate issue positions. While we do find outside-funded candidates who fit that description—either recently arrived reformers recruited from charter school networks and committed to choice, test-based accountability, and tenure reform; or former or current teachers, backed by unions, and committed to resisting the positions supported by reformers—we again find that the realities on the ground are less sharply etched than the typical script suggests. Reform-backed candidates are more likely to be drawn from the charter school sector, but they and union-backed candidates often look like one another in other ways, both demographically and in prior educational experience. Candidates with outside funding, especially those backed by reformers, are able to run more professional campaigns, but all emphasize that their funding primarily comes from local sources and are adamant that donors played no role in the development of their platforms. And while reform- and union-backed candidates differ in their policy positions—as would be expected—those differences are more nuanced than the positions typically expressed in the highly polarized national debates.

Chapter 6 asks the question, "What difference does it make?" Does outside money change the nature of local school elections, and if so, does it do so for better or for worse? Drawing on analyses of local candidate interviews, media coverage, campaign documents, and voting data, we look at four ways that local school board elections can be altered when outside forces intrude upon the local arena: (1) campaign sophistication and local representatives; (2) public attention and voter turnout; (3) displacement of local agenda items and local voices; and

(4) polarization and negative campaigning. As we demonstrate, attention does not always turn to the most well-funded candidates, and outside funding does not always lead overall campaign coverage to become overly negative. In some cases, though, outside influence has shifted the nature of school board elections in important ways. Candidates of all types tend to focus on the same set of nationalized issues, sometimes at the expense of what may be significant local issues. Further, attention in the election often becomes fixated on the money itself rather than on more substantive policy issues. We suggest that the influence of outside donations does not follow a guaranteed path, but rather interacts with local context in ways that can either fuel or dampen the effect of national forces.

Finally, in chapter 7, we take stock of our findings, what they suggest about the evolving nature of education politics, and how our results connect to other trends in national politics. We consider, but ultimately reject, the possibility that the nationalization of local school politics is a product of the moment rather than a fundamental reorientation. While there may be ebbs and flows, with punches and counterpunches still to come, we think the arc is more likely to be toward nationalization's continuation rather than its evanescence. That's because nationalization, as we see it, is not just a discrete reform idea, but a phenomenon with roots in changes in the institutions of politics and governance, as well as in culture, economics, residential and corporate mobility, and technology. The book concludes by discussing what this might mean for education policy and politics in the years to come.

CHAPTER 2

....

Localism
and Education
Decision-Making

OBSERVERS FOR YEARS have bemoaned the disconnect between Americans' professed love of locally controlled public schools and the reality of school board elections as typically low-interest, low-turnout affairs. In this chapter we chronicle the rise and fall of this love affair and begin to highlight the ways in which our attachment to local control is developing into a new and different relationship between local loyalties and voice, on the one hand, and the imperatives of national politics and governance on the other.

At any one time, there are conflicting views, patterned by variation in local realities and the fact that different groups can have radically different experiences even in the same time and place. During periods in which many were championing the triumphs of the US public education system, for example, others felt and were acutely aware of its shortcomings. While we keep this complexity in mind, it can still be useful to mark off four broad phases in the status of localism as a cultural and political answer to the question of where the goals and practices of public education should be determined and judged. Briefly, these phases can be characterized as follows:

- *Localism as a pillar.* For most of American history well into the twentieth century, the dominant perception and practice placed responsibility for shaping public education in the hands of local communities, where values were thought to be more homogenous and knowledge of needs and opportunities more accurate.
- *Localism as a problem.* Around the middle of the twentieth century, the tide of public opinion began to turn; various groups, for different reasons and in different ways, increasingly regarded local districts as flawed. Race and racial politics played important parts in this, as did the growth of urban education bureaucracies and more assertive teacher unions.
- *Localism left behind.* During the 1980s and 1990s, separate streams of dissatisfaction helped propel an era of centralization in which first states and then the national government became more aggressively involved in setting standards for local districts, monitoring their performance, and generally expressing interest and concern about outcomes and practices previously delegated to local communities. The drift toward centralization accelerated with the 2002 enactment of No Child Left Behind, as the national government and states moved from setting standards to enforcing accountability, and in the process became increasingly involved in setting guidelines for what happens inside schools and districts. In the minds of many, the real action of education reform was shifting up the ladder of federalism, with local jurisdictions relegated to more marginal decisions and the task of implementing policies they inherited from others.
- *Nationalization of local education politics.* Despite the relative centralization represented by the standards movement and No Child Left Behind legislation, local arenas remained an important venue for mobilizing the nation's energy and capacity for education politics and for shepherding policies from ideas to implementation. While local electoral participation remains low and public interest in local politics continues to decline, we argue that the political rationale for organized interests and donors to engage in local school board elections has grown. The result is a new phase during which local jurisdictions are neither ignored nor authoritatively dictated to, but rather emerge as important strategic

fronts in national contests over alternative visions of schooling. We do not mean that national actors and their interests will wash over ever-increasing numbers of local districts; the phenomenon we describe is deliberately selective, concentrating attention on a relatively small number of districts during any election cycle. While some major districts may find themselves regularly on the national radar screen, others may find themselves rotating in and out of the attention of national donors and interest groups, and the vast majority are likely to go on about their business with little outside notice at all. What makes nationally inflected local school elections important is not their number, but the fact that they have deliberately been targeted for influence precisely because events and circumstances make them important battlegrounds with the potential to shift momentum and power among competing visions of what American education should become.

The remainder of this chapter first fleshes out these four phases and the political forces behind them and then provides an overview of the research design and data that provide the grist for the chapters to come.

LOCALISM AS A PILLAR IN AMERICAN EDUCATION

Localism in general has long been a touchstone for American democracy. The notion that decisions made locally are better decisions draws from several streams of thought. These arguments in favor of localism are not specific to education. Indeed, they are part of an intellectual and cultural tradition of political decentralization that Alexis de Tocqueville, in the mid-1800s, identified as key to the nation's vitality and which helps to account for the fact that the United States continues to have one of the most decentralized systems of governance in the developed world.[1]

One argument emphasizes that the spatial clustering of populations into culturally homogenous groups means that decisions made locally will be more likely to *adhere to citizens' values*. A strong tradition in political science research focuses on ways that contextual factors shape political identity and preferences, resulting in shared clusters of political attitudes at the state, local, or even neighborhood level.[2] Local communities are a social incubator in which values, ideas, and beliefs are promulgated and reinforced. Local institutions like schools and places of worship play a role in this, as does proximity and face-to-face communication.[3] More recent research by Katherine Cramer on Wisconsin shows the ways in which rural identity formation shapes attitudes about the role of government and fosters divisions between urban and rural political identities.[4] Time and again, political science research has demonstrated that place-based context shapes political views. Thus, to the extent that localities represent clusters of shared values, localized democracy is more likely to be consensual and less likely to impose upon and constrain those with differing priorities.[5]

A second rationale for localism is the idea that, because the opportunities and constraints that governments face can differ from place to place, locally made policies are more likely to *respond to local circumstances*. "Historically," Asen et al. observe, decisions about curriculum, instruction, personnel, and finance "have been regarded as local matters, since each community presumably knows best how to educate its children."[6] Communities may differ, for example, in the nature of employment opportunities and the skills and knowledge they demand, and some would argue that curriculum and school policies should take this into account. Localities differ in other ways that may matter as well. School choice options like charter schools and vouchers that are viable in dense urban areas may be infeasible in rural areas where there are many fewer schools to choose from and they are much farther apart. By the same token, rural areas might be much more interested in online educational options as a way to bring a richer and higher quality array of instructional options to their students.

A third is the idea that, because local leaders are more known and accessible to voters, local decisions are more likely to *respond to democratically expressed desires*. Especially in smaller districts, but also in some large districts where school board members are elected by ward, it is common for citizens to run into their representatives in the course of their everyday lives. Both subjectively and objectively, that accessibility can create a bond and a channel of communication that is more intimate and effective than between voters and state or national leaders. And while the latter can and do make efforts to show themselves as well, formal political contacting, lobbying, and protests typically often require travel to state capitals or Washington, DC, which is too expensive and time consuming for most to pursue.

A fourth and final reason that some consider localized decision-making preferable is that locally made decisions are more likely to *engage citizens as coproducers* and thereby lead to better outcomes.[7] Policy outcomes can depend heavily on whether citizens and street-level bureaucrats resist, ignore, or actively embrace those policies. Whether students learn depends in part on what teachers do in the classroom, but it also depends on whether parents ensure that children come to school eager and prepared to learn, monitor students' attendance and assignments, and provide various enrichment opportunities. If, as seems likely, people are more likely to buy into and support policies and programs that they helped to shape, locally made decisions may lead to better outcomes.

Americans' general allegiance to localism as an ideal has been especially strong when it comes to public schooling in the United States. Public education historically has been more decentralized than decision-making about most other areas of social policy, and our arrangements for education governance are among the most decentralized of the developed nations of the world.[8] When Americans were asked which level of government should "take the lead" on delivering thirteen different kinds of services, for example, "providing public education" was the fourth most commonly assigned to the local level, following only urban development, crime reduction, and economic development.[9]

Americans consistently grade their local schools higher than those in the nation; in 2016 twice as many (48 percent) gave their local schools a grade of A or B than did for national schools (24 percent). Asked, in 2014, which level of government "should have the greatest influence," 56.7 percent said local versus 28.3 percent choosing state and 15.1 percent federal.[10] The notion that public schools as currently governed are "an expression of local democracy and a pillar of the local community" is so consistent, reflexive, and powerful that political scientist Terry Moe has labeled it the "public school ideology."[11]

Even in the early twentieth century, though, not everyone was on the localism bandwagon. While decentralization struck many as the most natural and democratic way to oversee public schools, some began to see localism as a shorthand for parochialism, amateurishness, and susceptibility to capture by interests with agendas of their own. "In 1913, on the eve of World War I, fully one-half of the nation's school children attended one of its 212,000 single-teacher schools."[12] This statistic changed dramatically in the wake of a national movement to consolidate many tiny school districts into a much smaller number of large ones. In 1939–40, there were over one hundred seventeen thousand school districts in the country; by 1973–4 there were fewer than seventeen thousand.[13] This meant that while localism remained the dominant norm until around the middle of the century, the local units of governance to which we delegated authority were themselves becoming larger.

LOCALISM AS A PROBLEM

By the middle of the twentieth century, America's schools had been on an upward march by many indicators and at least some observers were pointing specifically to urban districts as models of the kinds of comprehensive education to which the nation should aspire. More children were attending school; some gaps between the races were narrowing; classes were getting smaller; graduation rates were increasing; and the comprehensive American high school was being touted as an international model. But this was not destined to last for long.

School enrollment of five- to nineteen-year-olds had risen from 50.5 percent in 1900 to 86.2 percent in 1954, the year of the momentous *Brown v. Board of Education* decision. The gap between whites and blacks in terms of enrollment—not necessarily in access to quality education—had narrowed dramatically. In 1900 only 30.1 percent of black five- to seventeen-year-olds were in school, compared to 53.6 percent of whites, a gap of 23.5 percentage points; by 1954 the gap had narrowed to 80.8 percent for blacks versus 87 percent for whites, a gap of 6.2 points. Despite rising enrollments, during the mid-1920s, "a long-term pattern developed of a slowly falling pupil/teacher ratio. This slow movement picked up in the 1960s, when the pupil/teacher ratio fell from 27 to 23."[14] At the turn of the twentieth century, the number of high school graduates in the nation totaled less than 7 percent of the population of seventeen-year-olds. The number and proportion of graduates rose steadily, and by 1940, the ratio of graduates to seventeen-year-olds rose above 50 percent for the first time. After a dip during World War II, the graduation ratio resumed its upward trend, reaching about 60 percent in 1953-4 and just under 70 percent in 1959-60.[15] By the 1950s, James Conant, an authoritative voice who had served as the president of Harvard University, was speaking and writing consistently about comprehensive high schools, of the type pioneered in urban districts that had the size and money to support them, as models for the kinds of rich curricula and diverse student bodies to which the nation and the world should aspire.

During the second half of the twentieth century, however, the shimmering ideal of locally led public education increasingly diverged from a less flattering reality. The combination of demographic change, the civil rights movement, and efforts to desegregate schools spawned new images of localism that were tightly entwined with the nation's complicated and problematic relationship with race. For different reasons, some on the political left and some on the political right began to see local control of schools as a problem. In the process, localism came to be linked with two of the more divisive issues of national partisan and ideological debate: race and governance.

Race: Locals as parochial and racist. According to Michael Kirst, it was "during the 1950s that confidence in local school boards and administrators began to weaken."[16] One factor was the Soviet Union's 1959 launch of the *Sputnik* satellite, which prompted fears that the United States was losing its educational edge, especially in the sciences. This was the first major dent in the public's view that America's schools were indisputably the best in the world, and this meme that we were slipping down the ladder of international competition would reemerge with a vengeance with the publication of *A Nation at Risk* in 1983. More visceral and at least as consequential, however, was the growing prominence of racial inequity and defense of segregation as a defining feature of "local control" of education.

The Supreme Court's decision in *Brown v. Board of Education* started a slow-moving train of court-ordered desegregation that accelerated in the 1960s, when President Lyndon B. Johnson and Congress added muscle to the court's more tempered call for desegregation with "all deliberate speed," and spread into the north in the 1970s as the court expanded its definition of *de jure* segregation to include government actions more subtle than the formal enforcement of separate schools for whites and blacks. Many others have written vivid and revealing accounts of this period, but what's most relevant here is the way local resistance to integration led many Americans—including some political leaders—to associate local control with parochialism, bigotry, and the ability and willingness of local elites to use their political power to subjugate others.[17]

Race: Big cities as black dominated. For other Americans, localism began to take on a different meaning as they watched the ascension of blacks into leadership positions in many school districts. During the 1950s and 1960s, the enrollment in a number of large city school systems became majority black, and by the 1970s many of these school districts had black superintendents and majority black school boards.[18] This played a role in the politics of education in at least two ways. First, numerous studies have found evidence that white voters' support for various social programs tends to decrease when racial minorities are seen to be the primary beneficiaries of those programs; that big-city education came to be equated by many with the education of growing populations of minority children may have contributed to the erosion of political support.[19] Second, as black urban voters began to exercise their political muscle and wrest control of elected offices away from white leaders and interest groups, governors and state legislators were emboldened to intervene more directly into those districts, either by instituting stricter oversight and accountability or, more extreme, taking direct control over urban schools or entire districts.

New Jersey, in 1989, became the first state in the country to take over a local school district: Jersey City. As Domingo Morel explains in his book on state takeovers of school districts:

> Within 10 years, states took over another 39 school districts, including the Baltimore, Boston, Chicago, Detroit, and Newark public schools. By 2005, Cleveland, New Orleans, New York City, Oakland, and Philadelphia would also experience a state takeover

of their local schools. As of 2016, states have taken over more than 100 school districts and hundreds more have been threatened to be taken over.[20]

More recently, perhaps somewhat chastened by New Jersey's rocky record in taking over entire districts,[21] a handful of states have instead created districts designed to remove only low performing schools from local control.[22]

Poor student performance, suspicion of corruption, or perceived ineptitude most often are the stated rationale for state incursions on what had previously been seen as the province of local authority. But the fact that state policy makers are predominantly white and the targeted districts and schools predominantly black has raised the issue that state control is selectively applied depending on race and the political empowerment of blacks. Based on quantitative analysis, Morel finds that state takeovers have disproportionately impacted majority-black districts, and these districts typically experienced decreased levels of black political representation in education.[23]

Governance: Bureaucracies as new machines. Disaffection with local school governance also emerged from constituencies at the local level. Within large urban districts, many parents and activists were increasingly frustrated by what seemed to them to be sluggish, rule-bound, and unresponsive bureaucracies that had been allowed to grow in the name of expertise and professionalism but had become unmanageable power centers.

This critique had both a race-neutral and a race-infused version. Some analysts saw the growth of unresponsive bureaucracies through the lens of governance and organizational theory. Political scientist Theodore Lowi, for example, characterized urban bureaucracies as examples of "the new machines": the unintended stepchildren of the Progressive reformers' efforts to insulate good governance from political interference. To the Progressives, bureaucracies represented reservoirs of specialized expertise and, where they could, they instituted structural protections to limit the ability of elected leaders to corral them for political purposes. But, Lowi argued, the result was that city agencies and school districts pursued their own organizational interest and vision with no overarching framework for coordination and control.[24] Lowi's argument was not specific to education and did not directly wrestle with the politics of race.

Others saw the growth of unresponsive local education bureaucracies as intimately connected to changing demographics, race, and education professionals' unselfconscious insistence that they were the guardians of neutral expertise. Through this lens, school district bureaucracies were seen as dedicated to maintaining a status quo consisting of predominantly white administrators and teachers implementing a curriculum that was insensitive to the particular history and culture of its students and perpetuating mediocre performance based on low expectations for minority children. This line of cleavage between district-based educators and black parent and community activists erupted famously in the late 1960s conflict over community control in New York City. The point is not that localism, bureaucratization, and race-based tension over jobs and influence are inherently intertwined. Indeed, in a number of large cities, control of school district leadership and education bureaucracies eventually shifted to minorities, and minority parent and community activists have often rallied around local education bureaucracies when they perceive them to be threatened by outside forces.[25] Rather, what is represented here is further erosion of the historic constituency that celebrated and protected localism, one more strand unravelling and setting the stage for a broader backlash against local control of schools.

Governance: Amateurish school boards and policy churn. Still another chink in the armor of localized education decision-making was the growing sense that school boards were simply not up to the task of instituting needed reforms. Citizen school boards may have made sense in earlier days when districts were much smaller, local populations more homogeneous, and the challenges of global economic competition less intense. One version of this critique suggests: "Our system is, more than anything, an artifact of our Colonial past."[26] Partly by design, to avoid attracting "professional politicians," school board positions are typically part-time, unpaid, and poorly staffed. Boards today not only face more complicated challenges but also have to negotiate—and sometimes battle—with more and better financed entities like teacher unions, charter management organizations, and for-profit purveyors of educational products and services.[27]

Some have believed these shortcomings can be addressed by recruiting and electing better prepared candidates, arranging workshops and seminars to provide board members with better information about the problems they need to address, arranging board tours to visit cities with programs worth emulating, and the like.[28] The stronger versions of this critique have laid the fault at built-in structures and incentives. Because genuine engagement with the modern complexities of education requires long-term attention, but election cycles are short, critics like Hess have argued that boards tend to focus on superficial changes, hiring and then firing superintendents in order to maintain the appearance of activity but in the process only churning the surface.[29]

Governance: Low turnout and the faded promise of democratic vitality. Many of these apparent failings of school boards might be tolerated or taken in stride if seen as the necessary price to pay for the benefits they provide as "the ultimate expression of American democracy . . . operated by the people, for the people."[30] Yet rather than "the crucible of democracy," various reports have revealed school board elections are low turnout and dominated by a few highly mobilized interest groups. For example, in 2010 an op-ed in the *Austin Statesman* declared "democracy's most disgraceful day" after an election in which only 2.5 percent of potential voters took part, in which three precincts had no voters and two had just a single vote recorded.[31] In 2012, in the approximately 240 school board elections in Arkansas, only 36,000 voted, less than 1 percent of those eligible. In November 2015, more than half of the 1,528 open school board seats in New Jersey had one or no candidates on the ballot; 130 had zero candidates.

Partly because of such low turnout, some critics argue that school boards are easily captured by organized interest groups, especially teacher unions, that can use their money and other forms of support to ensure the election of candidates that would protect the jobs, pay, and standard working conditions of their members even when these might come at the expense of learning and well-being of students.[32] Rather than open forums for democratic expression, critics argue school board meetings are often highly managed and structured so that internal debates are hidden. Critics also claim that local boards are micro managing districts; for example, pressuring principals to hire local constituents or donors. Yet another line of critique emphasizes the failure of school boards to address upward mobility for less advantaged groups; instead, these local boards become nodes of resistance to equity-oriented goals.[33]

Within the swirls of national politics, disillusionment with localism was not exclusive to either Republicans or Democrats, liberals or conservatives, but instead affected subgroups within each of these broader categories. The reshuffled coalitions that coalesced around these critiques of localism helped create a movement toward centralization and the growing assertiveness of states and the national government.

LOCALISM LEFT BEHIND: CENTRALIZATION WITHIN THE FEDERAL SYSTEM

Although states and the national government began claiming a somewhat more proactive role in education policy more than a decade before it, President George W. Bush's 2002 signing of No Child Left Behind (NCLB) marked a sharp rebuke against the country's historical allegiance to local control of education. States still retained their Constitutional authority over public education and local districts retained most of their delegated authority to run schools day to day, but Congress used the leverage that comes with federal funding to steer state policies and induce states, in turn, to buckle down on low performing districts and schools. Among other provisions, the law required states to test every student in grades three through eight in math and reading, disaggregate testing data by subgroup (including nonwhite, low-income, and special education students), ensure progressively higher rates of academic proficiency across all subgroups with a goal of 100 percent proficiency by 2014, place highly qualified teachers in every classroom, and force districts and schools to face cascading consequences for failing to make sufficient academic progress.[34] The result was "a transformative shift in federal education policy—not merely a new policy."[35]

The political shifts that made this transformation possible are complicated but have been well chronicled elsewhere.[36] Two points stand out as relevant to the historical evolution of localism that we are sketching in this chapter. First, the bipartisan support that enabled the passage of NCLB was due in no small measure to the various threads of disillusionment with localism discussed previously. Second, NCLB changed the perception and, for a time, the reality of ongoing politics and policy around school reform: the action, it seemed, was moving to Washington, DC, and for reformers hoping to leverage change, that was the place to be.

The leadership from the Republican Party in enacting NCLB was something of a surprise. Historically, Republicans had been the party that championed states' rights and local control. That was still the case on most issues of domestic policy, but on education some important elements within the party had switched gears, and disillusionment with local districts—particularly in large central cities—was part of the explanation. One important subset of Republicans supporting strong national action comprised business interests. Since *A Nation at Risk*, leaders within the corporate world had connected education quality with global economic competitiveness, and they saw local districts as complacent in the face of mediocre student outcomes. Within the business sector, too, were investment firms and education entrepreneurs that were eager to see the private sector gain a larger share of the roughly $600 billion in public spending invested in K–12 education. They saw local districts as public monopolies that hoarded control of public dollars and resisted innovation, making them impervious to their efforts to open the K–12 market to private providers.[37] Also supportive were some Republican governors and other state-level leaders who wanted to partner with the national government to crack down on what they perceived to be wayward big city districts.

Democrats, for their part, were traditionally more open to strong national action, but Bush had made school reform a major plank in his campaign, and some in the Democratic Party were reluctant to give Republicans a big early win. National teacher unions, major donors to Democratic candidates and historically a key element within the party's constituency, were deeply skeptical of NCLB, seeing it as blaming teachers for past failures and unlikely to come with the funding they thought would be necessary to support meaningful change. Most Democrats in Congress, though, ended up supporting the bill, which passed by wide margins. Senator Edward Kennedy and Congressman George Miller were important shepherds of the Democratic vote, and while pragmatic calculations that this was the most politically feasible way to leverage some needed funding were part of their strategy, so too was their view that local districts had failed to vigorously address race- and class-based education gaps.

This impression that NCLB marked a "punctuation" in the previously stable regime of localism was further cemented when control of the White House shifted from the Republican Bush to the Democratic Obama administration, but the direction of national education reform leadership did not shift. Race to the Top (RTTT), initiated under Barack Obama, arguably ratcheted centralization a notch or two higher by strategically using competitive grants and selective waivers to induce states and localities to adopt a range of preferred policies relating to data-based accountability and charter schools.

While the centralizing aspects of NCLB and RTTT can be seen as the culmination of long-simmering frustrations with local control, these policies can also be seen as the starting point of a new era in which the importance of local venues for education decisions seemed permanently deflated. Two concepts from political science help explain how a sharp and self-reinforcing marginalization of local districts might have taken place. One concerns policy feedback; the other, regime transformation.

Policy feedback refers to the process by which a change in policy can alter the political landscape in which subsequent policies are shaped by influencing the political resources, mobilization, or incentives of constituencies, interest groups, or other actors involved in the political process.[38] Policy change also can empower or disempower the legitimacy and capacity of particular institutional venues for decision-making. By effectively framing the national government as the setter of goals and maker of rules, the state governments as their enforcers, and local districts as the subjects of accountability, NCLB sent a strong message that those seeking influence should aim their efforts higher up the ladder of federalism.

If policy feedback helps account for the downward shift in the stature of local districts, regime theory helps explain why that shift could be permanent. The concept of regimes underscores the ways that political arrangements—not only the formal institutions and powers of government but also the informal-yet-patterned interactions among government, business, unions, and the nonprofit sector—shape policy priorities and the prospects for getting things accomplished. In *No Child Left Behind and the Transformation of Federal Education Policy 1965–2005*, Patrick McGuinn developed a compelling argument about the ways in which new ideas, shifting interests, and reconfigured institutions coalesced into a new regime, focused at the national level, comprising a new set of political actors, and leaving some traditionally influential groups out in the cold. In the powerful and popular musical *Hamilton*, Aaron Burr laments the fact that, when a key decision is made, he is not one of those who had access to "the room where it happened." In the aftermath of NCLB and continuing through the Obama administration, it seemed to many that those in the room where key education policy decisions were being made included foundation leaders, education technology providers, and a new set of pro-accountability advocacy groups. Organizations representing teachers, superintendents, and school boards were not invited. In her 2007 analysis of the changing politics of federal education policy, Elizabeth Debray-Pelot identified seven interest groups as formerly—but no longer—influential in setting federal education policy, including the American Association of School Administrators, National School Boards Association, Council of Chief State School Officers, and the Council of Great City Schools.[39]

Making the story of the marginalization of local venues for shaping education more compelling is that it was reinforced by a broader argument—one that had been brewing for quite some time—about how a range of forces were undermining localism more generally and inevitably. This argument points to changes in transportation and communications technologies that make people and businesses more mobile and devalue the importance of geographic proximity. Improved communications and transportation technology means businesses and investors are able to find opportunities, move goods, and undertake financial transactions with little regard for the costs once associated with distance. And the expansion of national media as well as news and opinion sources on the internet means that localized images and values are less distinct and are forced to compete with images and values shaped by and for a much broader audience, appealing to common identities and eroding local loyalties. Local newspapers and television have increasingly come under the ownership of larger companies. Hopkins summarizes some of the trends and underscores their implications for a broader nationalization of Americans' knowledge and interest. As of 2014, he reports, twelve companies owned 589 local television stations compared with just 304 a decade earlier; newsroom employment in newspapers declined by over one-third between the mid-1990s and 2014. The result may be the substitution of national news for local news, whether in the name of responding to public interest in national news over local news, cost cutting, or to serve an ideological agenda.[40]

From this perspective, structural changes are well on the way to making localism obsolete. Its historical power over education policy in the United States may have meant that local dominance of education decision-making was more resilient and resistant than was the case in other areas of social policy, but it was time now for it to succumb.

NATIONALIZATION: LOCAL FRONTS IN NATIONAL WARS

Despite many appearances, the migration of formal power up the ladder of federalism did not make local governance and politics obsolete. Even as the momentum of centralization was building, some analysts began to push back on the notion that local districts have been marginalized. As Smrekar and Crowson observed: "Interestingly, although much of our national attention in educational reform has been upon national and state agendas, local (district- and community-level) action in educational policy has also been experiencing a revival."[41] They use the term *new localism* to characterize the ways in which local decision-making venues continued to be vital albeit in some new and different ways. This new localism highlights the fact that implementation of state and national programs still leaves considerable room for localities to make decisions that matter. Principal-agent theory and implementation research time and again have confirmed that the nominal agents of central policy makers can and do have room to reinterpret, adjust, co-opt, or stymie directives filtered down from above—including administrators in state governments, local jurisdictions, or street-level bureaucrats like police on the beat or teachers in their classrooms.[42]

Critically, the new localism also points to a political role for local actors and venues that goes beyond exploiting zones of administrative discretion and begins to recognize ways in which localities can actively push back against top-down pressures and at times force their reconsideration or reversal. Even as states and the national government have become active in setting the broad policy agenda on issues like accountability and charter schools, local jurisdictions continue to make many of the key decisions that determine how these policies become manifested at the street level.[43] Even as the debates over big policy ideas seem to eclipse local issues, national movements and actors increasingly are required to provide an evidence base to legitimate their arguments, and local districts remain as the gatekeepers that determine whether and how new ideas are tested. In addition, even as national political actors dominate the public's consciousness of who has power and influence over education—whether that be President Donald Trump, former president Barack Obama, Senator Lamar Alexander, Betsy DeVos, Randi Weingarten, or a pivotal member of a Supreme Court majority—local arenas retain the same kind of importance as the minor leagues in baseball, where new talent is identified and nurtured before being promoted to the big leagues.

Our characterization of "the nationalization of education politics" builds on the new localism literature but also opens up some new lines of thinking about the reciprocal relationship between national and local actors and venues on the changing landscape of education policy making. We posit that the involvement of outside donors in local school board elections reflects a growing realization on the part of well-resourced political actors that, rather than being parochial outposts or limited to administrative discretion in implementing policies set elsewhere, local arenas continue to be important as sites for agenda setting, policy coordination, evidence accumulation, and political engagement over national issues.

In redirecting some of their attention and resources to local school politics, wealthy individual donors and organizations involved in national debates are not turning back the clock to earlier eras of localism. It is possible that the 2015 passage of the Every Student Succeeds Act (ESSA) and the 2016 election of President Trump will initiate a period in which some degree of formal authority slides back down the ladder of federalism. Yet the phenomenon of nationalization has more to do with informal dynamics of politics than with formal authority, and the factors contributing to nationalization of politics can, and are likely to, continue even if Washington, DC, loses some of its centrality. In many cases, donors are supporting policy ideas they hope to see expand on a national scale, such as charter school expansion. Yet part of their strategy for achieving this goal involves direct engagement with local politics, rather than focusing their energies primarily on the federal government.

Thus, nationalization of education politics involves an effort by wealthy individual donors and organizations to expand the field of battle on which national contestation is being played out. Nationalization reflects their realization that gaining the balance of control over local school boards can supplement their efforts in state capitals and Washington, DC, in at least five ways:

- *Local implementation.* Education reformers are relearning a lesson that those who crafted liberal social policies at the national level learned in the 1960s and 1970s: policy victories at the federal level can be derailed by reluctant implementation at the local level. Installing sympathetic local school boards can increase the chance that policy victories won in Washington, DC, will be carried out in practice in schools and communities.
- *Local capacity.* Much of the financial and human capital required to bring about effective education still resides at the local level. Local sources account for about 45 percent of all K–12 public education revenues and an even larger proportion of person-power. Local governments, for example, employ three times as many people working on education as do states, and roughly three thousand times as many as the US Department of Education.[44] Paul Manna has used the term *borrowing capacity* to explain how national policy

makers commandeered states as partners in pursuing their goals.[45] By influencing the balance of local power that directs local revenues and personnel, national actors similarly can be seen to capture capacity to support their national agendas.

- *Evidence matters.* Capturing local arenas enables national actors to enlist them as sites for testing their policy ideas and building an evidentiary base to buttress their claims in national debates.

- *Locally enacted policies.* Local authorities are more than passive implementers; they also enact their own *policies that complement or counteract* policy initiatives coming from state and national levels. For example, while federal and state policies may promote the creation of charter schools, local districts are often in a position to craft their own policies dictating whether charter schools have access to existing school buildings.

- *Local government as political "farm system."* Local government and politics remain a critical arena for mobilizing citizens, creating advocacy organizations, and grooming future leaders. Just as professional baseball teams support so-called farm systems for identifying and nurturing talented young players and providing them with experience and coaching before they move to the big leagues, so do local government and politics create a farm system for national political actors concerned about recruiting the supporters and leaders they will depend upon.

Table 2.1 provides a summary overview of the historical stages of localism and the basic precepts that have dominated during each period. As indicated, the dates we ascribe to each period are meant as rough markers. Key events like *Brown v. Board of Education* (1954), *A Nation at Risk* (1983), and *Citizens United v. Federal Election Commission* (2010) offer convenient break points, but it's important to understand that rather than sharp punctuations, the temporal boundary lines are blurry and overlapping. While critiques of localism rose in volume and breadth beginning around the middle of the twentieth century, proponents of localism as a pillar did not disappear and many remain vocal and influential today. While states and then the national government grew more muscular and assertive beginning in the 1980s, and while some actors who promoted that centralization may now be

TABLE 2.1
Summary of historical stages of localism

STAGES	DOMINANT YEARS (rough markers)	DEFINING ELEMENTS
Localism as a pillar	1900 to 1954	*Most important decisions made at the local (district) level, maximizing the role of* Local values Local circumstance Democratic decision-making Local buy-in and engagement
Localism as a problem	1954 to 1982	*Some limitations of localism become manifest, although at times seen differently by liberals vs. conservatives. Local districts seen as* Parochial and racist Captured by racial minorities Bureaucracies as new machines Amateurish school boards and policy churn Low turnout and the faded promise of democratic vitality
Localism left behind	1983 to 2015	*Nation at risk and global economic competition help prompt centralization; first by way of state standards, then federal No Child Left Behind and Race to the Top. Bush/Obama years marked by* New education actors Unions lose some influence Test-based accountability Reform agenda including charters and choice
Nationalization	*2015 to >?*	*National actors rediscover local arenas as strategically important for national policy battles.* Locals as implementation managers Capturing local capacity Districts as laboratories; proof points for national debates Policies that complement or counteract Farm system for national politics

looking back to local arenas as meaningful venues for political engagement, that does not mean that those same actors will not continue to engage in tactical venue shopping, sometimes pushing for stronger national actions, sometimes steering decisions to the states. It is coalition building across levels of government that marks the contemporary political landscape.

If there is a bridge in time between the centralization of education policy through expanding federal involvement and the emergence of the actors and strategies that would spur the nationalization of education politics, the ED in '08 (Education in 2008) campaign could be that bridge. The ED in '08 campaign was an effort to increase the prominence of K–12 education issues in the presidential campaign, funded in partnership by the Bill and Melinda Gates Foundation and the Eli and Edythe Broad Foundation. The campaign responded to the imperatives of the era of centralization and the perception that the federal government should be the focal point for advocates interested in influencing education policy. The ED in '08 campaign established a headquarters in Washington, DC, sent staff members to follow presidential candidates on the campaign trail, and coordinated a debate for Democratic primary candidates.[46] The funders spent $25 million (considerably less than the $60 million that was originally promised), and in the end, the effort was largely criticized as ineffective or even laughable—"a dismal waste of time and money, an embarrassment whose name should not be spoken and whose memory would hopefully fade fast."[47] The funders had high expectations for making education a prominent issue in a presidential campaign where many other major issues dominated, such as health-care reform and the growing economic crisis.

Despite these critiques, many now recognize that ED in '08 laid some groundwork for future advocacy in education involving groups like Democrats for Education Reform and Stand for Children.[48] Although the Gates and Broad Foundations were disappointed with the outcome of the campaign, many other donors followed in their footsteps to get more directly involved in funding advocacy campaigns and engaging in electoral politics around education. The US Supreme Court decision in *Citizens United* supercharged their involvement by making it much easier for individuals to give large donations, especially through intermediary organizations. And rather than becoming small fish in the big pond of presidential politics, these donors found much smaller ponds where their dollars would make them into very big fish indeed.

CHAPTER 3

....

Who Are the Outside Donors?

DAVID TEPPER AND REID HOFFMAN are both billionaires. Tepper is founder and president of Appaloosa Management, a hedge fund. Born and raised in Pennsylvania, Tepper lived in New Jersey for decades and founded his company there but relocated to Florida (which has no personal income tax) in 2016.[1] Hoffman, who grew up in Berkeley, California, and currently lives in Palo Alto, is cofounder of the professional social network LinkedIn. Both Tepper and Hoffman have gained sufficient notoriety to be the subjects of long-form magazine articles sketching their personal lives and rise to wealth. In a *New York* magazine profile, Tepper, who earned nearly $4 billion in a single trade, cheekily exclaims to the reporter: "What do you think I should do with it? I could buy an island. I could buy a private jet—but I have NetJets. I could get myself a 22-year-old!"[2] Known for his outsize confidence, Tepper keeps a pair of brass testicles affixed to a plaque on his desk (a gift from former employee Alan Fournier). Meanwhile, an article in *Wired* magazine presents a decidedly contrasting portrait of Hoffman, who still drives the same car he bought ten years ago and earnestly muses, "I basically believe I can learn the skills to do most anything . . . but I'm paranoid that I'm not good enough."[3] His preferred splurge is fine dining, and the reporter describes a "five-hour molecular gastronomy dinner" featuring a "62-degree egg with green lentils in a vermouth zabaglione."

Their wealth places Tepper and Hoffman in a rarified category in the United States—not only as top earners and asset holders, but also as political contributors. In 2012, Hoffman contributed more than $1 million to candidates in federal elections; all of Hoffman's contributions supported Democratic candidates, PACs, and party committees. Like Hoffman, Tepper is also a top campaign donor in federal elections, though his $600,000 in 2012 contributions supported Republican candidates, committees, and PACs. Aside from their status as billionaires, it seems that Tepper and Hoffman could hardly be more different—the brash East Coast hedge fund founder Republican and the introspective West Coast foodie/techie Democrat. Yet Hoffman and Tepper have one more surprising similarity—both have been donors to school board candidates in Denver and New Orleans, cities far outside of their home states. Not only did Hoffman and Tepper support candidates in the same cities, but both billionaires contributed to the same candidates: Sarah Newell Usdin in New Orleans and Mike Johnson, Landri Taylor, Rosemary Rodriguez, and Barbara O'Brien in Denver. How did far-flung billionaires with sharply contrasting partisan politics, personalities, and professional backgrounds become contributors to the same school board candidates thousands of miles away?

Most research on school board elections provides little guidance on the factors that might motivate a donor residing in a different state to contribute to a school board election. While many studies point to teacher union fundraising and involvement in school board elections,[4] there is scarcely any systematic evidence or analysis of individuals living out of state as a substantial source of campaign funds. Adams conducted one of the few studies of the geographic distribution of local campaign contributions, showing that out-of-state contributions ranged from only 4 to 8 percent of total contributions for city council and mayor in four major cities.[5] Data limits may have played a role in discouraging research into local elections generally and school board elections specifically; it is painstaking and time consuming to compile local campaign finance data.

The data on federal campaign contributions is much more accessible and easily compiled, and a growing body of research has explored and described the behavior of big donors in national politics. Congressional candidates raise an increasingly large share of funds from out of state; a recent study showed that on average, incumbent senators seeking re-election in 2012 received almost half of their individual contributions from out of state.[6] Research by Rhodes, Schaffner, and LaRaja identifies a distinct category of donors that they call "nationalized donors." According to their research, "what really distinguishes extreme big donors is their ability to and interest in spreading their contributions over a wide range of targets and, in particular, [focusing] donations on out-of-jurisdiction House and Senate candidates."[7] They further argue that these donors are uniquely well positioned to gain "surrogate" representation from elected officials outside of their home states and suggest that this is a key source of political inequality.

In light of these trends, the school board contributions from Hoffman and Tepper could be seen as extensions of a broader trend in national politics—the expansion of out-of-jurisdiction contributing among very wealthy donors. School board elections are not isolated from this nationalizing behavior among major donors. School board elections were once low-profile, low-price, and highly localized affairs. For decades, strong norms, traditions, and protective institutions kept school politics buffered from many of the broader partisan and ideological battles swirling around Washington, DC. But that seems to be changing.

In this chapter, we explore the who, what, and how of individual national donors in local school board elections. Overall, our evidence paints a portrait of donors operating on a national political stage; we identify an elite group of nationalized donors in both federal elections and school board elections. Within the larger group of national donors in school board elections, our analysis gradually zooms in to focus on a smaller group of unique donors who are nationally active, contributing to school board elections in multiple places. We call these donors "strategic national donors." Local school board elections tend to be a very small investment in their political giving portfolios, but their contributions, which are given in amounts much larger than funds from the average local donor, can compose an outsized share of the funding raised by certain school board candidates. Meanwhile, there is a distinctly education-oriented flavor to the donors who focus on school board elections; this group is well represented on the boards of nationally prominent education nonprofits and charter schools such as Teach for America (TFA), New Schools Venture Fund, KIPP charter schools, and Democrats for Education Reform. Finally, if we analyze school board contributions as a network, in which donors are connected through contributions to the same candidates and committees, we find evidence suggesting coordination. Donors like Hoffman and Tepper are not merely isolated wealthy individuals with an interest in school boards. Instead, donors are linked by ties to other donors through education organization board memberships, suggesting that some donor mobilization may occur through social connections or information distributed by organizations.

This chapter begins with a discussion of donor mobilization based on existing research. Next, we provide a descriptive overview of individual national donor giving, including the amounts they give to school board elections and the recipients of their funds. Next, based on our analysis of campaign contributions and donor characteristics, we are able to sketch some of the mechanisms by which outside voices can penetrate the cocoon of localism. In particular, we show that national ties through board memberships and federal campaign contributing activities make these donors active and easier to mobilize for widespread engagement in local campaigns. Finally, we examine the role of local elite donors and whether their giving tends to support the same candidates and organizations as the large national donors.

DONOR MOBILIZATION: IDEOLOGUES AND NETWORKS

Much of what we know about campaign donors and their motivations from political science research is based on studies of legislative elections, especially Congressional elections. A common theme in this work is the importance of candidate ideology among donors.[8] Ideologically extreme donors tend to be among the most frequent contributors, and donors tend to rate ideological agreement as a top motivation for their donations. In the context of local education elections, traditional ideological alignments may not be clear cut, because many elections are nonpartisan. Furthermore, education politics has scrambled traditional partisan and ideological alignments, with intraparty disputes emerging in both parties (for instance, pro- and anti-charter school factions among Democrats, and pro- and anti-Common Core factions among Republicans). This is not to say that ideology is irrelevant, but rather that ideological conflict is not always split along the traditional Left to Right spectrum in educational politics. As the Tepper and Hoffman examples seem to demonstrate, large donors with vastly different ideological alignments in national politics are finding a way to support the same candidates in local school board elections. Thus, we approach the questions of the partisan or ideological motives of donors in an exploratory fashion, by gathering data on federal campaign contributions to learn more about the partisan preferences of the large national donor population. Further, we suspect that political ideology or partisanship is not a sufficient explanation for understanding the motivations of large national school board donors.

Meanwhile, new research on campaign contributions is beginning to examine the social aspects of contributing behavior.[9] For instance, Betsy Sinclair analyzes social networks of campaign contributors, conceptualizing individuals as "social citizens." Her research examines a network of donors within a single congressional district, and she shows that individual donations to a congressional campaign are positively associated with visible contributions from other donors in the same social network. Sinclair and others have argued that a network approach helps to account for the collective action paradox of individual campaign contributions: individual donations would seem irrational unless others with similar preferences also contribute; social networks help like-minded contributors to coordinate.[10] Networks can be based on social relationships, but networks can also indicate social, political, or ideological similarity between individuals who do not know one another. For instance, individuals who are members of the same corporate boards show greater similarity in contribution patterns to presidential candidates.[11] Additionally, some studies have examined how spatial proximity is related to campaign contributing.[12] Geographic proximity could suggest social contact; however, geographic proximity may represent only social similarity and common interests.[13]

Drawing on these findings on donor networks, we also explore the possibility that large national donors are connected or involved in organizations that could mobilize them to donate in school board elections. In particular, we focus on the possibility that the growing sector of educational nonprofits and political organizations could play a role in connecting donors to one another and to potential candidates. Especially when these groups involve individuals who support similar reform ideas in education, such as charter school supporters affiliated with the board of a charter organization, these groups might effectively help mobilize like-minded donors. Additionally, we use information about donors' geographical location, based on zip codes, to investigate whether large national donors are clustered within particular places or types of communities.

NOTES ON THE DATA

Before we turn to our findings, it is important to provide a sketch of our data and the definitions we use for identifying different categories of donors. For some purposes, it can make sense to think of the distinction between local and outside as a continuum. For example, there can be donors who live outside of the district but within the surrounding suburbs, donors who live outside the metro area but within the state, and donors who live outside of the state. For some purposes, it can make sense to look at different types of donors (e.g., individuals and various types of organizational entities), and for others, it makes sense to look just at individuals. Our data allow us to make these distinctions. Table 3.1 makes it clear, for example, that out-of-state donors give disproportionately large donations, and this is particularly the case when we focus on individuals, with out-of-state donors giving nearly $1,300 more than the average local area donor. Although out-of-state donors represent only 8.4 percent of all individual donors, those giving from out of state contribute 22.5 percent of the total dollars given by individuals in the elections we analyze. This result mirrors the findings of Rhodes, Schaffner, and LaRaja for nationalized donors in federal campaigns; although their numbers are small relative to other types of donors, they contribute a disproportionate share of the dollars.

We coded every donor in the dataset to identify the major individual out-of-state donors; these are individuals who contributed at least

TABLE 3.1

Comparison of donations by donor or organization location

FOR *ALL DONORS* (individuals and organizations)	NUMBER OF DONATIONS	PERCENT OF DONORS	AVERAGE AMOUNT	TOTAL AMOUNT	PERCENT OF DONATIONS
Local area	12,674	67.9	$1,647	$20,871,852	74.7
Metropolitan area	2,444	13.1	$575	$1,405,070	5
In state	2,223	11.9	$1,019	$2,264,208	8.1
Out of state	1,339	7.2	$2,529	$3,385,769	12.1
FOR *INDIVIDUAL* DONORS	NUMBER OF DONATIONS	PERCENT OF DONORS	AVERAGE AMOUNT	TOTAL AMOUNT	PERCENT OF DONATIONS
Local area	10,042	71	$554	$5,560,239	58.2
Metropolitan area	2,151	15.2	$551	$1,185,495	12.4
In state	775	5.5	$853	$661,157	6.9
Out of state	1,183	8.4	$1,814	$2,145,960	22.5

$1,000 in a given election year and supported at least one candidate or committee outside of their home state. We call these individuals "large national donors" or "national donors." Recall, local school board candidates historically raised relatively small sums for their campaigns, with more than 90 percent of large district candidates reporting that they spent less than $25,000. Thus, while a $1,000 donation would be relatively small in other elections, this donation is rather large in a school board election.[14] Donors were coded based on the address reported in campaign finance records. Once donors are identified as out of state, they maintain that classification in all elections because we are treating donors as our main unit of analysis. Thus, a donor residing in San Francisco who contributes to elections in New Orleans and Los Angeles would be considered a large national donor for both elections.

For the analysis of donor characteristics, we focus on 132 individual large national donors who contributed to school board elections in our dataset. We collected additional data on these large national donors to analyze factors that could relate to their involvement in funding out-of-state school board elections. First, we identified board member-ships with educational organizations (including state- and national-level advocacy groups, nonprofits, and think tanks), based on thorough web searches for each donor's name. Second, we compiled donor metropol-itan areas and zip codes based on their residential addresses. Third, we gathered data on 2012 federal campaign contributions from the Cen-ter for Responsive Politics website for each donor.[15] We recorded the political party affiliation of each federal candidate and committee that received money from our large out-of-state donors.

Finally, we also coded the campaign contribution data to iden-tify categories of candidates aligned with different organizations and policy positions in education politics. Each organization in our data (both contributing and receiving organizations) was coded based on the type of organization, including business, candidate committee, political party, labor union, trade association, teacher union, reform organizations, and other. We created a single "union" variable for all union-affiliated organizations and PACs. The coding of reform organi-zations was based on an analysis of each organization's website. Orga-nizations were coded as "reform" if their platform or mission included goals aligned with the Obama administration's Race to the Top pro-gram. RTTT provides a useful heuristic for identifying the core agenda items favored by educational reformers; scholars have noted the close association between the program and the educational reform movement.[16] Policies aligned with RTTT include expanding charter schools/innovative schools, using student data in teacher evaluation, using teacher retention policies such as merit pay and career ladders, employing data systems and accountability, turning around the lowest performing schools, and adopting Common Core standards. We used the coding of organizations as "union" or "reform" as the basis for coding candidates as "union" or "reform" or not affiliated. Candidate categories were determined based on the proportion of contributions the candidate received from reform organizations or teacher unions. Alongside our donor data, these categories for recipients of campaign contributions allow us to make systematic comparisons in the amount of donations to various candidates and organizations across all five of the cities included in our dataset.

HOW MUCH MONEY AND FOR WHOM?

Our campaign contributions dataset allows us to trace funds from specific donors to recipient candidates and committees across school board elections in five cities from 2008 to 2014. These data present a revealing picture of where and how money from large national donors is targeted in school board elections. Overall, we find that large national donors comprised a substantial share of campaign funds in each of the five cities in at least one election cycle, and their dollars overwhelmingly supported candidates and committees aligned with educational reform organizations.

Table 3.2 shows the proportion of campaign dollars from large national donors as a share of funds from all individual contributors, broken down by election cycle and city. All five cities had one election with individual out-of-state donor funds constituting 25 percent or more of individual contribution dollars. Yet these percentages do not reveal the overall amount of funds from large national donors flowing into school board elections in these cities. In the 2008–9 election years, large national donors gave a total of $38,725; this grew to $633,600 in the 2011–12 election years. By 2013–14, the amount more than tripled, to $2.6 million. This growth, however, is largely driven by funds focused on one city—Los Angeles.

As the graphs in figure 3.1 show, cities like Bridgeport, Denver, and Indianapolis did not continue an upward rise in campaign contributions from individuals in the most recent election cycle in our dataset. Yet Los Angeles, which is plotted on a different scale (since contributions there can be measured in millions, rather than thousands),

TABLE 3.2

Proportion of campaign dollars from large national donors as a share of funds from all individual contributors, by election cycle and city

ELECTION YEARS	BRIDGEPORT	INDIANAPOLIS	NEW ORLEANS	DENVER	LOS ANGELES
2008–2009	0%	0%	4%	5%	4%
2011–2012	66%	44%	25%	24%	13%
2013–2014	9%	25%	—	32%	48%

FIGURE 3.1   Total contributions from individual donors

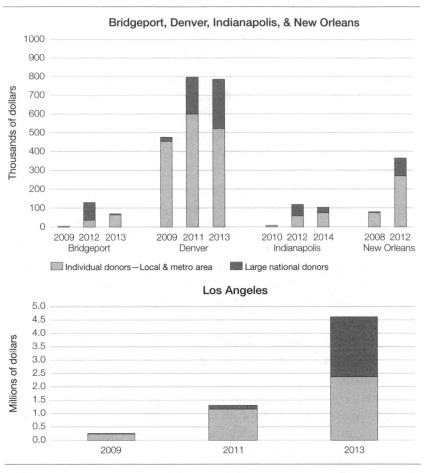

experienced a huge uptick from 2011 to 2013. These graphs represent funds from individual donors in each city, with the lighter portion of the bars representing the more traditional individual donors in
school board elections—those who reside in the local area or surrounding metropolitan region. We group together both local and metropolitan area donors based on the perspective that some residents in the
broader metropolitan area may have a direct stake in the local school
board election (for instance, as employees of the district or as former
residents of the city).

The darker portion of the bars represents the funds from large national donors. It is interesting to note that funds from individuals in the local/metropolitan area also grew as national donors became a larger proportion of the donor base. Overall, this creates a more sizable pool of funds for campaigns and suggests that the activation of a large donor base is not purely a national donor phenomenon.

Finally, we can examine the types of candidates or committees that receive funds from large national donors. We coded each recipient candidate and organization, with a focus on two major categories of interest for education politics: union supporters and reform supporters. Table 3.3 provides a summary of the funding from individuals for each category of candidates and election committees, as well as the uncategorized candidates and committees. According to the table, the overwhelming share of funds from all individual donors—not just large national donors—was raised by reform candidates, PACs, and independent expenditure committees. These candidates and committees raised over $8.4 million from individual donors, while union-aligned candidates and committees raised only a little over $600,000. Union-backed candidates certainly have other funding sources (including union organizations, which raise some political funds from their individual members), but this table highlights a distinct fundraising advantage among individual donors for the candidates and committees classified

TABLE 3.3

Share of individual donor funds for reform, union, and uncategorized candidates and committees

	TOTAL RAISED FROM INDIVIDUAL DONORS	PERCENT FUNDS FROM LARGE NATIONAL DONORS
Reformer-backed candidates	$3,363,046	17.8
Reform PACs and IE committees	$5,046,561	51.2
Union-backed candidates	$602,951	5.7
Union PACs and IE committees	$3,510	0
Uncategorized candidates	$481,174	4.3
Other PACs and IE committees	$56,809	29.9

as "pro-reform" in these cities. Within the individual donor category, large national donors also predominantly backed reform candidates and committees, with scarcely any funding for union-backed candidates and $0 for union-aligned PACs and committees. Of the $3.25 million in campaign contributions provided by large national donors in these elections, 98 percent of the funds supported reform-aligned candidates and committees. By comparison, 88 percent of funds from all individual donors supported reform candidates and committees. Thus, we find an enormous fundraising advantage for reform candidates and committees among all individual donors, but the advantage is tilted almost entirely toward reform candidates and groups among the large national donors.

If we drill down to specific candidates, we find that certain candidates raised a particularly sizable share of funds from large national donors. For example, in New Orleans, all three reformer-backed candidates in 2012 raised at least 20 percent of their funds from large national donors, and the most prominent reform candidate—Sarah Newell Usdin—raised 39 percent of her campaign cash from large out-of-state donors. In Indianapolis in 2012, Caitlin Hannon depended on large national donors for an even larger share of her funds, 62 percent. Nine other candidates across the elections we examined raised more than 20 percent of their funds from large national donors. While these candidates stand out and represent a significant shift in school board campaigns, it is important to remember that these individuals are still not the norm. The majority of school board candidates in our dataset, 69 out of 114, raised no money from large national donors. One particular characteristic unites the top two candidates supported by large national donors—Usdin and Hannon. Both women were Teach for America corps members before their entry into school board politics. Both Usdin and Hannon also occupy prominent reform-oriented positions in their respective cities. Usdin is founder and board member of New Schools for New Orleans (an organization that has supported the growth and expansion of charter schools in New Orleans), and Hannon is the founder and executive director of Enroll Indy (an organization focused on creating a single enrollment system for charter schools and traditional public schools in Indianapolis). TFA is one important organizational network that links the large national donors.

WHO ARE THE DONORS?

Who are the national donors contributing to far-flung local school board races? Some are billionaires well known to the public and visible actors in the world of education policy. Many became wealthy working in similar and highly lucrative professional fields, particularly finance and technology. Examples include Michael Bloomberg, former mayor of New York City and founder of Bloomberg Philanthropies; Eli Broad, the California-based philanthropist; and Laurene Powell Jobs, wife to the late Steve Jobs and founder of Emerson Collective, which funds educational reform organizations and the high-profile XQ Project—a $50 million competition to create new high schools. John Arnold is an investor and former hedge fund manager from Houston with a net worth of $2.9 billion. Along with his wife, who is also a donor to school board elections, he cofounded the Laura and John Arnold Foundation, which invests in projects that promote more school choice for families and increased flexibility and accountability for teachers. Arnold also served on the board of The New Teacher Project, a nonprofit that promotes teacher quality reforms. The Arnolds contributed to school board candidates in Denver, New Orleans, and Los Angeles. Others are generally familiar figures whose focus on education may not have been quite so apparent, such as Reed Hastings, CEO of Netflix, who has been active in supporting the development of new charter schools and founded educational organizations such as NewSchools.org and Aspire Public Schools. Still others lack a national profile, such as Alan Fournier, the founder of Pennant Capital Management, which manages $6 billion in assets, and who donated in Indianapolis, Los Angeles, and New Orleans; and Katherine Bradley, the president of CityBridge Foundation, which "finds, incubates and invests in the most promising practices in public education," who donated in Denver, New Orleans, and Los Angeles.

These donors are spread across metropolitan areas in more than twenty different states, but a greater density of donors exists in certain parts of the country. Figure 3.2 maps the locations of the large national donors by Core-based statistical area, a geographic designation used by the census that defines metropolitan areas. By far, the largest amount of donor money originated in the New York metropolitan area—more than $1.6 million in school board campaign contributions. Michael Bloomberg provided the predominant share of those funds (more than $1.4 million), but he is joined by more than twenty other large national donors based in New York, such as R. Boykin Curry, John Petry, Whitney Tilson, Mark Gallogly, and Margaret Chernin.

The next highest-ranking metropolitan areas for large national donors are Los Angeles, Denver, San Francisco, San Jose, and Santa Cruz. The division of the San Francisco Bay Area into three different core-based statistical areas may mask the overall amount of campaign contributions from that region of the country: the three CBSAs in the Bay Area combined provided $487,000 in contributions (more than Denver and slightly less than Los Angeles). Digging deeper into the geographic concentration of donors in the Bay Area reveals another pattern: a few zip codes have an unusually high concentration of donors. Four households with large national donors are located in Atherton, California, zip code 94027. According to *Forbes* magazine's ranking of the most expensive zip codes in 2017, the 94027 zip code was ranked number one, with a median home price of $9.68 million.[17] Based on American Community Survey estimates for this zip code in 2016, 90 percent of homes were valued at $1 million or more, and 33 percent had five or more bedrooms; additionally, 50 percent of households had three or more vehicles available. Several other zip codes are home to more than one national donor household, including zip codes in Greenwich, Connecticut; Palo Alto, California; New York, New York; and Washington, DC. In total, thirty-one of the large national donors live in the same zip code as at least one other large national donor (who is not a member of the same household). With more than thirty-thousand residential zip codes in the United States, that is a highly unlikely level of geographic concentration for a small group of people. Not surprisingly, many of the large national donors reside in extremely wealthy areas within these metropolitan areas. Prior research on the concentration of congressional donors within certain zip codes has referred to these areas as "political A.T.M.s,"[18] and it seems that school board campaigns can also look to certain wealthy enclaves for significant fundraising opportunities.

Wealth on its own does not imply an interest in contributing to distant school board campaigns, but it certainly does help as a

FIGURE 3.2 Large national donor locations by CBSA

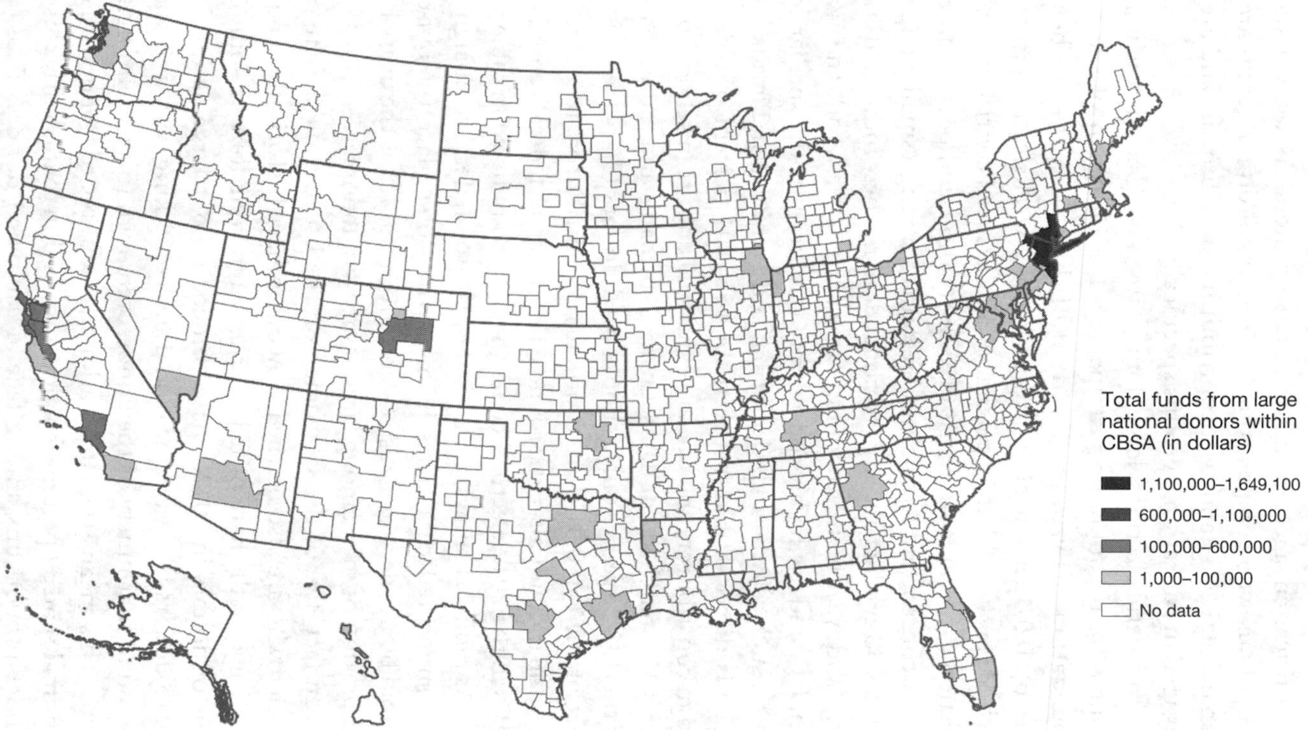

Total funds from large
national donors within
CBSA (in dollars)

1,100,000–1,649,100
600,000–1,100,000
100,000–600,000
1,000–100,000
No data

prerequisite. Beyond wealth, we might expect to observe a higher level of political engagement among active donors. As we will show, the individuals who compose our large national donor group are exceptionally active as campaign contributors more broadly and are highly engaged in educational groups specifically.

In federal elections, large donors are playing an increasingly dominant role in bankrolling campaigns. Lee Drutman of the Sunlight Foundation analyzed the 1 percent of the 1 percent—in other words, the top 0.01 percent of contributors to federal elections in the 2012 cycle.[19] He shows that 28 percent of all disclosed contributions in that election cycle came from just over thirty-thousand people—an extraordinary concentration of political resources among a small group of individuals. Much like our large national donors, these individuals reside in large and wealthy metropolitan areas such as New York and Washington, DC, and are highly concentrated in very wealthy smaller communities, such as Atherton, California, and Palm Beach, Florida.[20] In fact, there is direct overlap between the top 0.01 percent of federal campaign contributors and the large national donors in school board elections. We matched our dataset with Drutman's and found that 46 out of the 132 large national school board donors (35 percent) were also part of the top 0.01 percent of federal contributors in 2012. In total these 46 individuals gave around $17 million to federal candidates and PACs in the 2012 electoral cycle (the top 20 are listed in table 3.4).

As table 3.4 shows, about half of the top federal campaign donors also supported candidates in more than one place for out-of-state school board elections. Also evident from this list is the overwhelming proportion of men among large campaign donors.

In fact, five of the six women on the list in table 3.4 are married to men who are also on the list. Women have historically composed a relatively small share of federal campaign contributors—only 30 percent of donors in 2012.[21] Based on coding our large national school board donors by first name (and double-checking with web searches), we found that ninety of the donors were men (overwhelmingly white men). This means the large national school board donors are 68 percent male and 32 percent female, a proportion that is fairly close to the gender proportions among federal campaign donors. Thus, women

TABLE 3.4

The 1% of the 1%: Top twenty federal donors who are also school board donors

INDIVIDUAL	LOCATION	OCCUPATION (IF LISTED)	FEDERAL $ 2012	OUT-OF-STATE SCHOOL BOARD ELECTIONS	SCHOOL BOARD $
Michael Bloomberg	New York, NY	Mayor, City of New York	$13,703,720	Bridgeport, Denver, Indianapolis, Los Angeles, New Orleans	$1,475,000
Stephen Silberstein	Belvedere, CA	Retired	$1,091,599	Denver	$1,500
Reid Hoffman	Mountain View, CA	Executive, LinkedIn	$1,086,600	Denver, New Orleans, Indianapolis	$12,500
Alan Fournier	Far Hills, NJ	Investment Manager, Pennant	$606,050	Indianapolis, Los Angeles, New Orleans	$5,100
David Tepper	Short Hills, NJ	President, Appaloosa Management	$610,800	Denver, New Orleans	$9,400
Eli Broad	Los Angeles, CA	Founder, The Broad Foundation	$477,800	Bridgeport, (Los Angeles-in state)	$529,000
Michael Sacks	Highland Park, IL	CEO, Grosvenor Capital Management	$410,300	Los Angeles	$1,000
Stephen Sherrill	New York, NY	N/A	$207,600	New Orleans	$2,500
Mark Gallogly	New York, NY	Managing Principal, Centerbridge Partners	$127,630	Los Angeles	$25,000
Leo Hindery	New York, NY	InterMedia Advisors	$125,800	Denver	$5,000
Stephen Schutz	La Jolla, CA	Artist, SPS Studios	$118,300	Denver	$3,000
Susan Polis-Schutz	La Jolla, CA	Writer, Blue Mountain Arts	$114,800	Denver	$4,000

(continued)

TABLE 3.4 (*continued*)

The 1% of the 1%: Top twenty federal donors who are also school board donors

INDIVIDUAL	LOCATION	OCCUPATION (IF LISTED)	FEDERAL $ 2012	OUT-OF-STATE SCHOOL BOARD ELECTIONS	SCHOOL BOARD $
Albert Ratner	Cleveland, OH	Retired	$111,900	Denver	$1,000
Cari Sacks	Highland Park, IL	Homemaker	$95,932	Los Angeles	$1,000
John Arnold	Houston, TX	Founder, Centaurus Energy Management	$89,450	Denver, Los Angeles, New Orleans	$63,400
Charles Ledley	Boston, MA	Highfields Capital Management	$88,000	Denver, Indianapolis, New Orleans	$14,600
Jennifer Fournier	Far Hills, NJ	N/A	$84,120	Indianapolis, New Orleans	$3,100
Sheryl Sandberg	Atherton, CA	COO, Facebook	$77,300	Indianapolis, New Orleans	$3,500
Elizabeth Strickler	New York, NY	Retiree	$77,000	Los Angeles	$1,000
Michelle Yee	Mountain View, CA	Self-employed	$74,349	Denver, Indianapolis, New Orleans	$12,500

tend to be substantially underrepresented among large national school board donors.

Beyond the unique group within the top 0.01 percent, the other large national school board donors are also highly active federal contributors. Based on data we compiled from the Center for Responsive Politics, 80 out of the 132 donors (61 percent) contributed to federal campaigns in 2012; the median total contribution amount was $38,000 and the smallest amount given was $250.[22] This contrasts sharply with contributing behavior in the broader population: only 0.2 percent of voters reported giving $200 or more to a congressional candidate.[23] For every contribution in this dataset, we coded whether the candidates and PACs receiving the funds were Democratic, Republican, or

Independent. Based on these data, the large national donors in school board elections lean heavily toward the Democratic Party. Seventy-one percent of the federal contribution dollars supported Democratic Party candidates and PACs, whereas 24 percent funded Republican Party candidates and PACs.[24] There are some interesting implications from the prevalence of Democrats among outside donors in school board elections. These same individuals gave heavily to candidates facing off with union-backed candidates in local school board races, even though unions are a constituency that is traditionally closely aligned with the Democratic Party.

While federal contributions provide important information about a donor's propensity to give to political campaigns, and about their resources for political giving, this does not tell us much about interest in education specifically. For more background on this area, we turn to information we gathered on the board memberships of the large national donors. Among the 132 large national donors, 31 have a current or former affiliation as a board member of an organization focused on K–12 education. Some serve on boards of major national organizations associated with education reform alongside other donors involved with the same organization (see table 3.5); Teach for America and KIPP both have three or more donors currently affiliated with their organizational boards.

These groups are not primarily focused on political advocacy or promoting specific candidates in elections, but they are advancing a particular education policy agenda involving charter schools and alternative certification for teachers. Teach for America does have an affiliated 501(c)(4) organization, Leadership for Educational Equity. Other donors serve on charter school boards or scholarship foundations in their own local areas.

STRATEGIC NATIONAL DONORS

The background information related to geography, federal campaign contributions, and education board affiliations paints a picture of a group of donors who tend to reside in wealthy areas, engage actively as political contributors, and serve on boards of organizations directly involved with K–12 education reform—with some serving on the same

TABLE 3.5
Donor organizational affiliations

ORGANIZATION	DONORS SERVING ON BOARDS
Teach for America	Joel Klein, Greg Penner Laura Arnold (former member) Arthur Rock (former member) Katherine Bradley (DC regional board) Zack Neumeyer (former member, Colorado regional board)
New Schools Venture Fund	Chris Gabrieli, David Goldberg (in memoriam) Laurene Powell Jobs (former member) Jonathan Sackler (former member)
KIPP Charter Schools	Katherine Bradley, Reed Hastings, Mark Nunnelly
Charter School Growth Fund	Stacy Schusterman, Greg Penner (former member)
Education Reform Now	John Petry, Charles Ledley (former member)

organizational boards as other donors. Yet these characteristics do not describe all of the large national donors in our dataset. For instance, based on last name alone, a few donors are clearly family relations of the school board candidates they support. Others may be friends or other personal acquaintances. We do not assume that we can systematically explain all of the factors driving the contributions by every one of the 132 large national donors, yet we are particularly interested in understanding the most active donors. For our next analysis, we define most active national donors as those who contributed to elections in more than one of the school districts in our study. We call these donors to more than one out-of-state election "strategic national donors." Their participation in multiple out-of-state elections shows that their donation behavior is not a one-off occurrence, implying a strategic choice to contribute to specific school board elections on more than one occasion. We expect these donors, as a group, to be visibly politically active, involved with educational organizations, and possibly connected socially based on residence in the same locations.

In total, 30 individual donors are designated as strategic national donors.[25] These donors gave a disproportionate share of out-of-state election funds. The 30 strategic national donors contributed $2.96

million, and the median total contribution amount in this group was $125,000. By comparison, the other 102 national donors gave a total of $295,000; their median contribution was $1,000. Thus, although the large national donors are an unusual group overall, the strategic national donors are the most distinctive set of individual donors in our school board elections, and their funding across multiple districts plays a disproportionate role in funding candidates and committees.

Table 3.6 presents the results of two logistic regression models predicting which donors are strategic (i.e., multicity) donors; the table entries are reported as odds ratios because every independent variable is measured as a dummy variable. The independent variables include four possible factors associated with the behavior of strategic donors. First, we expect that donors involved in federal campaign contributing activity will be more likely to give in multiple school board elections. We use a dummy variable to indicate whether or not an individual was a donor in federal elections in 2012. In the second model, we focus on a more select group of federal campaign contributions: the 1 percent of the 1 percent from the Sunlight Foundation dataset for 2012. With this variable, we assess whether multicity school board contributing behavior is associated with particularly high dollar involvement in federal elections. Second, we expect that these donors are involved with educational organizations; we use (1) to indicate past or current membership on an education organization board and (0) to indicate no such membership. Third, we believe these donors might live in close proximity to other donors—in wealthy zip codes. Geographic proximity could also suggest social contact, particularly at a neighborhood level.[26] Once again, we use a dummy variable: (1) if the donor shares the same zip code as at least one other large national donor, outside of the household, and (0) if no other large national donor lives in that zip code.

As shown in table 3.6, federal campaign contributions and education board memberships are both positive and statistically significant predictors of strategic national donors. Moreover, when we compare the odds ratios for federal contributors and the 1 percent of the 1 percent of federal contributors, it is clear that the high dollar federal campaign givers are even more likely to be strategic out-of-state school board election donors. The zip code variable is positive, but not

TABLE 3.6

Logistic regression models predicting strategic donors

2012 Federal contributor	5.408* (-3.947)	—
1% of 1%: 2012 Federal contributor	—	6.941** (-40.13)
Past or current board membership: education organization	14.286** 0.000	13.747** (-7.715)
Residence in same zip code as another large national donor	2.385 (-1.346)	2.979 (-1.752)
Pseudo R²	0.357	0.398
N	132	132

Table entries are odds ratios with standard errors in parentheses. Odds ratios above 1.00 indicate a positive relationship with the dependent variable. For a two-tailed test of significance, *$p<0.05$; **$p<0.01$.

statistically significant. Education board membership is a particularly important factor, with an odds ratio of around fourteen in both models; this is roughly two times greater than the likelihood that the top 0.01 percent of federal contributors will be strategic national donors.

Based on this analysis, we can offer more informed explanations of the pathways that could mobilize certain individuals as long-distance school board election funders. First, these individuals are already politically active as campaign contributors. In many cases, their political activity is already unusual, and their willingness to put large sums of money into politics is exceptional. Second, these individuals have become involved in education through other means, especially by serving on the boards of nonprofits involved in education. Many of these organizations are involved with charter school operations or expansion, but some focus on teachers (Teach for America) or scholarships for low-income students. These explanations are not at all surprising: people with a great deal of money to invest in politics and an interest in education are willing participants in funding out-of-state school board candidates. Yet the predictability of the behavior also highlights another feature of these donors: they are not isolated and are unlikely to be one-off participants in education politics. Rather, these donors are likely to be connected to one another through well-established organizations within education and in the broader political system.

Our interviews with knowledgeable informants in education reform organizations supported this perspective. A reform leader described this process of sharing information about elections between donors:

> The most common [process] tend[s] to be, there is a particular donor that's already engaged in one place, and he seeks out other donors from around the country, basically says, "I'll help you with your race when it comes two years from now, if you help me with mine." And then you've got donors who are sending money to support school board candidates that wouldn't normally be on their radar screen, people they'd never heard of, and in some cases, would forget that they exist, but they write the check. But because they trusted the person, usually another donor, who put out the call.[27]

Thus, direct person-to-person connections play a role in spreading the word about giving donations to particular candidates and particular elections. Another informant mentioned how organizations also coordinate contributions and provide information to prospective donors. One example is through an entity known as Education Century, which is not publicly visible, but has a password-protected website at https://educationcentury.com/?act=login. Prospective donors can access this website to make contributions that will automatically be split into equal parts among a set of preselected candidates. The term *century* refers to the donation total that the site seeks to attract—$100,000. A total donation of that amount divided among three candidates would result in three contributions of $33,333.33. Interestingly, our data suggest that both Laurene Powell Jobs and Reed Hastings may have used this approach. Both gave exactly three contributions totaling that amount in 2013. The Education Century site is maintained by an organization called Impact for Education, which, according to its website, "engages forward-thinking philanthropists to catalyze systemic change in public education."[28] This provides a potential explanation for the relationship between Education Century and Impact for Education, since individuals like Laurene Powell Jobs are active as both educational philanthropists and campaign contributors. Thus, an organization dedicated to mobilizing activity on both fronts could work with the same individuals in both areas. The president and founder of Impact for Education is Alex Johnston, the cofounder of the Connecticut-based education advocacy organization ConnCAN.

If organizations like this exist to aggregate contributions from multiple donors, perhaps a substantial level of overlap exists in the contributions of strategic national donors across various school board elections. Figure 3.3 displays the thirty strategic national donors as a bipartite network. The donors represent one mode of the network, indicated with lighter circles, and the candidates and committees that received their contributions represent the other mode, indicated with darker circles. The candidates and committees are labeled only if they received funds from more than one strategic national donor.

The strategic national donors are entirely connected to one another; they all supported at least one candidate or committee in an election that is also supported by another strategic national donor. A few candidates in particular were supported by a large number of donors (shown by their central position in the network), including two who were mentioned earlier in the chapter—Sarah Newell Usdin (New Orleans) and Caitlin Hannon (Indianapolis). Usdin received funding from twenty-six out of the thirty strategic national donors. A set of candidates based in Denver—Landri Taylor, Rosemary Rodriguez, Barbara O'Brien, and Mike Johnson—also received contributions from twelve or more strategic national donors.

Our findings show how dozens of major national donors can be mobilized to support campaigns in distinct and widespread local school districts. In particular, affiliations through education organizations are significantly associated with school board campaign contributions. The significance of this indicator of membership as a key predictor of school board contributions suggests the emergence of a durable "education donor" social network that will influence future election cycles. These donors are not isolated individuals, and a highly active core group of donors is capable of sharing information and mobilizing others through their connections to educational organizations and charter school boards. Yet it is important to recognize that these elite national donors are not the largest source of individual

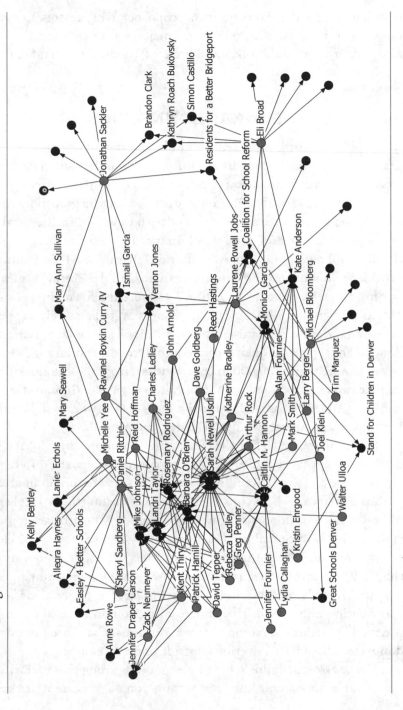

FIGURE 3.3 Strategic national donor network

contributions for the vast majority of school board candidates. In many cases, these national donors are one major source of contributions alongside a more traditional backbone of funding for candidates—local donors.

THE LOCAL CONNECTION

Although the contribution behavior of large national donors tends to draw more scrutiny and media attention, many of the candidates who receive these funds are also recipients of significant resources from local donors. We identified 847 individual donors who gave more than $1,000 in a school board electoral cycle who live within the locality or metropolitan area of the school district holding the election. Of the $2.3 million in campaign contributions that these 847 individuals provided to candidates and committees across all the election cycles in our five cities, 81 percent of the funds supported reform-aligned candidates and groups. Thus, local elite donors overwhelmingly support the same reform candidates and organizations as the large national donors. The top six candidate recipients of local elite donor funds each received more than $100,000 in contributions from these donors; they include two reform-aligned candidates in Los Angeles (Monica Garcia and Kate Anderson) as well as four in Denver (Mary Seawell, Jennifer Draper Carson, Allegra "Happy" Haynes, and Anne Rowe).

Furthermore, much like the large national donors, these local elite donors also appear to make overlapping contributions; the difference is that these clusters are confined within distinct metropolitan areas, as shown in figure 3.4. To construct figure 3.4, we limited the local and metropolitan area donors to a highly elite group—the fifty-seven individuals who have contributed at least $10,000 to school board elections in our data (excluding four candidates who contributed more than $10,000, mostly to support their own school board campaigns). We have records of these individuals (unlike the national donors) contributing only within their home metropolitan area; however, it is entirely possible that some of these individuals have been national donors to school board elections outside of our five cases.

The network in figure 3.4 is single mode, meaning that each circle represents a donor, and lines connecting donors indicate that those

FIGURE 3.4   **Local elite donor networks**

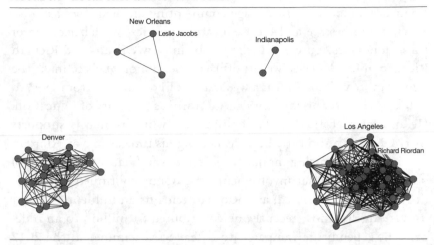

individuals supported at least one candidate or committee in common. As figure 3.4 clearly demonstrates, all of the local elite donors in four of our election sites—Denver, New Orleans, Indianapolis, and Los Angeles—are supporting similar sets of candidates and committees as other local elite donors. Not surprisingly, the largest cities (Denver and Los Angeles) also have the largest clusters of local elite donors. Bridgeport is not represented because no donors within the local or metropolitan area contributed enough to meet the $10,000 threshold.

A few interesting patterns of contributing behavior do emerge from examining the identities of the donors. First, some clustering occurs within certain zip codes of elite donors. For instance, four elite Denver donors live in the suburban Denver zip code of 80113, which includes the community of Cherry Hills Village, recently named the "second richest city in the U.S.," according to Mansion Global website.[29] Based on employment information provided in the campaign donation disclosures, these individuals are mostly local business elites, including the president of a financial investment firm, the wife of a health-care company executive, and the chairman of a local construction company. In Los Angeles, donors are clustered in wealthy zip codes on the west side of the city, as well as Beverly Hills (including the well-known 90210 zip code). In addition to this geographic clustering, some elite donors are recognizable as figures mentioned frequently in local news coverage commenting on their roles as influencers in both state and local education politics. We labeled two of these donors in figure 3.4: Leslie Jacobs in New Orleans and Richard Riordan in Los Angeles (we left off the other donor labels to make the figures more visible). Riordan was mayor of Los Angeles from 1993 to 2001, and he later briefly served as California's Secretary of Education. He also founded the Riordan Foundation, which primarily supports K–12 education and early literacy. During his time as mayor, Riordan was involved in raising money for slates of candidates for the school board.[30] His personal involvement as a donor continued well after his mayoral career ended, and Riordan remains an influential donor in Los Angeles. Most recently, he contributed $1 million to an independent expenditure campaign to defeat Steve Zimmer in the 2017 Los Angeles school board election.[31] In New Orleans, Leslie Jacobs is well known and frequently cited for her influence in education; one recent article called her the "godmother of the local charter school movement."[32] She's also been called the "bulldog of education," and she was "instrumental in passing the Louisiana constitutional amendment that created the Recovery School District."[33] Jacobs, who worked as an insurance executive, is a New Orleans native who has served on the Orleans Parish Board as well as the Louisiana State Board of Elementary and Secondary Education. In 2008, she started a New Orleans education reform nonprofit organization called Educate Now! As the Riordan and Jacobs examples demonstrate, local political influentials sometimes find ways to extend their political influence beyond the formal boundaries of office holding and into the more informal realm of donor mobilization.

Overall, the importance of elite donors within the local and metropolitan area shows that national donors are not acting alone to bankroll reform candidates for school boards. Their funding comes alongside a substantial investment of resources from donors locally, and many of these donors are highly active. Some, like Jacobs and Riordan, are clearly invested in educational policy and politics broadly, including their own political careers. Others seem to fall in the more traditional donor category of wealthy members of the business community who are willing to provide large sums to local candidates. The combined behaviors of both sets of donors suggests that reform candidates and organizations are able to draw from a local-national alliance of elite donors. In other words, the nationalization of school board elections through donors appears to be closely linked with local elite mobilization.

DOES MONEY MATTER?

School board elections have become much more expensive in some places, and national donors are playing a role by injecting significant resources. Our research suggests that many of these donors are motivated by their high level of engagement in politics more broadly as well as their specific interests in education, often through affiliations with education reform-aligned organizations. Furthermore, national donor resources supplement substantial amounts of campaign contributions provided by local elites for many reform-aligned candidates and organizations.

A more challenging question for any study of money in politics is this: does money matter? Do these donors gain outsized representation for their views? Can they influence the outcome of school board elections with money alone? Do candidates feel beholden to outside donors? We later attempt to explore some of these questions of consequences, though we acknowledge that causal links are difficult to establish. One initial way to explore these consequences is by considering the policy preferences of the donors. Scholars have discussed the notion of surrogate representation—that donors who live outside of an electoral district could gain representation through their financial contributions.[34] Recent research on members of Congress provides some evidence that surrogate representation—through donations—can impact the policy positions of representatives. Members of Congress with greater dependence on out-of-district contributions tend to be more extreme as either liberals or conservatives and further from the ideological preferences of their district residents.[35]

In the context of school board elections, the role of large national donors raises the question of whether or not these donors prefer educational policies that are out of step with the preferences of the voters in the local school district. We do not have a direct way to test this proposition. Prior research does suggest, though, that very wealthy individuals hold attitudes about education that differ somewhat from the general public. Gilens finds several divergences in the policy preferences of the wealthy and the general public where the wealthy favor market-based solutions to policy problems. For example, Gilens shows that "school vouchers, which would help parents pay for private-school education, were opposed by the poor and favored by the affluent."[36]

Focusing on a wealthier population, Page, Bartels, and Seawright's survey of the top 1 percent of earners compares the views of the super-wealthy to the general public on several aspects of education policy. Their findings fit the pattern of greater support for market-oriented reforms among the rich. The authors conclude

> Our data suggest that the great enthusiasm of wealthy Americans for improving the US educational system mostly focuses on improving effectiveness through relatively low budget, market-oriented reforms, not on spending the very large sums of money that might be necessary to provide high quality public schools, college scholarships, or worker retraining for all Americans.[37]

Thus, we have reason to consider the possibility that candidates supported by large national donors have divergent or distinct preferences compared to the local district public they seek to represent.

CONCLUSION

A simple assumption that national elite donors are taking over school board elections and bulldozing local politics is not supported by our data. The reality is that reform-aligned candidates do receive more money from individual donors across the board, and this includes a large share of local funds. Local elite donors, including many who are wealthy and white, are not representative of the families with children in these urban districts. Nonetheless, critics of teacher unions and their involvement in electoral politics would similarly argue that union preferences can also be contrary to the policy preferences of the broader public and the families of public school children.[38] In other words, it is not likely that the absence of large national donor involvement in local school politics would produce an idealized form of local representative democracy; other types of elites, including local wealthy donors and organizations like unions, are significant power brokers. Yet it is possible that large national donors amplify a more nationalized agenda within local campaigns. As our analysis of individual donors demonstrates, school board elections are no longer buffered from the strategic choices of elite donors who have also contributed to tremendous spending in national elections.

CHAPTER 4

....

Unions Versus Reformers

COMBATANTS IN major political and policy debates typically frame their arguments with appealing ideas and motivating values. They reference ideas like school choice, teacher accountability, mayoral control, standards, professional development, and community schools while linking these to animating values such as "what's good for children," "expanding family options," "taking advantage of expertise," "evidence-based decision-making," and "getting more bang for the buck." But in American education politics today, many see the real battle as pitting teacher unions against those who see unions as the enemy of needed reform.

The charge that teacher unions are the key enemy of reform has been leveled forcefully by advocates of causes the unions oppose. Calling them the "800-pound gorilla," for example, a source from the conservative Heritage Foundation asserts that "[b]reaking the stranglehold from these unions is the first step toward making long-term, meaningful education reform."[1] AFTFacts.com, a somewhat slyly named anti-union website, charges that the American Federation of Teachers, the nation's second largest teacher union, "militantly opposes the vast majority of credible education reforms," defends incompetent teachers, and is "a political animal, donating millions of dollars to left-wing advocacy and front groups," whose "stock-in-trade is conflict, hostility, and distortion."[2] Some of these charges are markedly ideological and partisan in motivation.[3] But, as we will elaborate, this view also has heft as a scholarly argument, backed by theory and some evidence.

To their critics, the damage that teacher unions do is intimately entwined with the privileged status of localism. "Local control essentially surrenders power over the schools to the teachers' unions," journalist Matt Miller wrote in the provocatively titled article "First, Kill All the School Boards." Low levels of local participation, attention, and institutional competence make districts vulnerable to unions, including national unions that can funnel in money and expertise. "Union money and mobilization are often decisive in board elections," he continued. "And local unions have hefty intellectual and political backing from their state and national affiliates. Even when they're not in the unions' pockets, in other words, school boards are outmatched."[4]

Outside donors that support school choice, accountability, and related strategies for education reform often say they are simply trying to rebalance a scale that has been heavily weighted in favor of teacher unions. "The teachers unions spend $300 million a year on political races," charter advocate Jeanne Allen complained to the *Hollywood Reporter* while criticizing a Matt Damon documentary that she argued presented her as a money-wielding villain while treating AFT leader Randi Weingarten as a hero. "We don't have that kind of money."[5] Democrats for Education Reform (DFER) was formed in 2007, in large part as a counterforce to the perceived overdependence of the Democratic Party on the unions.[6] Appraising its early efforts, one education reformer made the case that, as important as the effort might be, it was still overmatched by the dominating unions: the teacher unions were "printing money and DFER is doing cocktail parties."[7]

Critics of the efforts by national reformers to influence local elections argue that something else is going on. They portray these approaches to school reform as elements in a broad strategy of privatization: a strategy that targets public employee unions less because of the specific education reforms they support or oppose than because those unions are a last bastion of organizational muscle supporting extensive governmental involvement in addressing social problems. They charge that, rather than champions of children and the public good, the deep-pocketed financial supporters of the so-called education reform movement are pursuing their own economic, ideological, and partisan interests. Rather than the most powerful actor, they see teacher unions as David confronting a Goliath comprising a nexus of billionaire donors, pro-market foundations, right-leaning think tanks, profit-seeking corporations, and Republican tacticians.[8] From this perspective, the battle within the education sector is just one front in a larger political battle in which weakening public sector unions is in itself a motivating force.[9]

Advocates on both sides of this issue tend to offer single-actor narratives about power in education politics. Either teacher unions *or* reformers are the Goliath, with other stakeholders marginalized or in relatively minor supporting roles. While qualitative case studies portray a much more complicated multiactor game, almost no quantitative studies directly juxtapose unions and reformers to examine how they compete, who punches and who counterpunches, and how they measure up against one another in the resources they bring to play. In addition, both sides in this debate ignore or offer overly simplistic portrayals of the intergovernmental politics around the teacher union versus reformer battle for influence. Critics of teacher unions typically discuss union power as a local phenomenon in which the absence of mobilized challengers allows unions to substitute their interests for those of children and the community at large. Critics of national reformers typically present them as moneyed and muscled interlopers, able to overwhelm local voices and impose an agenda from the outside. Missing are portraits of how both reformers and teacher unions may reflect and connect with those of local organizations and individual donors.

This chapter begins by further detailing the two clashing perspectives that currently dominate discussions of the role of interest groups in local education politics. Taken alone, each offers a narrative that overstates the extent to which power is dominated by a single actor. Stitched together, they offer a two-actor story that leaves unexplored the motivation and influence of many other organizations that get involved in local school-related campaigns. Whether taken alone or stitched together, both encourage a narrative focused on one level of our federal system, with the main action being either in local arenas that favor unions or national arenas dominated by wealthy donors and the reform organizations they support.

Following reviews of these perspectives and their limitations, we turn to an empirical analysis of organizational donations to school elections across our five cities. We have already shown that wealthy outside individual donors do get involved in local campaigns, contribute money far disproportionate to their numbers, and seemingly act with some coordination to focus their attention on particular races. In this chapter we focus on organizations rather than individual donors. In this arena teacher unions have historically been seen as the dominant actor, but we will show that the organizational landscape is more complicated than that. When local elections get on the radar screen of national attention, teacher unions face off against an array of reform groups that match or exceed them in spending and that have some tactical advantages in their ability to pick and choose campaigns with which to get involved. The unions are no pushovers: they have deep pockets also, they are more or less equally attuned to the tactical questions of when and how to spend, and the candidates they back win as often as they lose. In addition to wealthy individuals from outside the community, the political landscape includes groups that are not irrevocably in either the teacher union or reform camp, and the degree and direction to which these groups mobilize can also play important roles. Rather than two behemoths slugging it out head to head, the story that emerges is one of building and mobilizing coalitions across levels of government leading us toward a more complete and more dynamic lens for understanding the ebbs and flows of education politics today.

CLASHING PERSPECTIVES

Unions as Powerful Veto Points

Coincident with—and related to—the relative decline in the centrality of local school districts has been the dissemination of a strong critique of teacher unions. Political scientist Terry Moe has been the most influential articulator of the version of the "unions are the problem" perspective. Moe argues that teacher unions are "the most powerful groups in the politics of education. No other groups have even been in the same ballpark."[10]

Moe's influence is due, in large measure, to his ability to interlace established theory about political institutions and interest groups with original empirical work. Moe starts with principal agent theory, which in turn begins with the assumption that rational agents of various kinds—from the person you might hire to help you sell your house to the bureaucracy the legislature relies on to enforce its laws and regulations—have the incentive to substitute their interests for those they nominally work for. Not only do they have the incentive, but their superior supply of information about the work they do (or don't do) gives them the power to substitute their interests for those of their nominal bosses and to avoid or repel efforts to hold them accountable. Principal agent theory has been applied and tested in a wide range of contexts from the behavior of for-profit firms, to nonprofits, to government, and from education to health care to science policy. While controversies about its universality and accuracy certainly exist, many scholars and policy analysts find it can generate useful insights in at least some contexts at least some of the time.[11]

Teachers also are a kind of super-agent, Moe suggests, with an additional form of power that other agents typically lack. This additional power stems from their role as political actors who can affect who gets elected to school boards and other positions of governmental authority.

> Since the unions first got established, they have had millions of members . . . astounding sums of money coming in regularly (mainly from dues) for campaign contributions and lobbying . . . well-educated activists manning the electoral trenches—ringing doorbells, making phone calls. They have been able to orchestrate well-financed media campaigns on any topic or candidate. And their organizations have blanketed the nation, allowing them to coordinate all these resources toward their political ends.[12]

Moe and others present evidence that unions use this power to block initiatives that infringe upon the well-being of their adult members, even when those initiatives would benefit the children they are meant to serve.[13] Among the things that unions typically and strongly resist are charter schools (because charters often do not have unions and might draw funding away from traditional public schools), test-based accountability (especially when applied to evaluate, reward, or punish individual teachers), school closures, differential salaries, and efforts to forcefully reassign teachers to high-need schools.

Moe believes teachers are powerful at all levels of government, but his argument is especially strong when applied at the local district level. Using data on California school districts, Moe has demonstrated that teacher union support is a powerful predictor of who gets elected to school boards; candidates' chances of winning increase by 47 percent if they are incumbents, by 56 percent if they get union support, and by 76 percent if they are incumbents who also have union support.[14] It is not, however, the symbolism of the endorsement that matters so much as it is the support that comes along with it, in the form of campaign contributions, teachers' votes, and teachers' willingness to do the work of placing campaign signs, making calls, canvassing door to door, and getting supporters to the polls. Here it matters, Moe finds, whether teachers have the kind of direct interest that comes from actually living in the district in which they work. In the seven school districts he examined, teachers who lived in the districts were two to seven times more likely to vote in school board elections or school bond measures than other citizens were. Rather than an abstract appreciation for public education or a political allegiance to the union and its leaders, Moe's analysis suggested that teacher involvement primarily was driven by a direct personal interest in the policies school board members would determine. The evidence to support this was the finding that teachers who worked but did not live in the district voted at lower rates than the teachers who both lived and worked there, in some instances by wide margins. For this and other reasons, Moe speculates that, as a rule, it may be that "the power of public sector unions tends to be greater the lower the level of government. For as governments in the United States get closer to where the bureaucrats in those governments live, the numbers and resources of bureaucrats become more politically effective and their interests more coherent."[15]

Moe's analysis allows for some nuance and complication. For example, he acknowledges that teacher unions do not win on all issues and that they have been suffering more defeats in recent years. He thinks unions have less leverage at the state and national level than locally, and less ability to promote policy changes they favor than to block those they oppose. He acknowledges that other interest groups give substantial amounts of campaign funds, although he emphasizes that those other organizations have a broad range of agenda items extending beyond education while teacher unions can be more focused and effective as a result.

Bows to nuance aside, however, Moe's basic argument is clear: when it comes to local education politics, unions are operating on a different level than other local actors. Their resources and focused commitment allow them to outmuscle any challengers and usually are sufficiently intimidating that potential challengers decide that taking them on is not even worth the effort. Teacher unions use that power to promote the interests of their members and do so even when their members' interests run counter to those of the public and the children in their classrooms.

Reformers as Powerful Privatizers and Interlopers

Critics of the national school reform movement tell a different story. Rather than the most powerful actor, they see teacher unions as David confronting a well-financed right-leaning Goliath. Where principal agent theory presents teachers and their unions as motivated by material self-interest, they argue that educators know the most about instruction and learning and have the fullest understanding of the developmental needs and varying learning styles of the nation's young people. If unions are often on the winning side of elections, they argue the reason is that voters respect their expertise and because the unions speak to issues that the public cares about. It is the so-called reformers, they argue, who are putting the public good at risk by pursuing their own interests; rather than champions of children and the public good, the deep-pocketed financial supporters of the so-called education reform movement are attending to their own economic, ideological, and partisan concerns.

If Terry Moe stands as the foremost academic critic of teacher unions, Diane Ravitch arguably stands as the most well-known and influential voice on the other side of the battle. Ravitch is an education historian who also served as an assistant secretary of education under

President George H. W. Bush. She was at one time a champion of standards-based accountability, testing, and school choice but has come to see these as at best misguided, and often little more than weapons in a cynical effort by private profiteers to access the roughly $650 billion in public money that supports K–12 education and roughly $160 billion for higher education.[16] In 2017, according to one assessment, Ravitch was ranked the most influential person or organization in social media visibility and impact.[17]

There exist both restrained and sweeping versions of the critique of the education reform movement. The restrained version portrays reformers as technocratic, impatient, misguided, and yet holding unwarranted confidence in their own vision and capacity. According to this view, contemporary education reformers are the heirs to the Progressive movement of the early twentieth century. The Progressive reformers denigrated the urban politics of the day, attacking big city machines for putting political party, patronage, and their own control of power above the common good. "There is no Democratic or Republican way to pave a street" was a slogan of the time, with the implication that there was instead an objectively correct way, best determined via technical and scientific expertise. Like their predecessors, critics argue, today's education reformers see themselves as champions of data and evidence locked in battle against entrenched defenders of the status quo. Whereas the historical progressives portrayed professionalism and bureaucracy as the solution to the problem of politics, however, the contemporary reformers see professional educators and district administrators as the problem and place their bets, instead, on strong executive management, strict accountability, technological innovations, and relentless focus on improving measured outcomes. Among the problems with the reformers' efforts, four stand out according to this critique. First, in their readiness to portray teachers as defenders of the status quo, reformers needlessly cut themselves off from valuable information about learning, instruction, and the complexity of serving student populations with complex and heterogeneous needs. Second, in their zealous insistence that the crisis of poor and unequal education leaves no time to spare, reformers have been willing to bypass the slow but ultimately critical process of building grassroots support. Third, in promoting the idea that better schooling will close education achievement gaps, reformers have dismissed the role of broader, nonschool forces such as concentrated poverty, poor health care, institutionalized racism, and attenuated social welfare programs. Finally, despite their self-confidence, more than two decades of the ascendancy of their reform agenda has produced only spotty, limited, and contested evidence that performance is being improved.

The more sweeping critique accuses education reformers of complicity in a broad assault on traditional institutions of public sector capacity and democratic control. While conceding that many education reformers are well intentioned, Ravitch has characterized the movement as a "reign of error," a "hoax," and a "danger to America's public schools."[18] According to this perspective, the real drivers of the reform movement are a combination of profit-motivated corporations and investors, and ideologically motivated philanthropists and foundations, amplified by think tanks and advocacy groups that they initiated and sustain with their dollars.[19] Rather than a toolbox of discrete proposals for improving education, these critics see reform proposals for charter schools, vouchers, test-based accountability, portfolio-management models, modifications of tenure, and school closures as complementary elements of a broad privatization strategy to invest in individual choice, competition, and market-based solutions over strong government anchored in institutions of democratic control. In this formulation, teacher unions serve as the foil less because of their stance on education per se than because the union movement has been a critical ally of liberal Democrats and the growth of the welfare state. From this perspective too, localism stands as an impediment to the momentum that reformers have gained by leveraging their greater political access in state capitals and Washington, DC.

When the Union Versus Reform Discourse Goes National

Thinking, talking, and strategizing about school reform can take different forms at the national and local levels. Both policy needs and political pressures force national actors to a higher level of abstraction. Policy needs force abstraction at the national level because variation in demographics, values, and need across roughly 13,500 school districts makes it impossible to offer solutions tailored to local context. Political pressures encourage reliance on abstractions because partisans and movement leaders at the national level are charged with the task of mobilizing publics—a task that often requires simplifying models rather than reasoned appeals nested in complicated considerations of context and policy detail. In contrast, local actors operate in a more concrete arena in which context, personalities, and parochial idiosyncrasies loom large.[20]

This discrepancy can affect the way people think and act on issues involving teacher unions, reformers, and local school politics. At the local level, perceptions of teachers and their unions are largely driven by the impressions people have formed about specific union leaders and the experiences they and their children have had with real-life teachers. At the national level, key perceptions are shaped by ideas about unionization and public education more generally. This distinction is important because public opinion polls consistently show that Americans are much more positive and trusting toward teachers and schools in their community than they are about teachers and schools nationally. This phenomenon can help explain why the public and political leaders in conservative states like West Virginia, Oklahoma, and Arizona largely rallied to support "their" teachers when they walked out for higher wages in the spring of 2018, while those same citizens and leaders have proved hostile to teacher unionism and especially militant teacher actions as a national phenomenon.[21]

In a similar fashion, local perceptions of reform initiatives such as charter schools can hinge on the particular attributes of charter providers in a community. "The primary difference between national and local elections," Eric Oliver writes, "is that while the former are highly ideological, the latter are managerial in character."[22] Consistent with this, Henig and Stone observe: "At the national level, the debate about charter schools is framed in terms of markets versus government or perhaps professional educators versus parents and communities. . . . Framed thus, the stakes are extraordinarily high."[23] The charter school issue is less freighted when left to unfold on its own terms in specific school districts and communities.

There, charter schooling is less a symbolic abstraction that stands in opposition to an idea of public education and more a set of specific charter school providers, often with track records and constituencies already in place; there, the traditional public school system is not a stand-in for heroic visions of democracy and the public good but, rather, a familiar institution with a particular history of successes and failures. National debates can acknowledge that local conditions vary, but, to maintain traction, they minimize the same particularities upon which local perceptions and decisions typically hinge.[24]

When drawn into the vortex of national politics, sparring between teacher unions and education reformers may more readily be infused with ideological and partisan polarization rooted in historical clashes over the proper role of government versus private markets. The decline of unions in the private sector has made public employee unions, and especially teacher unions, important foot soldiers and piggy banks for the progressive left. While membership in private sector unions has declined precipitously and now sits at under 7 percent, over one-third of public sector workers are now unionized. Within the public sector, the union membership rate was highest in local government (40.1 percent), in particular among teachers, police officers, and firefighters.[25] Conservative networks of funders and think tanks, it is suggested, intentionally have pushed policies and lawsuits that they know are likely to weaken public sector unions, including right-to-work laws, limitations on collective bargaining, and the ability of public employee unions to charge "agency fees" to nonmembers.[26]

Contributions and Limitations of the Two Standard Models

Each of the two standard portrayals—the one emphasizing unions as the dominant and dysfunctional force and the one emphasizing reformers as powerful and problematic—illuminates some important elements of the politics of education. Both, appropriately, remind us that organized interests can be more influential than atomistic donors and voters, by virtue of their more sustained focus and greater capacity to mobilize and target resources strategically. As Moe and others underscore, teacher unions have been disproportionately powerful, especially in the historical environment of localized, low-turnout elections. As Ravitch and others point out, over the past two decades private for-profit and nonprofit firms, foundations, ideological and partisan advocates, and deep-pocketed donors have become more active and influential in setting the terms of the national education reform debate.

On their own, the standard models each have serious limitations, and the dichotomous and polarized debate between them has obscured as much as it has illuminated. Advocates on both sides of this issue tend to offer single-actor narratives about power in education politics, each with implications about where the politics of education should (or should not) take place. Critics of the teacher unions generally emphasize the local arena, where they think unions are especially strong. Critics of the reformers generally emphasize national politics, where they think corporations, national foundations, and billionaire philanthropists rule the roost. While proponents of both perspectives generally recognize that the politics of education occurs at the national, state, and local levels, they do not have fully developed theories about how the groups act tactically and strategically across the levels. Both models presume that unions and reformers are rational, tactical, and strategic—that they have goals they seek to maximize, that they act opportunistically to take advantage of favorable openings for influence, and that they strategize about how to allocate their resources and energies with a long-term perspective in mind. Yet media and popular accounts describe battles in which leaders' personalities and ambitions loom large, cleavage lines are infused with racial overtones, and short-term objectives swamp long-term ones. Neither provides a fully realized account of how rational interest-based strategies and emotional appeals for mobilization converge. Finally, most of the rigorous studies still focus on *either* the unions *or* reformers with few keeping both in the picture and almost no studies considering the broader ecology of both individual donors and other organizations whose willingness or failure to respond to the appeals of the major combatants may be decisive in determining who wins and who does not.

PATTERNS OF ORGANIZATIONAL CONTRIBUTIONS ACROSS CITIES AND ELECTIONS

Individual donors, particularly large donors and those who contributed to elections outside of the states in which they lived, are an important part of the story of school board politics—but not just the wealthy ones. While most individual donors give only small amounts, donating is a stronger form of political participation than simply voting, and the act of contributing is part of what binds citizens to the democratic system. It is also important to understand organized interest groups like teacher unions and reform groups like DFER and Stand for Children. While fewer in number than individual donors, organizations that channel money into local school elections account for a disproportionate amount of funds: they are more focused in their giving, more fully mobilized to spot tactical openings and move their giving to candidates and places where it can be most effective, and more able to attach their money to strong preferences in terms of policy priorities. Often, too, organizations play a key role in recruiting individual donors, so some proportion of individual contributions are likely following the lead set by organizations.

How Organizational Donors Differ from Out-of-State Individual Donors

One way that organizational donors differ from individual donors is in the scale of their giving. In our data, across the fourteen elections in five cities 14,165 donations were made by individuals, more than three times as many as the 4,524 by organizations.[27] On average, the organizations made contributions that were 125 times as large as those made by the average individual. Individuals gave an average $674 per donation and on average gave $4,771 across elections and cities; each organization gave an average $4,061 per donation and on average gave $598,036 across elections and cities.

Another way that organizational donors differ from individual donors is that it is trickier to distinguish those that are authentically local from those that have local addresses and names but may be helped by or even dominated by larger organizations that operate on a state or national scale. In working with individual donors, we could identify outsiders by simply comparing their home addresses to the district where the election was being held. When we applied that same approach, 58 percent of the organizational contributions originate from organizations within the district, with most of the rest from state-based organizations. For some organizations—especially for the teacher union and reform organizations that are our primary focus—simply looking at the originating address can be misleading.

Locally based union and reform groups often have national roots and support. Local teacher unions may benefit from funding, in-kind contributions, and borrowed expertise from their state and national affiliates. In 2017, for example, the National Education Association gave $1 million to the NEA Advocacy Fund, which in turn gave just under $950,000 to support state and local races, including $600,000 for two school board candidates in Los Angeles (Padillo and Zimmer) and $250,000 for a cluster of candidates in Denver (Every Student Succeeds).[28] The AFT, AFL-CIO Committee on Public Education disbursed over $6 million, but almost exclusively for national elections.[29]

This complicated relationship between national and local organizations applies to reform organizations also. Stand for Children, a major reform organization, was active in Denver, Indianapolis, and New Orleans, for example, but most of its giving was channeled through state affiliates such as Stand for Children–Colorado, Stand for Children–Indiana, and Stand for Children–Louisiana. Overall, reform groups, including those that had local affiliates, received more than $3.2 million from out-of-state individual donors, comprising just under half (48.5 percent) of the donations they received.[30]

Families for Excellent Schools, a reform organization that was for a time extremely powerful in debates about charter schools in New York, provides an interesting case study of how out-of-state money can flow through seemingly localized groups. In 2016, charter proponents initiated a referendum in Massachusetts intended to raise the state's cap on the number of charter schools. Families for Excellent Schools became a favored instrument for funding to support the referendum, channeling the money through a newly established group: Families for Excellent Schools–Advocacy, which in turn passed a little over $15 million to Great Schools Massachusetts. Subsequently, the state's Office of Campaign and Political Finance concluded that Families for Excellent Schools–Advocacy had violated the state's campaign finance law by using this pass-through as an effort to hide the identity of donors that it would have had to provide if it funded the campaign directly. As a result of the violation, the group was fined $426,466, and the state released information about donors that otherwise would have been kept secret. This information revealed the group had raised and spent $20 million for the last six months of 2016. While many of the donors were Massachusetts residents, the list included fourteen separate donations from New York City–based organizations (likely channeling money from other donors especially in NYC), totaling just under $2.5 million. Also on the list were out-of-state individual donors, including Doris Fisher and her son John, major donors to KIPP charter schools ($500,000); Jonathan Sackler, whose wealth comes from the pharmaceutical industry, and who has provided support and leadership to the Achievement First charter school network; the New Schools Venture Fund, 50CAN, a national school reform advocacy group, and Students for Education Reform ($70,000); and Alice Walton, an heir to the Walton family fortune and a donor to multiple pro-charter causes around the nation ($750,000).[31]

Although we have collected information on secondary donations and will draw on those selectively, we cannot be confident in our ability to trace all organizational donations to their ultimate source. Thus, in this chapter, we will focus on union and reform organizations—and their allies—regardless of whether their donations came from a local or outside address.

Which Organizations Get Involved, and How Active Are They?

Conventional portrayals feature either the unions or reformers as dominant actors. Combining them gives us a two-actor story, as if the future of education is being battled out by two muscle-bound boxers trading punches in an otherwise empty ring. But education increasingly is a multiactor game. Moe acknowledges that organizations other than teacher unions are sometimes involved in education politics, but he emphasizes that such organizations typically are not focused on education alone, as teacher unions are, and therefore must spread their money and attention across a wider range of issues and campaigns. Looking at the top twenty-five all-time donors in federal elections, he concludes that, other than the NEA and AFT, not one of the other large donors "has a special interest in education. There is no group representing parents. No group representing taxpayers. Not even a group representing administrators or school boards. . . . *As education interest groups, the unions are in a league of their own*" (emphasis in the original).[32]

Things look quite different when you zero in on local school board elections with a national profile. Table 4.1 shows the different kinds of organizations and the number and average size of their contributions to school board elections in our five cases. Organizations were labeled as "reform" if their platform or mission included goals aligned with the Obama administration's Race to the Top program. RTTT provides a useful heuristic for identifying the core agenda items favored by educational reformers; scholars have noted the close association between the program and the educational reform movement.[33] Policies aligned with RTTT include expanding charter schools/innovative schools, using student data in teacher evaluation, using teacher retention policies such as merit pay and career ladders, employing data systems and

TABLE 4.1
Organizational donors by type and activity

	NUMBER OF SEPARATE CONTRIBUTIONS	PERCENT OF CONTRIBUTIONS
Teacher union	1,599	35.3%
Reform	939	20.8%
Misc. business/nonprofit	834	18.4%
Other union	716	15.8%
Political parties	224	5.0%
Other	88	2.0%
PACs	53	1.2%
Candidate committee	52	1.2%
Trade association	19	0.4%
Total	4,524	100.1%

(*continued*)

accountability, turning around the lowest performing schools, and adopting Common Core Standards. For the most part, we look at all organizational activity without distinguishing between those that are formally inside or outside of the districts and states.

Let's begin by comparing the two types of organizations—unions and reform groups—that are the primary focus of our concern. Among other things, table 4.1 highlights the importance of distinguishing between simple activity (the number of donations) and the amount of money contributed. Some organizations—and some broad types of organizations—make much smaller contributions than others. Measured simply by the number of donations made, teacher unions are indeed major actors, but they are far from alone. Teacher unions account for just under 36 percent of all organizational donations, the largest share, and they made 1.7 contributions for every one made by reform groups. Reform organizations also are active; at 21 percent, they are the second most active type of organizational donor. Reform organizations, moreover, tend to make substantially larger contributions, and they give more in total as a result. The average contribution per donation by reform groups was 2.6 times as large as those by teacher unions. Overall, reform groups in our database provided $2.5 million more than did teacher unions.

TABLE 4.1 (*continued*)
Organizational donors by type and activity

AVERAGE CONTRIBUTION AMOUNT	TOTAL CONTRIBUTED	PERCENT OF TOTAL AMOUNT
$2,890	$4,621,110	25.2%
$7,595	$7,131,705	38.8%
$1,535	$1,280,190	7.0%
$6,822	$4,884,552	26.6%
$678	$151,872	0.8%
$1,672	$147,136	0.8%
$1,746	$92,538	0.5%
$933	$48,516	0.3%
$603	$11,457	0.1%
$4,061	$18,371,964	100.0%

Nonteacher unions are also active donors. They include public employee unions but also trade unions that provide services or work in school construction and rehabilitation. It's easy to imagine that these unions work in concert with teacher unions; after all, unions share common interests in a range of issues such as promoting higher minimum wages and opposing right-to-work laws. If one assumes that's the case, it is tempting to simply add the dollars contributed by other unions to those contributed by teacher unions. Looked at that way, it would seem as though unions and reform organizations are fairly evenly matched with unions holding the edge ($9.5 million to $7.1 million for reform organizations). Yet, as we will see, the assumption that other unions universally ally with the teacher unions does not hold.

The other types of organizations included in table 4.1 do not contribute as much individually, but that does not mean they should be ignored. The category labeled "Misc. business/nonprofit," for example, includes a large number of law firms, architects, real estate developers, builders, banks, public relations firms, graphic designers, and the like. This category also includes some nonprofit organizations, like hospitals. While many of these are making small donations, they can be important representatives of the local civic community. Of course, many may also have a direct stake in the local district because they do contract work, for example, related to building or rehabilitating school facilities. In some instances, the amounts given by these businesses and nonprofits are far from trivial. In Bridgeport, for example, eight of these types of organizations gave donations of $10,000 or more to support the reform-backed referendum for mayoral control of the schools. This category included two banks and two medical centers, but also Bridgeport and Port Jefferson Steamboat Company ($14,000), Harbor Yard Sports & Entertainment LLC ($14,443), and The United Illuminating Company ($10,000). In Denver, it included Oakwood Homes LLC, which gave $15,000 to Great Schools Denver. In California, where much bigger sums of money are in play, Zenith Insurance Company gave three separate donations to a reform candidate slate in 2011 adding up to $100,000, as did The Anschutz Corporation, a large investment company headquartered in Colorado. News America Marketing, headquartered in New York City but with an office also in Los Angeles, gave three contributions totaling $250,000 to a different reform slate in 2013.

The PACs represented in the table include at least one in every city, but they are relatively minor actors (PACs that are more directly associated with unions or reform organizations are included in those categories). The exception is Indianapolis, where the Chamber of Commerce is a major donor through its own PAC. Political party donors, similarly, are relatively minor actors overall, with a major exception being the Working Families Party in Bridgeport.

While teacher unions and reform organizations are the primary focus in the national debate, and while they are indeed the most important actors across the cases we consider, other types of organizations are important in specific elections and as representatives of an underappreciated part of local civic capacity. They also are important as allies and amplifiers of unions and reformers. It matters, therefore, whether they primarily ally with the teacher unions or with reformers or whether they divide their allegiance evenly.

What Kinds of Candidates Do Organizations Support?

Table 4.2 shows how the various types of organizations targeted their giving among candidates who were generally aligned with the teacher union, aligned with reformers, or not categorizable. This categorization of the candidates is inductively based on which candidates the teacher unions and reform organizations supported. Candidates disproportionately supported by the teacher union, with minimal or no reformer support, are assumed to represent the teacher union priorities. Those disproportionately supported by reform organizations are assumed to represent the reform agenda. Just under 8 percent of organizational contributions went to candidates who could not be categorized, either because they received little funding by either teacher unions or reformers or because both types of organizations supported them.

Reform-backed candidates took in almost $3 million more from organizational donors than those that were predominantly backed by teacher unions: capturing 46.9 percent of the dollars versus 30.7 percent for teacher union–backed candidates and 22.5 percent for candidates who could not be categorized.[34] The biggest surprise provided by

TABLE 4.2

Organization contributions by candidates' stance

	TEACHER	REFORM	NOT CATEGORIZED
Teacher union	$4,363,920	$6,828	$250,803
Reform	$681,492	$5,698,280	$752,424
Other union	$382,976	$2,206,114	$2,295,302
Misc. business/ nonprofit	$71,824	$475,116	$733,248
Other	$70,016	$24,651	$52,486
Political party	$41,184	$74,240	$36,531
Candidate committee	$10,348	$34,290	$3,897
Trade association	$6,696	$4,753	$0
PAC	$3,000	$87,240	$2,272
Total	$5,632,384	$8,611,968	$4,126,896

the table is that nonteacher unions actually gave more contributions to candidates supported by reformers (55.6 percent) than they did to those supported by teacher unions (35.8 percent). This is not attributable to them giving larger donations to teacher union–supported candidates; indeed, on average, their contributions to reform candidates were substantially larger, averaging $5,543 versus $1,496. This counterintuitive finding is driven largely by several high-profile elections in Los Angeles, where two things came into play. First, some nonteacher unions split with others and provided donations to candidates aligned with reformers. Second, nonteacher unions gave heavily to a few candidates in high-profile campaigns who attracted enough support from both teacher unions and reform groups that they fall into our "not categorizable" group.

Businesses and nonprofits also were much more likely to support reform rather than teacher-backed candidates, as were PACs, which in our data are all business related. Political parties gave more frequently to candidates aligned with the teacher unions, but here again the matter looks different when you consider the size of donations.

What is clear overall is that the landscape of organizational involvement in local school elections is more diverse and evenly balanced than implied in the literature. Moe is right that teacher unions are major actors. Ravitch is right that reform groups are major actors, and this is especially the case when one considers the extent to which major individual donors lean toward the reformers. If public unions consistently supported teacher unions, the organizational balance of power would be relatively even, but that turns out not to be the case. The organizational landscape in general is much more diverse than even a two-actor model suggests.

Tactical Targeting Versus Playing for Ongoing Access

While both teacher unions and reform organizations are working with large pots of resources, they are not necessarily playing the same game. Reform organizations appear to be free to be more tactical in targeting their funds to a smaller number of races and a smaller number of candidates chosen to maximize their chance to capture seats and create or defend reform-oriented majorities. Teacher unions are also strategic, but because they have a range of bargaining and other interests that are ongoing, they need to worry more about long-term access to local board members. As a result, they may need to devote some of their resources to supporting incumbents in safe seats and newcomers who may not be facing strong challengers.

Interviews we conducted with high-level officials in the national reform and union camps make clear, nonetheless, that both types of organizations self-consciously consider their opponents' actions as they selectively and strategically allocate funds to elections across the national map. As one leader in the national reform movement explained, organizations like Democrats for Education Reform "are doing one-on-one meetings with philanthropists and making the case that they ought to have a certain percentage of their overall giving be going toward the political activity." Even when these donors are tremendously wealthy, they are highly attuned to making sure that they are getting a good bang for their buck. Many of the funders at DFER are "investors, hedge fund managers, so they looked at the world in terms of some losses here, some wins there, they hope you have more wins down the road. They're willing to make some risky bets 'cause for them those are the ones that are fun and they pay off but they don't get depressed if they don't." But others "like a lot of data. They're looking for me to assess risk and they can afford it, but they don't wanna put themselves in risky situations." As this leader at DFER went on to explain:

> We tried to be able to tell a story to donors, that you're not just supporting a candidate for a school board election in Denver; you are helping to keep a national narrative moving forward. And certainly, when you're raising money for these kinds of races, *if you can point to the likelihood that the teachers union or somebody else will be spending a lot of money on the other side, it amps up the pitch a little bit. It gets the adrenaline flowing for the donor.* (emphasis added)

Speaking about counterparts in the teacher union, this reform leader observed that "their money is not infinite, so they've gotta make smart investments themselves," and added:

> They're doing polling in the same places that we're doing polling. And in the same way that we used the threat from a union investment in a race as a way to raise money, they do the same thing to justify. They'll get money over there and they'll say, "Look, Eli Broad is gonna be putting in a half million dollars in this race, we can't let him go unmatched."[35]

A top national organizer on the union side provided a similar story, although one that even more emphatically presented the union as having been drawn reluctantly into a fight the other side had initiated. According to this person, the union had not been involved in local school board races until around 2012 when a couple of high-profile elections in which national reformers made huge investments forced them to sit up and take notice.

> We saw in Douglas County [Colorado] in one election, the very next day or within a few short days of the new school board coming in, seventy-five years of labor management cooperation that was unparalleled in most quarters of the country, which was a really great relationship and decades of high-quality professional development that our union members provided each other, wiped away. . . . And it was a real reality check like, "Oh! These guys are

not messing around." They're not just sinking tons of money into the federal elections.[36]

Significantly, both the reform and union strategists emphasized that other concerns, including national elections for nonschool offices, constrained them in terms of how much they could invest in local politics generally and school board elections more specifically. Both felt the other had advantages they did not. Viewed from the reform side, the teacher unions have the advantage of being "able to play what they know is gonna be long game." As this reform leader put it:

> Every time we raise a lot of money on the reform side, you sort of have this feeling that this is the last time you're gonna be able to raise that money either because it goes really well and they don't feel like that they need to do it again when this person is up for re-election in a couple years, or it goes so horribly that they're like, "Oh, I'm out." So where the unions, they know they've got a set stream, they can afford to be patient, which I think helps them to be strategic over the long haul.[37]

From the perspective of the union, the short-term tactical approach of the reformers may give them an advantage:

> When they don't come from the community, they pop up and then they shut that down. It's like playing whack-a-mole, right? It was the same ultimately, if you were able to trace back to what the parent funder was, a lot of it is coming from the same sources, but they have different names and they pop up and then they go away, unlike us. . . . Even if we do invest in independent expenditures, at some point you see a clear line to AFT. So we're not popping in and out. We live with and work in these places, so we're there.[38]

Timing

Timing of union and reformer contributions is important for at least two reasons. First, it has the potential to shed light on the conflicting narratives between those portraying unions as the driving and dominant force versus those arguing that it is outside reform groups and wealthy individual donors who are calling the shots. Proponents on both sides tend to present themselves as counterpunchers, mobilizing their resources primarily in response to efforts by "the other side." Second, timing of donations can be important for logistical reasons. By delaying donations, strategic givers may be better able to determine where their giving will be most needed and consequential. "These people don't like giving their money away for the sake of lowering their balances in their bank account," a national reform leader explained. "Potential large donors would ask 'One, is this gonna be a real battle? And two, can they win it?' They wanna know that there's an opponent that they're helping the candidate beat, but they also wanna know that it's remotely winnable."[39] Potential donors often wanted to see late polling numbers before opening their wallets to the full extent.

As indicated in figure 4.1, organizational donors and out-of-state individual donors are much more likely than individual donors to make their contributions in the waning days of the campaign.[40] In the last couple of weeks before the election, fundraising looks completely different than previously, with organizations generally eclipsing individual donors, especially those that live in the state. Teacher unions and reform organizations appear to hold back until fairly late in the election cycle, but this is especially true of the reform groups that dominate in the final two weeks. Just under one in three donations (32.6 percent) by individuals was made more than sixty days before the election, compared to 2 percent for teacher unions, 6 percent for labor, and 5 percent for reform groups. Teacher unions were more likely to give earlier than other union and reform groups: 43 percent of teacher donations were made more than thirty days before the elections versus 23 percent for other unions and 18 percent for reform organizations.

Such tactical lurking makes sense for organizational and out-of-state donors that are trying to be efficient in allocating funds across candidates and elections, but it is not necessarily good from the standpoint of cultivating deliberative democracy at the local level. Late money cannot be used by candidates for patient strategies of meeting with and listening to voters in order to better understand their priorities. It cannot be used for deep voter education about the issues. It cannot be used for the recruitment of local citizens for positions that will give them more exposure to politics and genuinely develop their skills. Instead, it must be turned to short-term media blasts to raise

FIGURE 4.1 **Amount donated by time**

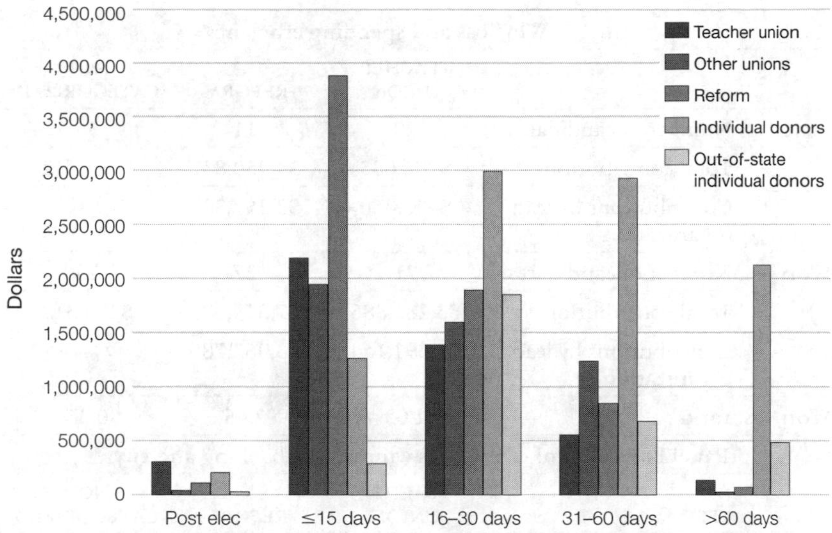

name recognition and brand candidates in simple terms or to fund a last-minute army of get-out-the-vote recruits targeted on potential voters known to be likely supporters. These may be smart strategies for winning votes, but they are not strategies that cultivate the kind of deep engagement needed to sustain strong, public institutions.

Winners, Losers, and Efficient Targeting of Funds

Panel A of table 4.3 summarizes the win/loss record of reform-backed versus teacher union–backed candidates across our cases. Overall, reform-backed candidates have compiled a stronger record, winning about 2.5 times as often as they lose, while teacher union–backed candidates basically break even. Teacher unions, on the other hand, arguably have been more efficient in their use of funds.[41] The row labeled "Contributions by lead organization" refers to the amount specifically donated by teacher unions or reform organizations. Teacher unions spent much less in losing causes ($413,460) than did reform organizations ($2,357,307). Unions spent just 15 percent of their donations on candidates who lost versus 43 percent for reform organizations.

TABLE 4.3
Win/loss record

Panel A: Win/loss and spending efficiency				
		TEACHER UNION	REFORM	NOT CATEGORIZED
Lost	Number of candidates	20	11	36
	Total contributions	$706,685	$4,250,832	$331,712
	Contributions by lead organization	$413,460	$2,357,307	—
Won	Number of candidates	21	27	13
	Total contributions	$3,281,886	$7,314,673	$223,312
	Contributions by lead organization	$2,391,144	$3,063,788	—
Won/lost ratio		1.05	2.45	0.36
Panel B: Percent of candidates winning, by backing and city				
CITY		TEACHER UNION	REFORM	NOT CATEGORIZED
Bridgeport		89%	0%	75%
Denver		30%	70%	17%
Indianapolis		0%	100%	15%
Los Angeles		57%	60%	0%
New Orleans		40%	88%	24%

Exploring the results for candidates who could not be categorized as either teacher or reform backed is interesting as a window into what local school board elections are like when they do not become the focus of national organizational attention. The thirty-six losing uncategorized candidates averaged $9,214 in total donations; the thirteen winners, $17,178. This compared to the average total of $196,887 contributed to candidates backed by either teacher unions or reformers.

Panel B breaks down some of this information by city. Teacher union–backed candidates had their greatest success in Bridgeport, and they have a losing record in Indianapolis. Los Angeles is revealed as a tight battleground with reformer-backed and union-backed candidates winning and losing at relatively similar rates. Reformer-backed candidates usually win in New Orleans and Denver, but union-backed candidates also have some victories in those places. Even in cities touched by nationalization, in other words, local context can have quite a bit to say about how school board elections play out.

Importance of Local Context

Throughout this chapter, we have primarily looked at data aggregated across our multiple cities and elections. This approach helps from the standpoint of capturing broad patterns, but it risks obscuring some important local peculiarities and, when we are discussing total dollars donated, it risks letting a few very high-spending elections overwhelm what happens more typically. The late Congressman Tip O'Neill famously once declared that "all politics is local," and while the thrust of our argument is that this is no longer the case, cities and districts do vary substantially in the rules that govern their elections, in the norms that influence local engagement, in the history and capacity of organizational activity across different types of groups. In this section we review some of the ways our cases differ in terms of the confrontation between teacher unions and reform organizations, the organizational allies they align with, and the scale of the funding that comes into play.

Before looking at our own data, let's consider some national data that help put our cases into context. Figure 4.2 shows the level of union membership from 2000–16 for the United States and each of the states represented by our cases. California and Connecticut have a substantially stronger union presence than is the case nationally. Indiana and Colorado are close to the national average, but union membership in Indiana has been declining rather steadily while it has been increasing slightly in Colorado since 2010. Louisiana has a very low level of union presence, and it has been declining.

Table 4.4 presents information specifically about the states' teacher unions. The rankings of influence on various dimensions were generated by the Fordham Institute, an organization generally skeptical of teacher union influence. Fordham found the teacher unions in California and Connecticut to be the strongest overall, with Louisiana weakest, consistent with the data on overall union strength. When it comes to campaign funding and political influence, however, the five states at times look quite different depending on which particular dimension one considers. The teacher unions in California are

FIGURE 4.2 **Union membership all industries, 2000–2016**

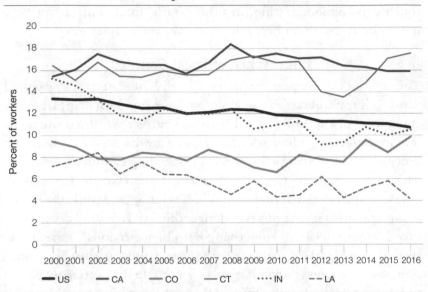

especially highly ranked in their giving to political parties and in their perceived influence on education policy compared to other groups. They are closer to the middle of the pack among states when it comes to campaign giving to state candidates, reflecting the fact that there are other big donors in the state as well. Colorado, in contrast, ranks low in overall union strength (reflecting low membership rates and relatively weak financial strength), but quite high among states in giving to state candidates; their contributions accounted for 2.1 percent of all the funds received by state-level political candidates and "a whopping 25.8 percent of all money donated by the ten highest giving sectors in the state came from teacher unions, the largest such proportion in the country."[42] Indiana is relatively active in giving to state candidates but is low in overall strength and influence on policy, reflecting matters like the state's laws limiting the scope of collective bargaining, teacher employment, and charter schools.

Turning to our own data, which focuses specifically on local school elections, table 4.5 summarizes the amount of organization contributions by city and type of organization. The broad patterns make it

TABLE 1.4
Teacher unions in the five districts

	BRIDGEPORT	DENVER	INDIANAPOLIS	LOS ANGELES	NEW ORLEANS
Local teacher union name	Bridgeport Education Association	Denver Classroom Teachers Association (DCTA)	Indianapolis Education Association	United Teachers Los Angeles (UTLA)	United Teachers of New Orleans
State	Connecticut Education Association (CEA)	Colorado Education Association	Indiana State Teachers Association[a]	California Teachers Association; California Federation of Teachers	Louisiana Federation of Teachers
National	NEA	NEA	NEA	NEA/AFT	AFT
Political involvement and influence of state unions based on Fordham Institute report					
State union overall strength[b]	17th	35th	31st	6th	42nd
By rank, what percentage of the total contributions to state *candidates* was donated by teacher unions?	35th	6th	3rd	21st	45th
By rank, what percentage of the total contributions to state-level political *parties* was donated by teacher unions?	14th	28th	45th	2nd	24th
By rank, what percentage of the contributions to state candidates from the ten highest-giving sectors was donated by teacher unions?	47th	1st	5th	22nd	43rd
How do you rank the influence of teacher unions on education policy compared with other influential entities?	Second- or third-most influential	Second- or third-most influential	Third-most influential	Most or second-most influential	Fourth- or fifth-most influential

Source: http://www.edexcellencemedia.net/publications/2012/2012 1029-How-Strong-Are-US-Teacher-Unions/20121029-Union-Strength-Full-Report.pdf

a: Indiana has two statewide teachers unions. The larger is the Indiana State Teachers Association, which is affiliated with the National Education Association. ISTA has about 40,000 members who belong to 331 local unions. The smaller union is the Indiana Federation of Teachers, affiliated with the American Federation of Teachers. It has about 5,500 members; http://www.chalkbeat.org/posts/in/2013/12/22/the-basics-of-teachers-unions-in-indiana-facing-tough-times/.

b: http://www.edexcellencemedia.net/publications/2012/2012 1029-How-Strong-Are-US-Teacher-Unions/20121029-Union-Strength-Full-Report.pdf

TABLE 4.5

Organization contributions by case city

ORGANIZA-TIONAL TYPE	BRIDGEPORT	DENVER	INDIANAPOLIS	LOS ANGELES	NEW ORLEANS
Teacher union	$450,261	$434,622	$5,001	$3,729,024	$2,500
Reform	$678,468	$315,360	$37,080	$6,082,896	$18,139
Misc. business/ nonprofit	$138,006	$30,448	$300	$991,468	$120,267
Labor union	$6,741	$16,320	$8,400	$4,846,895	$6,000
Political parties	$102,550	$636	$253	$48,576	$0
Other	$6,128	$101,968	$9,594	$24,192	$5,286
PACs	$3,000	$2,000	$76,260	$10,500	$750
Candidate committee	$1,000	$868	$200	$36,120	$10,350
Trade association	$0	$4,200	$0	$7,249	$0
Total	$1,386,165	$906,444	$137,104	$15,776,464	$163,280

clear that local giving is in part a reflection of the states' overall environment for unionization generally and teacher unions specifically. Just as California and Connecticut emerge as strong union states, so do Los Angeles and Bridgeport show the greatest union giving in school-related elections. But, as we saw in the aggregate data, these active teacher unions operate in political ecologies in which reform organizations match or exceed them and other donors are also active.

Two idiosyncrasies are important in understanding the Bridgeport results. The first is the fact that we include the referendum on establishing mayoral control: a referendum that attracted huge outside interest and that was defeated. Over $1 million of the $1.3 million included for Bridgeport was given for that election. Second is the large amount given by a specific and unusual political party: Working Families (WF). Working Families characterizes itself as a "growing progressive political organization that fights for an economy that works for all of us, and a democracy in which every voice matters." The group "recruits, trains and elects leaders who share our mission to local and state office in a growing number of cities and states."[43] It currently has chapters in Connecticut, Maryland, New Jersey, New

York, Oregon, Pennsylvania, and Washington, DC. Although WF does not neatly fit into the union versus education reformer narrative—it is a multi-issue organization that focuses most of its energies on general-purpose elections and labor-related issues such as minimum wage—it has some links to the national union movement and includes battles against "school privatization schemes" among its accomplishments.[44] It also played a major role in working against the Bridgeport referendum to replace the elected school board with a system of mayoral control. Across four campaigns, WF made 155 separate contributions totaling just under $60,000.[45] More than eight of ten of these contributions went to candidates also supported by teacher unions, and none went to candidates supported by reform groups.

Indianapolis is another city with some idiosyncratic variations. There is almost no teacher union presence. The Indiana Political Action Committee for Education (I-PACE), which is associated with the Indiana State Teachers Association, made three donations to three different candidates in 2014. Non-teacher unions, particularly American Federation of State, County, and Municipal Employees (AFSCME), were more active. It is the involvement of the local Chamber of Commerce that especially stands out. The Chamber's PAC gave only one donation of $2,000 in the 2012 school board election, but in 2014, the Chamber (or the Chamber's Business Advocacy Committee) gave just under $30,000—all to candidates supported by national reform groups. In Indianapolis, it was the alignment between the Chamber and wealthy individuals from outside of the state that provided much of the funding contributed for reform-oriented candidates. Large national donors who also gave in Indianapolis include Michael Bloomberg, Charles and Rebecca Ledley, Reid Hoffman, Sheryl Sandberg, Greg Penner, Kent Thiry, Alan and Jennifer Fournier, and Arthur Rock, among others.

Denver stands out as being the only one among our cases in which the teacher unions outspent reform groups. Moreover, most of the donations classified as "Other" in our database came from a small donor committee associated with the Colorado Education Association. More than in the other cases, teacher union giving in Denver had both a local and a state component. Compared to our other cases, Denver's union involvement primarily is from the local rather than state level. Almost $375,000 was given by the Denver Classroom Teachers Association (DCTA). AFT–Colorado gave two contributions of $1,500 apiece in 2009. Delta 4.0, a union-supported 527 organization, was active in 2011. It was funded by both DCTA and the state-wide Colorado Education Association.

Los Angeles stands out as having by far the most money in play. Part of the explanation for this is the district's size; measured in enrollment, it is about 3.5 times as large as the other four districts combined. California is also a strong union state overall; it is home to many of the wealthy individuals who also give to reform candidates in other parts of the country, and LA's high profile makes it an important battleground in education politics. While both the local (UTLA PAC) and state-level teacher unions (both NEA and AFT affiliates) were involved, other unions were especially active. The Service Employee International Union (SEIU) gave almost $2 million through various locals, and AFSCME gave around $180,000, but overall about seventy-five unions contributed.[46] The Los Angeles County Federation of Labor, AFL/CIO gave almost $900,000, but other donors included unions representing plumbers, construction workers, transit workers, police officers, firefighters, nurses, and sheet metal workers.

In New Orleans, organizational giving was minor, both on the union and reform side. The relatively low level of organizational giving in New Orleans is partly a consequence of the fact that the United Teachers of New Orleans, the teacher union, was decimated when all teachers were fired and the local school board largely disempowered in the aftermath of Hurricane Katrina. Outside education reform organizations have been extremely important in New Orleans, but until recently their attention was more at the state than local level and more channeled into developing private networks of school and service providers. The various business and local nonprofits that dominate the organizational giving comprise around 125 separate organizations, by far the bulk of which gave only one time.

Most of the activity summarized in table 4.5 occurred in general elections, but also included are the referendum and a primary in Bridgeport,[47] a recall election in Denver, and a runoff in Los Angeles. Compared to individual donors and other organizations, teacher and reform organizations concentrated more of their resources on these special elections. Among individuals, 88 percent of the donations took place in general elections compared to 76.4 percent for teacher unions and 67.6 percent for reform organizations, likely another indication that organizations are more strategic in focusing on special situations where their dollars are more likely to have an influence.

CONCLUSION

The reality of organizational involvement in funding local school elections is more complicated than either of the two standard models reveals. Teacher unions are not a Goliath that dominates the local landscape unchallenged. While active and still powerful, teacher unions face not only wealthy out-of-state individual donors but also national reform organizations that serve to guide those donors toward races that will matter. While teacher unions can count on other unions—especially public sector unions and those representing service employees in the private sector—for additional support, such other unions do not consistently align with them in their choice of races and candidates, and they sometimes side with reform organizations to support candidates that teacher unions do not.

Nor is it the case that the combination of wealthy out-of-state donors and national reform organizations can count on their deep pockets to have their way. While they do outspend the teacher unions in most of the elections in our sample, unions also have resources to bring to bear, and they win their fair share of head-to-head matchups. The most dramatic example is Bridgeport, where the state union and Working Families Party fought and defeated a well-financed effort to fundamentally reshape public school governance by establishing mayoral control, a structure that both reformers and their opponents expected would have been much more receptive to the reform agenda. Local context and civic infrastructure matter here: the reform groups have had their greater successes in places like Indianapolis and New Orleans where unions generally are weaker; in California and Connecticut, with stronger unions, their victories are costlier and fewer.

It is tempting to view the union versus reformer battle as a case of elephants dancing among the chickens: large and well-resourced national forces transferring their battles from Washington, DC, to local arenas with local leaders and citizens forced to retreat into their coops lest they get trampled in the fight. With the two major national forces facing off against one another, however, it also is possible that the two may cancel each other out. As the national reform leader we quoted earlier put it: "Yeah, sometimes it feels like mutually assured destruction in a way." Where that is the case, the balance of interest and mobilization of local actors may be determinative.

CHAPTER 5

....

The Candidates and Their Campaigns

IN AUGUST OF 2012, Sarah Newell Usdin announced that she would run for the District 3 school board seat in New Orleans. While this announcement marked Usdin's entry into electoral politics, she had been engaged in local school politics as the director of New Schools for New Orleans (NSNO), a nonprofit she founded shortly after Hurricane Katrina. Her entry into the election was, initially, surprising. After all, the Orleans Parish School Board (OPSB) controlled just six traditional public schools and oversaw only twelve charter schools. Usdin, whom *Education Week* called "one of the city's most visible charter school supporters," seemed an unlikely candidate for a traditional school board seat.[1] Despite the fact that the immediate stakes in the school board election seemed rather low, the District 3 race, and Usdin's candidacy in particular, would attract national attention. Usdin's campaign received large outside donations from around the country, amassing a campaign war chest more than three times that of the next largest, which belonged to incumbent Lourdes Moran (District 4), and more than four times that of Brett Bonin, the incumbent Usdin was challenging. These figures were publicized by local and national media, which highlighted not only the amount of funding she had received but also the long list of prominent reform donors who were supporting her bid for a school board seat. "It's not what you expect to see in a local school board election: generous donations from Joel Klein, the former New York City schools chief; Reed Hastings, the founder of Netflix; and New Orleans' own Walter Isaacson, the former *Time Magazine* editor and author of a recent best-selling biography of Steve Jobs," wrote Andrew Vanacore, reporter for the *Times-Picayune*.

In some ways, Usdin represents the popular image of the school reform movement. She began her career in education in 1992 when she moved to Louisiana to teach as part of the first cohort of Teach For America (TFA), where she taught fifth grade. Like many TFA corps members, Usdin quickly moved into a leadership position. She became the executive director of TFA in Louisiana and then served as a partner for The New Teacher Project (TNTP), a nonprofit founded by fellow TFA alumna, Michelle Rhee. After Hurricane Katrina, Usdin founded NSNO, which initially worked to support the effort to rebuild schools but quickly became involved in the reform efforts to promote charter schools and school choice as an alternative to traditional local school board control. Working with the Recovery School District, NSNO trained charter school leaders and "acted as gatekeeper for millions of dollars in federal grant money earmarked to help get new schools off the ground."[2] Usdin stepped down from this position before announcing her candidacy.

Brett Bonin, the incumbent whom Usdin was challenging, represents a different type of candidate. He was relatively new to education politics when he first ran for the local school board in 2008. Bonin, a Republican, has deep roots in the New Orleans community; he is a native of New Orleans, completed both his undergraduate degree and his legal degree at Loyola University, New Orleans, and currently practices family law in New Orleans. While on the board, Bonin had been a critic of state interference in local school districts. While he did not oppose charters and choice, he was a strong advocate for local control.

The third candidate for the District 3 school board seat, Karran Harper Royal, is also a life-long resident of New Orleans who was known for challenging state officials at public gatherings on education. She worked as an advocate for parents of disabled children through a local community resource center. Unlike Usdin and Bonin, Royal was critical of charter schools, especially of their self-appointed charter boards that she felt were accountable to no one. Her concerns about local control and transparency became a main focal point in her criticism of Usdin. Royal was also the only black candidate in this race. As an outspoken advocate for her community, she had previously criticized the state takeover for denying power from locally elected black leaders. She saw the actions of the state and white reformers as analogous to the period after the Civil War when, as she saw it, "African-Americans began to get some amount of political control, and then after that, whites basically pushed them out of office and enacted laws to keep African-Americans down."[3] Royal's campaign typifies the traditional school board election. She relied primarily on donations from friends and family that were frequently for no more than $20 or $25.[4] She thought her stature in the community would be able to serve as a primary vehicle for campaigning. But in the end, Royal never received the same level of visibility as Usdin and Bonin, possibly because she was never able to raise the kind of funds needed to launch a realistic challenge.

The battle in District 3 would become heated and at times nasty, and outside donations would come to dominate the coverage in the last days of the election. In the end, Usdin would win by a significant margin with some crediting her funding advantage.

Some celebrate Usdin's victory as a win for those fighting to change the status quo, who feared the looming return of schools from the state-run RSD to the local OPSB could destroy the city's burgeoning charter and school choice reforms, turning the clock back on the progress that had been made. Others see her win as exemplifying how homegrown locals, like Bonin and Harper Royal, are no longer able to compete because their fundraising capacity is no match for the deep pockets of national donors. Still others see Usdin as an outsider and her win as a sign that local black leaders, sensitive to the needs and wants of parents of children who attend the local schools, were being shut out of political positions as white reformers with a national agenda take over the city.

How much do these three candidates reflect the broader pool of candidates who participated in the election cycles we studied? Are black candidates being pushed aside by white reformer candidates? Are long-time residents finding themselves battling outsiders who can easily outspend them? Are reform-backed candidates being urged to unequivocally support a national policy agenda with donations being tied to their pledge for support? In this chapter we shed light on the candidates, their background, their connections to donors, and their policy positions to understand how outside funding is shaping the candidate pool and, ultimately, the types of representatives running our schools. Further, by speaking with candidates themselves, we were able to learn how they became connected to their donor base, what strategies they employed, and how funding shaped (or didn't shape) their policy positions. While some of the images sketched here are true, we found that our candidate pool is diverse with the white reformer image not holding in many cases. Further, in our discussions with candidates about their donor base, most candidates seemed genuinely surprised that they attracted such large donations from prominent reformers and reported virtually no contact with donors other than to send short thank-you notes. Finally, the candidates with whom we spoke hold a wide range of policy positions with reform candidates being more ideologically consistent (or rigid depending on your perspective), but all candidates insist that they came to their positions on their own and that the outside donors who came to support them had no influence on their platforms.

WHO ARE THE CANDIDATES?

If school board elections are rarely studied, the candidates themselves receive next to no scholarly attention. Outside of a small handful of studies, we know little about the men and women who seek to oversee the $634 billion spent annually on the day-to-day running of 98,271 public schools.[5] Further, most research in this area relies on national surveys that are useful when seeking to understand the broad picture of school board members but less useful when seeking to understand the basis for their thinking and actions. Another significant limitation to existing research on school board candidates is that only current or former board members have been surveyed. Thus, we know nothing about candidates who lost. Our study design allowed us to improve on this research base by both painting the broader picture of all of the candidates who participated in the elections between 2008 and 2014 in our five cities and providing in-depth understanding of school board candidates' motivations, fundraising strategies, and policy priorities. To describe our larger sample, we relied on extensive internet searches, including news biographies that profiled candidates during the election, social media searches (e.g., LinkedIn and Facebook), and other online data. While we were not successful in locating all of the candidates, we are able to confidently describe 101 of the 122 candidates that participated in the races we examined. We also conducted twenty-six interviews with a diverse set of candidates—some who won, some who lost, some who were well funded, and some who relied primarily on small donations from friends and family.[6] We interviewed at least 3 candidates in each of our case cities, and the interviews lasted, on average, about one hour. The candidates with whom we spoke were from all three candidate types—reform, union, and unaffiliated in roughly equal proportions. Finally, our candidate sample is racially and ethnically diverse—17 of the 26 candidates are people of color. The variation in our sample makes us confident that the insights we drew from our interviews reflect the experiences of many candidates in school board elections. See table 5.1 for further details about our interview sample.

Just as studies of state and national elected leaders show more of them to be male, white, wealthy, and to hold more advanced degrees than the populations they represent, previous work has also found this to be true of school board members.[7] Hess and Meeks found in 2011 that 80.7 percent of their school board member respondents were white. Black school board members were just over 12 percent of their sample, with only 3 percent being Latinx. Our sample looks different from this national picture. In part, this discrepancy is likely due to the fact that we examined only urban school districts, but even when we examine Hess and Meeks's data for school districts that enroll over fifteen thousand students, our sample is much more diverse (see table 5.1). Just over one-third (34.4 percent) of the candidates who participated in the elections we examined were white. Black candidates were actually more prevalent than white candidates, composing 40 percent of our sample. Latinxs too were well represented, and at rates six times that of the national elections previously studied (18 percent) There is some variation by city; for example, Los Angeles has a large percentage of Latinx candidates while Indianapolis and New Orleans have zero, reflecting the larger demographics of the city, but

TABLE 5.1

Demographics and affiliations of candidates for all elections from 2008 to 2014

	INTERVIEWED CANDIDATES		BRIDGEPORT CANDIDATES		DENVER CANDIDATES		INDIANAPOLIS CANDIDATES		LOS ANGELES CANDIDATES		NEW ORLEANS CANDIDATES		ALL FIVE CITIES	
	Number	Percent	Number	Percent	Number	Percent	Number	Percent	Number	Percent	Number	Percent	Number	Percent
Number of unique candidates			16	100%	24	100%	29	100%	29	100%	24	100%	122	100%
Number with complete information			12	75%	23	96%	21	72%	26	90%	20	83%	102	84%
Number of candidates interviewed	26		3	12%	9	35%	3	12%	5	19%	6	23%		
Election year														
2008	0	0%									14		14	
2009	7	27%	2		9				4				15	
2010	1	4%					13						13	
2011	1	4%			9				12				21	
2012	9	35%	5				10				16		31	
2013	8	31%	10		8				14				32	
2014	0	0%					10							
Incumbent	4	15%	2	13%	5	21%	5	17%	6	21%	8	33%	26	21.3%

(continued)

TABLE 5.1 (continued)

Demographics and affiliations of candidates for all elections from 2008 to 2014

	INTERVIEWED CANDIDATES		BRIDGEPORT CANDIDATES		DENVER CANDIDATES		INDIANAPOLIS CANDIDATES		LOS ANGELES CANDIDATES		NEW ORLEANS CANDIDATES		ALL FIVE CITIES	
	Number	Percent	Number	Percent	Number	Percent	Number	Percent	Number	Percent	Number	Percent	Number	Percent
Candidate classification based on donations received*														
Reform	9	35%	3	19%	10	42%	7	24%	7	24%	5	21%	32	26.2%
Union	10	38%	5	31%	9	38%	1	3%	11	38%	4	17%	30	24.6%
Unaffiliated	7	27%	8	50%	5	21%	21	72%	11	38%	15	63%	60	49.2%
Race/Ethnicity														
White	9	35%	6	38%	9	38%	9	31%	8	28%	10	42%	42	34.4%
African American	11	42%	8	50%	11	46%	13	45%	3	10%	14	58%	49	40.2%
Latinx	6	23%	2	13%	4	17%	0	0%	16	55%	0	0%	22	18.0%
Other	0	0%	0	0%	0	0%	0	0%	1	3%	0	0%	1	0.8%
Missing	0	0%	0	0%	0	0%	7	24%	1	3%	0	0%	8	6.6%
Gender														
Male	11	42%	11	69%	11	46%	17	59%	15	52%	16	67%	70	57.4%
Female	5	19%	5	31%	13	54%	12	41%	14	48%	8	33%	52	42.6%
Education level														
Less than a BA	2	8%	1	6%	2	8%	3	10%	1	3%	0	0%	7	5.7%
BA or above	22	85%	10	63%	21	88%	15	52%	24	83%	19	79%	89	73.0%
Missing	2	8%	5	31%	1	4%	11	38%	4	14%	5	21%	26	21.3%

(continued)

TABLE 5.1 (*continued*)

Demographics and affiliations of candidates for all elections from 2008 to 2014

	INTERVIEWED CANDIDATES		BRIDGEPORT CANDIDATES		DENVER CANDIDATES		INDIANAPOLIS CANDIDATES		LOS ANGELES CANDIDATES		NEW ORLEANS CANDIDATES		ALL FIVE CITIES	
	Number	Percent	Number	Percent	Number	Percent	Number	Percent	Number	Percent	Number	Percent	Number	Percent
Other affiliations and background experience														
Union member	5	19%	1	6%	1	4%	6	21%	12	41%	2	8%	22	18.0%
Current or former teacher	6	23%	1	6%	1	4%	5	17%	13	45%	3	13%	23	18.9%
Work experience in district	7	27%	2	13%	4	17%	6	21%	14	48%	2	8%	28	23.0%
Charter affiliation	7	27%	0	0%	6	25%	5	17%	1	3%	14	58%	26	21.3%
Teach For America	1	4%	0	0%	0	0%	2	7%	1	3%	1	4%	4	3.3%
Lived more than ten years in district	24	92%												
Self or cids in district	22	85%												

*Our union and reform categorization is well supported by the information on reform and union endorsements in these elections. Twenty-one out of the twenty-five reform candidates received endorsements from either Stand for Children or Democrats for Education Reform, two prominent reform organizations in the dataset. Twenty out of the twenty-nine candidates that were labeled as teacher union received endorsements from their city's teacher union.

generally, all five of our case study cities have diverse candidates running for the school board.

Moreover, despite the white reformer image that is often promoted, our reform-funded candidates were also racially and ethnically diverse. In table 5.2 we look only at those candidates for whom we have complete information.

While the funders themselves may be overwhelmingly white, the candidates they supported were far more diverse. Just under half (43 percent) of reform-backed candidates were black, and another 14 percent were Latinx. Unaffiliated candidates also look very much like the reform candidates with only a slightly higher percentage of black candidates (48 percent) running for school board. Finally, union-backed candidates were also quite diverse, especially when it came to Latinx candidates. Nearly one-third of the union-backed candidates were Latinx.

One reason that the stereotypical portrayal of white reform candidates taking on black and brown competitors with more locally authentic roots does not always hold is that in some cases both reform and union groups support minority candidates. For example, the District 6 election in 2013 pitted Antonio Sanchez against Monica Ratliff. Sanchez was the candidate favored by the reformers, and he had by far the greater financial support. Ratliff, running a low-budget campaign, had only nominal contributions from the teacher unions, in which she was a member, and could not afford a paid staff. According to a story in the *Los Angeles Times*, to make sure Latinx voters recognized that Ratliff shared their ethnicity (her mother was a Mexican American immigrant), she sent a letter to Latinx parents that included mention of the fact that she won a college scholarship available only to Latinxs and, based on the advice of a political consultant, on the refrigerator magnets that she distributed "there was an accent over the o in Monica."[8] This LA race also shows another reason that the color line between reform- and union-backed candidates can be blurry: while reformers like Michael Bloomberg and Eli Broad threw their financial support exclusively to Sanchez, the local teacher union hedged its bets by making donations to both Ratliff and Sanchez. This case demonstrates how lines of race/ethnicity do not follow neat patterns but does reinforce the continued potency of race/ethnicity in local elections as

TABLE 5.2

Characteristics of candidates by candidate type
(Incomplete background candidates removed)

	UNAFFILIATED		REFORM		UNION	
	Number	Percent	Number	Percent	Number	Percent
Total	42		28		32	
Race/ethnicity*						
White	16	38%	11	39%	10	31%
African American	20	48%	12	43%	12	38%
Latinx	5	12%	4	14%	10	31%
Other	0	0%	1	4%	0	0%
Missing	1	2%	0	0%	0	0%
Gender*						
Male	26	62%	15	54%	18	56%
Incumbent*	3	7%	3	11%	1	3%
Education level*						
BA or above	37	88%	24	86%	27	84%
Less than BA	1	2%	2	7%	4	13%
Missing	4	10%	2	7%	1	3%
Other affiliations and background experience						
Union member*	7	17%	5	18%	10	31%
Former teacher*	6	14%	6	21%	11	34%
Work experience in district*	7	17%	10	36%	11	34%
Charter affiliation*	4	10%	15	54%	1	3%
Teach For America*	0	0%	3	11%	1	3%
Kids in school district**	8	80%	8	89%	3	43%
Self in school district**	1	10%	0	0%	1	14%

*Data are from internet searchers
**Data are from personal interviews with candidates

candidates seek to demonstrate their connections to local parents and voters.

Our sample of candidates in our five cases closely matches the national profile of large enrollment districts along other dimensions, however. For example, when we looked at gender and educational attainment of candidates, our sample is similar (44 percent nationally are female, 43 percent of our sample is female; 75 percent nationally hold a BA or above; 73 percent of our sample hold a BA or above). The gender distribution between cities remains roughly balanced, with Bridgeport and New Orleans having more male candidates and Denver having more female candidates than the national average. We did find that unaffiliated candidates are slightly more likely to be male, but this difference is substantively small, about two candidates.

Because we tracked multiple election cycles in each city, some of the elections included in our study were not highly visible contests that attracted outside funders. By comparing these low visibility races to the others, we can cautiously make some claims about whether and how funders shaped the pool of candidates. Table 5.3 looks at this issue in two slightly different ways. First, we compared candidates in high-profile election years to those who ran in years in which the city attracted little outside attention or money. Because the number of candidates in any particular election is relatively small, we cannot say for certain how increasing campaign costs and donations shaped the types of candidates who run for school board, but generally, we found that candidates look quite similar with regard to race/ethnicity (see table 5.3). Unlike what we might assume, candidates in higher profile years were slightly *more* diverse with a slightly higher percentage of black and Latinx candidates.

Second, we also examined whether candidates in later elections looked different from candidates in earlier elections, ostensibly before public awareness of large national donor engagement in school board elections. It may be that once potential candidates become aware of this phenomenon, a different pool of individuals chooses to run for the school board regardless of whether outside donations become a reality. However, we again saw little difference between our early election candidates and our later election candidates. At least in our cases and during the period we studied, the involvement of national

TABLE 5.3

Composition change in candidate demographics

	WHOLE SAMPLE	CANDIDATES IN HIGH-PROFILE YEARS*		CANDIDATES IN MORE TRADITIONAL YEARS		CANDIDATES IN 2008–2010		CANDIDATES IN 2012–2014	
Total**	122	84		66		42		87	
Race/ethnicity									
White	34.4%	29	35%	25	38%	16	38%	30	34%
African American	40.2%	37	44%	25	38%	18	43%	39	45%
Latinx	18.0%	15	18%	10	15%	4	10%	15	17%
Missing		3	4%	6	9%	4	10%	3	3%
Gender									
Male	57.4%	45	54%	40	61%	23	55%	49	56%
Female	42.6%	39	42%	26	39%	19	45%	38	44%

*This includes Bridgeport 2012, Denver 2011 and 2013, Indianapolis 2012 and 2014, Los Angeles 2013, and New Orleans 2012.
**The total in the comparison categories exceeds the total number of candidates because some candidates ran in multiple elections and thus appear multiple times.

donors did not have much, if any, impact on the racial/ethnic composition of the candidates. Finally, we compared the gender composition of the candidate pool. In this case, we again saw no difference between early and late races, but we did see an increase in male candidates in more traditional years. This increase was relatively small, so we caution against too strong a conclusion. Overall, we did not find large or systematic differences in candidate race/ethnicity or gender corresponding to a rise in outside donations.

AFFILIATIONS AND MOTIVATION TO RUN

Our background searches also yielded information about other affiliations that candidates held. In one thesis, developed by Moe and others, local control has created opportunities for teacher unions to co-opt school board races. Taking that into consideration, we might expect to see a large number of candidates who are members or affiliates of unions, especially among candidates who received active union backing. Hess and Meeks, looking at a broad national sample in 2010, before outside money became a prominent feature, found that about 18 percent of their sample were current or former members of a teacher union and that about 27 percent of their sample listed their profession as "education." Our review of candidate profiles found somewhat fewer teachers: only 19 percent of candidates across our five cities could be identified as current or former teachers, but there was significant variation across the cases (see table 5.1). Union membership and experience in the classroom as a teacher are especially high in Los Angeles, where just under half (45 percent) of the candidates have teaching experience and 41 percent are affiliated with a union. Not surprising, however, we found that candidates who received union funding were more likely to be union members and more likely to be teachers, about one-third each with substantial overlap between the two groups (see table 5.2). When choosing where to invest their campaign support, unions strategically target candidates who are teachers with union affiliations, but in this era of greater nationalization of school board races, where unions are competing with reformers who are also attempting to have influence, unions may be having more difficulty in shaping the configuration of the overall candidate pool.

Diane Ravitch and other critics of outside reformers suggest that outside interests are seeking to advance an agenda of privatization including the promotion of charter schools. Taking that into consideration, we might expect to see reform-backed candidates affiliated with the charter school sector. Indeed, we did find that a number of candidates were linked to charter schools and the broader charter sector, with reform candidates being far more likely to possess this affiliation. While about a fifth (twenty-six candidates, 21 percent) of our sample overall had a charter connection, the differences between candidate types was large. We could find just one union-backed candidate and only four unaffiliated candidates with a charter affiliation. For reform candidates, over half (fifteen candidates, 54 percent) were affiliated with charters. In Denver, for example, one reform-backed candidate had been a founding member of a charter school while another was a charter school principal. These connections provide not only direct financial support and a network of potential donors, but it would seem that these networks may be acting as important sources for encouraging their members to run for office. While the majority of those we interviewed indicated that they self-selected to run, others indicated that affiliations, such as being on a charter board, served as important venues for recruitment. One Latinx candidate, who described himself as new to the K–12 policy arena before his run for school board, explained that it was his charter school connections that prompted him to even consider becoming a board member. A local leader from Building Excellent Schools, a national organization that trains school leaders to "take on the demanding and urgent work of leading high-achieving college preparatory urban charter schools," said to him, "Man, I really would love to see you [on the board]" and this suggestion spurred him to give it a try.[9] We know that recruitment is a key step to any political engagement and that when an organization takes a stand on political issues, recruitment requests increase.[10] Thus, the fact that many reform-affiliated and charter organizations are becoming increasingly engaged in local education politics may mean that requests such as the one here are likely to become more common.

The importance of recruitment by organizations also makes the *lack* of requests from unions extraordinary. Not a single candidate we interviewed indicated that the union played a role in motivating him or her to run for the school board. Certainly, we found that a sizable number of candidates were affiliated with unions, but no interviewees mentioned the union or union members as encouraging them to join the board. While unions and reform groups seem to both engage heavily in some types of political activities, our evidence suggests that reform or charter networks are more proactive in candidate recruitment.

Another affiliation that might motivate a person to run for the school board is direct, personal affiliation with a child's local school. Deckman found in her study of school board members that many had been active in their local PTAs and it was this affiliation that sparked their run for school board.[11] Nationally, about one-third of board members and about one-quarter of those in large districts have children currently enrolled in the local school district.[12] We asked candidates two slightly different questions—do you, or did you, have children in the local school district, and did you attend school in the district?—so our responses cannot serve as a direct comparison to national data. Interestingly, and in contrast to the image presented in the Usdin–Bonin–Harper Royal election, we found that reform candidates were actually more likely to have a direct connection to the local schools either through their own education or the education of their children.

The Usdin profile also highlights another group that could act as an important recruiting agent for candidates, especially reform-backed candidates. There has been some speculation that TFA might serve as a recruiting pool for national reform interests looking to recruit candidates for office. Such speculation was bolstered when TFA launched Leadership for Educational Equity (LEE), a spinoff of TFA specifically designed to expand the number of TFA alumni in public office. While TFA is restricted in how much political and legislative activity it may conduct because of its status as a 501(c)(3) organization, LEE is a 501(c)(4) social welfare organization that may engage in partisan political activity as long as it is not the primary activity of the organization. Among the cities we examine, New Orleans has been an especially prominent site of active TFA involvement, with Usdin fitting the popular image. Yet, overall, only four of the candidates in our data appeared to have TFA roots.

When we spoke to the candidates about their motivation to run, candidates expressed a wide range of reasons for their interest in becoming a board member, with nationalized policy issues often serving as a driving factor. Unaffiliated candidates, though, were more likely to state that they were interested in the school board because of their own children's education. The image of the mama bear (or papa bear) is a fitting description for how these parents explained their motivation. One candidate in Bridgeport was especially clear about her intentions when she said, "I'm not a politician. I never said I was a politician. I was a mad mother. That's what I was. I was fighting as a mother for my children."[13] A parent in New Orleans said he was "hell-bent on making sure my children were afforded a quality public education."[14] For these candidates, their own children—not ideological or partisan principles or interests—served as the spark for their candidacy. Another parent in Bridgeport explained that her child was an initial catalyst, but her concern quickly spread to all children in her community and prompted her to run for the school board. She explained that she had expressed concern about her daughter's education, specifically that her daughter had experienced twelve different math teachers during a single school year. This candidate recalled that district leaders "made every excuse in the book," and she believed the response was "pathetic." She was outraged for her own daughter's education and made sure to let school leaders know, "I hope you understand that there are one hundred children matriculated into this class. It's not just my child."[15] Her anger and outrage at the response she received not only for her own child but for all children enrolled in the local schools motivated her to run for office.

A focus on serving the broader community through the school board was also found in previous research, which documented that a sense of civic duty was often the primary factor motivating board members, rather than political gain or the desire to begin a political career.[16] Among the candidates we interviewed, only a few stated their motivation in terms of citizenship and duty. One candidate that stood out, however, was a black candidate in New Orleans, who explained, "I would never have considered running for public office, except that the stakes seemed so high that I felt that as a citizen and as a public school parent, I had to do something to try to impact the outcome. I really felt duty-bound to run. I felt like this wasn't really my choice. I felt like I had to do it, you know?"[17] It seems possible that the changing nature of school board elections and the rising price tag for a competitive campaign may be discouraging candidates who are more focused on civic duty. While nationally this motivation may still be the primary motivation for school board candidates, we did not find that the candidates we interviewed referenced this factor often as part of their reasoning for entering the school board race in contrast to earlier research.

Instead, the nationalized education reform debates frequently motivated candidates of all types to run. In this regard, it seems that nationalization and the engagement of large national donors is shaping the motivations of school board candidates, and ultimately their members. Rather than an emphasis on one's civic responsibility to the community or the children of the community, candidates in our sample more often stated that they were motivated by a desire to shape the nationalized policies being enacted in their local district. Some candidates sought to ensure that current reform efforts would continue. One reform-backed candidate in Los Angeles explained that "[it was the] policy that was very exciting, that was worth the challenge, and I was surrounded by community members who wanted to see the implementation happen. That was really the motivation."[18] Others expressed a desire to see a change in the policy direction, away from nationalized reform priorities. One Denver candidate was concerned "about the direction that Denver Public Schools . . . [were] head[ed] in terms of what I see as privatizing public education."[19] A New Orleans candidate who was not affiliated with any specific funding source stated that "there were too many special interests. The individuals who were [involved] were interested in the office [because] they had special interests."[20] Certainly, one can imagine that pursuing specific policy items could be related to one's sense of civic duty. After all, many reformers frame their policy agenda in terms of educational equity and social justice, yet this motivation was always secondary to policy goals, if mentioned at all.

STRATEGIES FOR FUNDRAISING AND CONNECTIONS TO DONORS

The affiliations and motivations that lead people to become candidates also prove important for fundraising efforts once they make the commitment to run. Once interested, candidates had to quickly start fundraising in order to gain visibility in the election. Some were unprepared for this reality, as one unaffiliated candidate from New Orleans explained: "I thought for certain me being a public school parent—an active public school parent—would give me the upper hand. Apparently, I did not take into consideration the role that money plays in elections."[21] Candidates of all types described, often in great detail, the hard work that goes into running even a modest campaign. For some, reflecting on their campaign in our interview left them in awe of their own past efforts. While the image of the heavily funded reform candidate being able to outspend opponents is sometimes true, our examination of candidate donations reveals wide variation in fundraising, sometimes with candidates in the same city running successful campaigns with vastly different amounts of money.

School board races in high-profile elections are indeed more expensive, although the impact of outside money is selective with many candidates—including some successful ones—still running relatively low-cost campaigns based on local giving. In their 2010 survey, Hess and Meeks found that even in large districts, 33.2 percent of candidates spent less than $1,000, and over half (58.7 percent) reported having spent less than $5,000.[22] Across all of our races, 100 of the 130 candidacies we tracked had total contributions that exceeded $5,000. Yet the variation in spending was large, even within the same city and same election cycle. For example, in the 2012 Orleans Parish School Board elections, Sarah Newell Usdin raised nearly $200,000, surpassing her opponents by a large margin. Combined, the three candidates for the District 3 seat raised over $260,000 while the three candidates for the District 7 seat raised just under $50,000. Further, more money does not always lead to a win. Leslie Ellison, an unaffiliated candidate for the District 4 seat, who raised just $16,700—well below the $66,000 raised by her opponent, Lourdes Moran—also eked out a win.

Candidates running for re-election when outside money is present often find that they must raise significantly more money to run a competitive campaign. In Bridgeport, Sauda Baraka was able to successfully win her seat in 2009 by raising $11,000 but had to double this amount in 2013 when she was running for re-election. While elections in Los Angeles, compared to our other four cities, are quite expensive, they became far more so in 2013 when outside money was flowing into the election. Because of campaign rules, donors are limited in how much they can donate directly to candidates but can make unlimited donations to independent expenditure groups. In 2009, when Steve Zimmer first ran for the school board, a total of just over $405,000 was spent on his election. Four years later, in the highly publicized contest between Zimmer and Kate Anderson, this figure doubled to just over $803,000.

Finally, in Indianapolis, where outside funding was heavily present in the 2012 election cycle but then dropped in the 2014 cycle (from 44 percent of all individual donations coming from outside funders to 25 percent; see table 3.2), the amount of fundraising remained high, well above the levels in the 2010 election. In 2010, Justin Paul Fork, an at-large candidate, raised the most funding with just $7,633.71. In 2014, all three candidates who won their seats spent over $50,000, vastly more than any campaign had cost just four years prior. Despite these variations across distinct electoral contests, in every election cycle we examined, reform-backed candidates had higher average total levels of contributions than those with union backing or those not affiliated.

While our data clearly show that some candidates received significant contributions from large national donors, candidates almost universally expressed what seemed to be a sincere belief that their donor base was predominantly local. In fact, sometimes when we mentioned particular names of funders that we knew had donated to their campaigns, the candidates seemed surprised, as they weren't always aware of these donors. The reform-backed candidates were more likely to acknowledge the funding they had received from outside sources but nevertheless insisted that they had a "mostly local donor base."[23] One reform candidate explained that his strategy was to "attract local donors. Period."[24] Another stated that she "took pride knowing that 80 percent of [her] donations were local people."[25] While this candidate did acknowledge that she had received funding from Michelle Yee, wife of Reid Hoffman, and Sheryl Sandberg, Chief Operating Officer of Facebook and author of *Lean In* (both are top twenty donors listed in table 3.4 and two of the strategic national donors included in figure 3.3), she added, "It's not like they're close, personal friends."[26] Reform candidates were also aware that some of their individual donations from large national donors came about because of connections to national organizations or funding groups such as Democrats for Education Reform, Stand for Children, or Democracy Engine, a "fundraising tool to empower donors to support the organizations and issues they care about at any level, in any party, in any state."[27] But such acknowledgments were always couched as the exception, not the rule, to their donor base. In some cases, candidates seemed completely unaware of how those large national donations came to be. "I got a contribution from Mr. Hoffman [cofounder of LinkedIn] two or three days before the election. That's one I didn't ask for—somebody just dropped it off at the office. I never quite understood how that came about but appreciated the contribution."[28]

Union-backed candidates were similarly aware that unions were an important source of their donations, but also frequently followed this acknowledgment with a statement that the majority of their funding came from local individuals. "I had more individual donations than any other candidate" was how one union-backed candidate in Denver opened his discussion of his donor base, and it wasn't until the end of his comments that he added, "I also got the endorsement of the teachers union, and they provided significant funds, but I was outspent by significant margins."[29]

Despite this near universal insistence on emphasizing that their funding was primarily local, when we looked closely at how candidates described their donors, we saw that the unaffiliated candidates utilized a somewhat different definition of "local donations." Their local donations were truly from the average community member, not local elites or locally affiliated national organizations. For many unaffiliated candidates, local was synonymous with those who were part of their daily lives. Unaffiliated candidates described neighbors, friends and family, relatives, and individuals "from my years in school and livin' in the city" as their local donors. One unaffiliated Bridgeport candidate explained that "my hairdresser gave me $50, and my gas station I've been goin' to for sixteen years, he gave me $150. Like, that whole list is what I worked off of."[30] Another candidate in Indianapolis described her base as "very homespun."[31] Thus, while all candidates claim to have a "local donor base," the definition of local donor varied significantly between candidate types, with reform- and union-backed candidates more often referring to geography, and unaffiliated candidates referring to those they interacted with in their daily lives.

To locate these donors, candidates utilized a wide range of strategies, with reform-backed candidates more often referring to the role that their campaign manager (or team) played in assisting their fundraising efforts. Candidates reported that they found and connected to donors through a range of mechanisms, including cold calls, fundraisers, one-on-one meetings, online marketing and social media, personal connections, and elite connections. However, at the end of the day, fundraising often comes down to asking someone personally for money, and nearly all of our candidates said that this was their primary mode of fundraising. As one candidate explained, "I spent a number of afternoons calling people and asking them for their support."[32] Most candidates with whom we spoke relied on their own list of personal connections as their primary contact list. One candidate said he called "anybody I could think of. It was a really creative list."[33] Some candidates would snowball outward from their own connections, asking those that donated to either share names of other potential donors or asking donors to solicit donations on their behalf. A few reform candidates also discussed their connections to elites within the city as another list of potential donors. A reform candidate in Denver explained, "friends of mine are governors, US senators, state representatives, US Congresspeople, that I can call. Many of those I have a personal cell phone number I can call."[34] While this individual is an exception in the breadth of his elite connections, we did hear more reform candidates mention their use of elite contacts to help them raise campaign funds.

Candidates also used their personal connections to ask friends and family to host a fundraiser. Over half of our candidate interviewees described having some type of fundraising event. Sometimes these fundraisers were "more grassroots"—such as a neighborhood house party with homemade food and eight to ten friends—while others held more elaborate events that included catering and guest speakers.[35] While candidates of all types utilized the same basic strategy of holding a fundraiser, the nature of the events could vary dramatically with unaffiliated candidates relying on more modest efforts to attract donors.

In addition to these more personalized efforts, candidates also connected with donors through an online presence. Social media sites, such as Facebook, and candidate websites served as points of contact with donors who could then make direct donations through these portals. Who created and managed these sites did differ, however, with better-funded candidates able to hire professional support, whereas less-well-funded candidates, especially those unaffiliated with either union or reform donors, relied on friends to manage their online presence.

While all candidates referenced a similar set of fundraising tools, candidates expressed different explanations for why donors were interested in supporting their candidacy. Over half of the reform-backed candidates explained that they received donations specifically because of their policy priorities. While some spoke more generally about being supported because of their policy agenda or policy positions, others were more explicit about the fact that donors were interested in specific issues, with charter schools and choice being the issue mentioned most often. One reform candidate stressed that some donors "saw it as a real fight between change and the status quo."[36] Another reform candidate stated matter-of-factly that donors supported him because "I was not anti-choice." He went on to explain that he didn't have any "inner qualms about that, I understood that." Because he was "very much aligned with charters in theory" even if he saw room for improvement in the way that the policies were executed locally, he did not see a problem accepting donations that were tied to this issue.[37] Both union- and reform-backed candidates were also more likely to state that donors gave to their campaign because of their prior work in education, while only one unaffiliated candidate mentioned this as a reason for receiving donations. One reform-backed candidate in Los Angeles stated that some donors gave because they thought, "I like what she does," while another reform-backed candidate in Denver stated, "I was experienced in working on high-profile and education issues . . . and had done quite a bit of volunteering on school issues."[38] One candidate even encouraged us to Google him to see all of his policy accomplishments prior to running for school board. These candidates believed that donors were supporting them because of their track record.[39]

When asked why donors were generally interested in the election overall, we again heard about the importance of "the reform agenda" with nearly half of all of the candidates we interviewed using this exact phrase. One unaffiliated candidate stated that Bridgeport is "ground zero," "the epicenter of the reform movement in Connecticut," and thus donors were attracted to the election.[40] One reform candidate in Denver stated that "school board elections are still important because it's about the debate around education reform and what's going to be the future of education." Candidates also mentioned specific issues that they felt were driving donor interest in their local school board election. Just over 70 percent of all the candidates (eighteen) we interviewed included at least one nationalized issue in their discussion of donor interests, with charter schools and privatization driving the vast majority of this discussion. In New Orleans, candidates referenced the future return to local control as being tightly bound with the future of charter schools in the city. One unaffiliated candidate who was very concerned about transparency and local control believed that donors were seeking to support candidates who, if elected, would ensure that as schools returned to OPSB, "everything is in place so that charter leaders can sleep at night, let them know that everything is not going to change tomorrow because the board changes."[41] A different unaffiliated New Orleans candidate further explained that in his view, donors were interested in the election because the school board "could smooth the way, to give away buildings, sell property at cheap prices . . . to open the door for further expansion of charter schools."[42] A union-backed Los Angeles candidate also explained that donors were looking to maintain an "ally" on the board, while a reform-supported candidate in Denver thought our question was a bit silly because "obviously, they were interested in getting a representative on the board that would be open to allowing more charters to open."[43] Some candidates believed that donors from outside of the community were especially motivated by these policy issues, whereas local donors were more interested in "their children in schools." In Indianapolis, a reform-backed candidate believed "parents, community members, [and] teachers have different hopes and dreams for the district than the outsiders."[44] These candidates believed outside donors were interested in their election because their city was just one battleground in a larger national fight about the future of the nation's education.

One point on which candidates we interviewed, regardless of type, unanimously agreed was that the donors themselves had absolutely no influence on their policy positions or beliefs about education reform. Candidates explained in our interviews that even when they met with donors one on one, they never experienced donors suggesting they adopt particular policy priorities or stating that a donation would be tied to the candidate adopting a particular position. Candidates at times described to us donors asking a "litany of questions to [act as] a kind of litmus test" before providing a donation, but this was never followed by any additional contact or encouragement to say something specific while on the campaign trail.[45] More often, candidates stated that "very rarely did we hear from them."[46] After a donation, the only contact candidates had with donors was initiated by the candidates when they wrote a thank-you note.

In general, we find limited evidence of either top-down pressure by donors to alter candidate agendas or interest among donors in learning about local issues and how candidates may propose context-specific policies associated with the more general policy agenda. While some fear that donations enable a donor to "purchase access" to a candidate, we found that in the case of the school board elections we studied, at no time did donors follow up with candidates to shape their strategies, messaging, or policy priorities. While donors may do this once a candidate is serving on the board, we did not find signs of donor interference during the election cycle, nor did candidates express reservation about accepting a donation due to what it may mean in the future. Rather, it seems that large national donors, which are nearly all reform focused, strategically sought out candidates through groups such as Stand for Children, Democrats for Education Reform, and through tools such as Democracy Engine, to locate and support candidates that were already aligned with their policy views.

IDEOLOGICAL RIGIDITY VERSUS PRAGMATIC DECISION-MAKING

School board members have been both praised and criticized for their slow, often pragmatic approach to decision-making. Supporters of the national reform movement tend to argue that local officials have become unresponsive and beholden to special interests (i.e., teacher unions), failing to enact the kind of change that is needed to address the serious issues facing public education. From this perspective, outside money can be seen as a liberating force, opening opportunities for a new breed of candidate less constrained by stale ideas and less dependent on institutions of recruitment that favor those unlikely to "make waves."[47] Proponents of this perspective also argue that there is a growing local constituency for such change—comprising frustrated parents, local leaders, and young and idealistic teachers who consider the local union unreflective of their views—for which outside funding can provide an amplified voice.

To reform critics, on the other hand, the drive to see sweeping changes reflects dogma rather than careful consideration of community wants and needs. Outside money, in this narrative, becomes an inducement to candidates to import ideas ill-suited to local norms and needs and to make them indebted to outside organizations with missions and interests at odds with those of local voters or even the instincts and proclivities of the candidates themselves. This is the concern raised by Diane Ravitch and others who worry that a "billionaire boys club" of wealthy donors will substitute its agenda of privatization, testing, value-added assessment of teachers, and school choice for one more focused on community-based schools, homegrown teachers, and investment in professional development to make stronger teachers rather than simply weeding out those whose students are not doing well.[48]

In our conversations with candidates, we asked them to express their point of view on the set of nationalized issues included in Race to the Top: charter schools, testing, holding teachers accountable by using test score data, tenure, and the Common Core State Standards.[49] In these policy conversations, we heard a range of viewpoints expressed by all candidate types with far less ideological rigidity from all types of candidates than popular narratives suggest. Caveats to support or opposition were often provided, with candidates sometimes stating that responding to our general prompt was difficult because the details mattered. Overall, however, our reform-backed candidates expressed more ideologically consistent positions that align with the national reform agenda. Only once did a reform-backed candidate express a position on a nationalized issue we discussed that was not in line with the reform agenda. Union-backed candidates were more diverse in their responses, frequently expressing moderate support (as opposed to strong, unilateral support) for their positions, and about half expressed some support for positions that are frequently characterized as reform policies. Finally, the unaffiliated candidates also expressed less ideologically aligned positions across the policy issues we discussed and more frequently stated they were uncertain or did not have an opinion on a particular policy issue.

Given the prominence of charter schools on the national school reform agenda, it should come as no surprise that all reform-backed candidates expressed support for expanding charter schools with three expressing unequivocal support—for example, stating "That was definitely one of the issues that I was pretty strong about in my candidacy."[50] Other reform-backed candidates were supportive but provided a caveat to their support, such as stating that charters needed to be "high quality" or that assurances needed to be made for children with disabilities.[51] One candidate even framed the popular debate as a "tug of war between charter schools and traditional public schools" but went on to explain why she didn't see the issue in these terms. She believed it was "more nuanced" and that "we needed to try to figure out how to work collaboratively because I think we all wanted the same thing."[52] While the reform-backed candidates we interviewed were primarily supportive of charters, most wanted to address some limitations and challenges they believed their district faced with regard to current charter school policy.

Most reform-backed candidates also supported accountability testing and using those tests to evaluate teachers' performance, stating things such as "we need to be informed by data" and "we need standardized testing so that we know how our district and particularly the minority kids in our district are faring."[53] However, they also expressed reservations about relying on test scores as the *sole* indicator of performance, advocating instead that test scores be used as "a piece of the evaluation, not necessarily the only piece."[54] While these candidates believed "it is very difficult to hold a system accountable without data," they were not blindly supportive.[55] A Latinx candidate, for example, believed "you always have to measure how much our children have learned" but worried that "students from a different culture or recent arrivals from other countries" would not possess the same "educational social capital" or might face language barriers that could lead to inequities in the system.[56] Thus, while generally supportive, reform-backed candidates also expressed a diverse range of issues that needed to be considered when enacting accountability testing policies.

Unlike how the reform-backed candidates discussed expanding charter options, applying accountability testing, and using those data to evaluate a teacher's performance, these same candidates often lacked any nuance in their discussions of teacher tenure. Instead, they almost universally expressed a strong desire to see tenure protections either limited or removed entirely, often relying on simple statements such as "I disagree with tenure protection" or "I don't understand why there was a need for tenure protection."[57] Referring to popularized images of tenure protections resulting in "complacency" or an inability to fire a bad teacher was common among their discussions of tenure.[58] "It may be a great tool for adults that wanna stay in a job that they're mediocre at, but it's not a good tool for students" summarized how strongly reform-backed candidates felt about tenure.[59] Thus, there was a stark contrast in how these candidates spoke about tenure policy as compared to other policy areas.

Union-backed candidates, on the other hand, were less consistently aligned with the national union policy agenda. Only three of the union-backed candidates expressed points of view across the policy issues we discussed that are consistent with established union policy positions: supporting tenure, opposing using test scores to evaluate teachers, opposing charter school expansion, and believing testing needs to be curbed. Unlike the nearly unanimous reform-backed candidates, however, the remaining four union-backed candidates expressed a wide range of opinions, sometimes agreeing with established union positions and at other times disagreeing. For example, two of the union-backed candidates were quite supportive of standardized testing, stating: "There has to be some way to gauge what's going on."[60] Despite their general support, where they may have differed with some of their reform-backed counterparts was on how often tests should be given or how much testing should be used to sort students and teachers. Similarly, while some union-backed candidates were vehemently opposed to charter schools, with one candidate asking us, "What's the strongest disagreement level that I can choose?" others gave responses that were remarkably similar to those we heard from the reform-backed candidates.[61] "There are some good charter schools. However, especially now, I am really concerned about the oversight" is how one union-backed candidate in Los Angeles explained her policy position.[62] Another stated "to charter or not to charter for me is a question of who's driving it? Who was asking for it? Was the community involved? That's not a clear yes or no answer."[63]

While we may have expected that charters would be a wedge issue creating a deep divide between candidates, it seems that reform- and union-backed candidates are more closely aligned than would be expected given the polarized rhetoric in the national battles. This even applied the issue of tenure and job security, bedrock issues for teacher unions. While some union-backed candidates spoke passionately in support of tenure, stating, for example, "protections for teachers are extremely critical," others considered the issue to be a "tough one."[64] While most acknowledged some rules should be followed to dismiss a teacher, several thought existing rules ought to change to ensure poorly performing teachers could more easily be dismissed. One union-backed candidate was highly critical of those teachers she believed "sit back and glide through things because they're so-called protected" but thought "eliminating protections without considering other due process considerations is a mistake."[65] The diverse set of views held by union-backed candidates challenges the assumption that, in seeking to broadly protect their interests, unions always apply a rigid test of candidate loyalty to a set of antireformer positions. Instead, union-backed candidates were much more ideologically diverse, often holding positions that are contrary to those supported by the unions.

Even more diverse are the points of view of the unaffiliated candidates. When these candidates took positions on the major national issues of contention, they tended to more closely align with unions than reformers, but they were also more likely to state that they did not hold a position on particular issues. Rarely did reform- or union-backed candidates state that they were uncertain or didn't know, but half of the unaffiliated stated they didn't have a position on at least one of the major policies we discussed. Also surprising is that unaffiliated candidates on the whole were both more likely to oppose charter schools and to express this view more strongly than the union-backed candidates. "I don't believe the school choice model works," "I don't believe they should be expanded," or "Absolutely not. Close every single one that's open here" is how these candidates responded to our inquiries about charter schools.[66] This seems to be a main policy area driving their interest in local school politics.

CONCLUSION

In idealized portrayals of democracy, candidates are the linchpin between the public's values and the government's agenda. It's candidates who knock on doors, attend community meetings, and win or lose based on their success in articulating the message voters want to attach to their ballot choice. The linchpin role of candidates has been especially important in local school board elections, which are often nonpartisan formally or by custom, so that individuals running for office stand more on their own. Given their critical role, it's surprising that so little scholarly attention has been paid to the candidates themselves. We hope that this chapter in particular can provide some much-needed insight into the men and women who make important decisions that shape local school district policies.

Those most critical of outside donations fear that candidates will become puppets to wealthy outside donors who pull their strings to push a nationalized policy agenda. Others believe that for too long, school board members have already been beholden to special interests—teacher unions—and that outside money is simply correcting this imbalance. Our review of the candidates who participated in both more traditional and high-profile elections demonstrated that neither of these images is accurate. The candidates are more pragmatic in their policy opinions than simplified caricatures imply. Many candidates, even those heavily supported by union funding *or* reform donor funding, expressed reservations about adopting an all-or-nothing stance to most policy issues.

Candidates also were steadfast in their belief that they were not influenced by outside donors. It's possible, of course, that this is rationalizing or dissembling on their part; most people prefer to consider themselves the arbiters of their own opinions and positions, and to admit to being influenced by campaign funds would be personally painful as well as politically harmful. Yet it is also worth recognizing that in almost every instance it is still the case that most of the candidates' funding comes from more local sources. The expectation that disproportionally large contributions will give those outside donors disproportionate influence may rest at least in part on the expectation that those donors make the effort to extract a quid pro quo. As far as we were able to determine, outside donors had relatively little communication with the candidates they supported though two incumbents did mention feeling as though they received less support in subsequent elections after making decisions that may not have been in line with the reform agenda. Local donors—including some who made quite large contributions—might loom larger because the candidates expect and experience more ongoing contact from those quarters. As one reform candidate summarized, "Local donors mean local votes. I could've [attracted more outside donations], if that had been my strategy, but dollars don't vote. People vote." Thus, even candidates who receive national donations recognize that they serve at the junction between local constituents and the schools, despite the attention and support from a wealthy national constituency. The next chapter considers this further, by examining a range of consequences that infusions of outside money may have.

CHAPTER 6

....

The Impact of Outside Money on Local Elections

"MAY YOU LIVE in interesting times." This expression, often presented as an ancient Chinese curse, has an uncertain provenance, but its double-edged message is clear. Interesting times may be stimulating but also unsettling, liberating but also a threat. Something similar is in play when we think of the possible consequences of outside money in local school elections. Some, who think American education has become stale and complacent, see nationalization as a bracing breath of fresh air. Outside money may elevate the visibility of school board elections, potentially engaging more citizens to participate in local education politics and increasing the often abysmally low voter turnout rates. The influx of funds may also lead to a more sophisticated candidate who can run a more serious campaign that is no longer tied to just friends and family.

Some who think of localism as the anchor for community, continuity, and pragmatic problem solving, however, see nationalization as an ill wind that blows no good. They fear that outside money may be used to capture the local policy agenda, pushing aside local issues or dropping them altogether. Increased funding for elections may fuel this agenda shift by providing candidates who support national reform issues with added capacity to produce more campaign

143

literature, make more phone calls, and hire more workers to knock on doors, all of which then focuses the election on a narrower set of educational issues. Candidates with more locally driven concerns who are unable to attract such funds may struggle to compete and muster a competitive campaign. Additionally, just as national politics has become increasingly polarized, some see the rise in outside donations as the first step toward polarization at the local level. To attract campaign funds, candidates may find they are unable to take more moderate, pragmatic positions on issues, resulting in not only more polarized elections but also potentially a more polarized board.

In this chapter we probe the consequences of outside money as a first step toward determining how alarmed or hopeful we should be about this trend. Our study's research design put limits on our ability to tease out the consequences in a way that might support strong causal claims that extend broadly. We selected our cases because we knew they had experienced outside funding and therefore lack a clear counterfactual case—cities where elections occurred outside the limelight and without involvement by national donors. Nonetheless, we can circle in on some answers to the question of "what difference does it make?" by comparing what we found to patterns described in other places, by looking at trends in our cities that correlate with increases or decreases in outside funds, by leveraging the fact that some of our candidates did not receive such funding and that some ran in district- or ward-based elections with little outside attention, and by drawing from interviews with candidates and other local knowledgeables. We focus on four areas of potential consequences: (1) professionalizing school board elections; (2) media attention; (3) displacement of local agenda items and local voices; and (4) polarization and negative campaigning.

PROFESSIONALIZING
SCHOOL BOARD ELECTIONS

School board elections have been repeatedly criticized for being amateurish affairs.[1] Images of campaigns run out of kitchens and poorly produced candidate interviews airing on public access television abound. After all, campaigning of this style is about all one can afford on the typical budget of about $1,000. This type of campaigning has changed, however, for many of the candidates that we interviewed, some of whom raised tens of thousands of dollars with the help of contributions from outside their district and state. These school board candidates now run a more professionalized campaign with better messaging, glossy campaign materials, and a campaign manager who handles the candidate's appearance schedule, arranges meetings with donors, manages volunteers, tracks fundraising goals, and may even oversee other campaign staff.

While not universal, campaigns with professional staff were more prevalent among candidates who received outside donations. Candidates from Denver who received outside donations described an entire "fundraising committee," and another estimated that his team was "approximately eight people" with a senior campaign manager who made sure the team stayed focused on "how much money we could raise and all the other aspects of the campaign."[2] *Chalkbeat Colorado* reported that "those with the most money are not hesitating to pay for high-end consultants" and explained how the Haynes campaign had retained Terra Strategies (located in Des Moines, Iowa), a firm that has handled presidential campaigns including John Kerry and Al Gore.[3] Several of the candidates we interviewed stated that their campaign manager was a full-time position. For one especially well-funded candidate in Los Angeles who received funding from several outside donors, her team included a campaign manager, a campaign consultant, a fundraiser, and a treasurer. Such support enabled candidates to run a more professionalized campaign.

Confirming the adage that sometimes you need to spend money to get money, hiring a campaign manager sometimes paved the way to additional funding. For the candidate who is relatively new to education politics, it can be difficult to find one's way into donor networks. Having a professional campaign manager with long-standing relationships to key stakeholders can quickly get a new candidate into meetings with individuals who possess political and fundraising resources. This was the experience of one candidate in Denver who received funding from national donors. He stated, "I think that's probably the only reason [I was supported.] I was so new to the race, or even to K–12 politics, or school board races, that I think a lot of the trust was given to my senior campaign manager." He imagined his campaign manager was able to say to these individuals, "Hey, we vetted him. We know that he's pro-charter, that he's supportive of the superintendent, that this, and that, and the other" and this opened doors for him.[4] Even though not all reform candidates were able to or chose to invest in a professional campaign manager, large outside donations enabled many candidates to hire experienced staff who implemented more strategic campaigning as a result. For example, one senior campaign manager for a reform candidate in Denver provided a strategic plan including a list of who had voted in prior school board elections, which enabled him to better target his messaging and canvassing.[5]

In some cities, union candidates were also able to access more professional campaign support. In Bridgeport, where candidates are affiliated with a political party, a Working Families Party candidate explained how he was able to use the party's fundraiser to assist him.[6] In other cases, union-affiliated candidates used their own networks to seek professionalized campaign advice and support, leading them to also run a more professionalized campaign. Not all union candidates had access to or funding for such support, but several utilized professional guidance for their campaigns. This professionalized campaign support stands in stark contrast to the criticism often leveled at school board elections. Certainly, some candidates, many of whom were not affiliated with either the reform movement or the unions, ran less sophisticated campaigns that relied on friends and family serving as their campaign managers or as treasurers. However, our interviews suggested that, at least in high-profile districts like those we studied, the amateurish kitchen-table campaign is changing, with many showing elements of professionalism.

MEDIA ATTENTION TO ISSUES AND CANDIDATES

Better-funded and more sophisticated campaigns can lead to greater visibility through candidate outreach, advertising, and public debates. Greater visibility, at least in theory, may stimulate more public engagement and participation. We explore the extent to which attention was related to the incorporation of national money into local school board elections across our five cities using electoral news coverage as a proxy for attention.

By employing a systematic search for news related to school board elections in our five cities, we were able to locate a total of 225 media reports focused on school board elections between 2008 and 2014. We located articles using a defined set of search terms in Google News, Google search, and LexisNexis. We included all forms of print media, including major newspapers, secondary newspapers, as well as education-specific online news media (e.g., *Chalkbeat*), and other online coverage by community or individual bloggers. In some cases, public radio and local television news also provided a written summary of their coverage and, where that was the case, we also included these media sources. We then utilized a content analysis coding scheme that included a focus on campaign fundraising, donations and costs, campaign issues, and candidates. Using this coding scheme, we were able to examine how campaign coverage was related to large outside donors both across our cities and within each city over time.

Table 6.1 shows the coverage of school board elections by city, year, and type of media. A number of findings regarding overall campaign coverage are worth emphasizing. First, with the exception of Denver, media attention to the school board races was disappointingly low. Across the United States, many school board elections take place in small communities; nearly three out of four school districts in the country contain five or fewer schools, and just a little over 4 percent have more than twenty.[7] In those intimate communities, word of mouth, personal reputation, and small-scale candidate forums might suffice to give voters a sense of the people and issues at stake. In larger districts, like those considered here, voters—especially those who do not currently have children in the system—need more if they are going to exercise their vote responsibly. Local media, at least local print media, do not seem to have stepped up to the plate in that regard.

Second, the attention paid by national donors was not, for the most part, joined by national media. National news outlets only very occasionally covered some of the school board elections in our study. When they did so, however, their coverage was almost exclusively driven by the fact that outside interests were engaging in the local elections. (See appendix B for a complete list of media sources.)

TABLE 6.1

Media coverage of school board election by city and year and news type

CITY	YEAR	PERCENT OF ALL INDIVIDUAL DONATION DOLLARS FROM LARGE NATIONAL DONORS	NATIONAL NEWSPAPER	MAJOR NEWSPAPER	SECONDARY NEWSPAPER	EDUCATION-SPECIFIC BLOG	INDIVIDUAL BLOG	OTHER	TOTAL MEDIA
Bridgeport	2009	0%	0	1	0	0	0	0	1
	2012*	66%	0	6	0	0	1	0	7
	2013	9%	1	12	2	1	5	1	22
Denver	2009	5%	0	29	0	4	0	1	34
	2011	24%	0	34	0	8	2	0	44
	2013	32%	0	29	0	3	2	0	34
Indianapolis	2010	0%	0	0	0	0	0	0	0
	2012	44%	0	0	0	0	0	0	0
	2014	25%	0	5	1	14	0	0	20
Los Angeles	2009	4%	0	3	1	0	0	0	4
	2011	13%	0	5	1	0	0	0	6
	2013	48%	4	7	7	5	5	1	29
New Orleans	2008	4%	0	0	0	0	0	0	0
	2012	25%	0	14	4	2	0	4	24
Total Coverage			5	145	16	37	15	7	225

*Special election

Third, one predictor of media attention is the presence of online media outlets that specialize in education. Denver (*Chalkbeat Colorado*), Indianapolis (*Chalkbeat Indiana*), and Los Angeles (LAschoolreport.com) have such outlets, which provide an active online education news community with regular, professionalized coverage of education-related issues, including school board elections. They not only offer a growing proportion of the school board coverage but also arguably increase the pressure on the more mainstream general print media outlets to pay attention to the elections themselves.

Fourth, while low overall, media attention to school board elections is increasing over time. Early election cycles in each of the cities showed extremely low levels of media coverage; indeed, in Bridgeport and Indianapolis, elections that preceded the appearance of outside donors received almost no coverage at all.

Finally, while growing attention roughly coincides with the growing involvement of outside donors, the pattern is not one to one. Contrary to our expectations, we did not always find increased attention in the years where outside money comprised a significant percent of the total individual donations received. While outside funding and attention more or less rose together in Denver, Los Angeles, and New Orleans, in Bridgeport and Indianapolis the rise in coverage appeared to come about in years subsequent to the initial infusion of national contributions.

One possibility is that a high-profile election with lots of outside money trips a wire that has a persistent effect on local engagement even in subsequent elections when outside attention may wane. This appears to be the case in Bridgeport, where media attention was significantly higher in the 2013 election despite the presence of little outside funding. Another possibility, though, is that the outside actors that originally are drawn to a local election also make investments in the local media that result in ongoing coverage. In August 2015, the Broad Foundation, established by philanthropist Eli Broad, joined with others to contribute nearly a million dollars to the *Los Angeles Times* to enable it to expand its education coverage. *Chalkbeat*, which tends to establish its local outposts in cities with high levels of involvement by national education reformers, is supported by a wide range of donors, but among them are the Gates and Walton Foundations, which have generally aligned with a reform agenda of charters, choice, and accountability. Indianapolis provides an especially good example of how national donor interest may combine with changes in the media environment to have lasting effects on the level of attention accorded to previously low-key school board elections. During the 2012 election cycle in Indianapolis when 44 percent of all individual donations were from large national donors, there was no coverage of the school board elections; however, in the following election cycle, we saw a large spike in coverage across multiple media types even though individual donations from large national donors were only 25 percent. In part, this additional attention was due to *Chalkbeat*, which began reporting on Indiana in October 2013. *Chalkbeat* not only covered the events in the election but also provided a complete profile of each candidate, followed by a Q&A where candidates were able to share their views on a range of issues. The arrival of *Chalkbeat* in Indiana not only increased attention to school board elections but also is itself a signal that Indiana generally and Indianapolis specifically are important sites of reform activity. *Chalkbeat* is currently located in only a handful of select states and cities, all of which are or have been targets of focused education reform efforts (Chicago, Colorado, Detroit, Indiana, Newark, New York, and Tennessee).

In addition to changing the amount of coverage, outside money could also impact the content and tone of the coverage. For those who have lamented the low visibility of school board elections, it is debatable whether the coverage that resulted was the type of attention they were hoping to garner. While educational issues certainly were discussed in the school board election coverage, attention often shifted to focus on the money itself. As one union candidate explained, "There was definitely a shift in focus to the idea that our schools were being bought by billionaires with ulterior motives."[8] One reform candidate in Indianapolis who had received outside funding similarly expressed frustration that the only coverage she felt she was getting in the media was about her campaign donations. As we spoke with her about this issue, she became especially animated saying, "Can we talk about *policy* also when we we're talking about the money? Because to me, the policy and what people stand for [are] more important."[9]

To examine these claims more systematically, we coded all news articles for their focus on campaign donations and donors. We found that the frustrations expressed here are borne out in the news coverage. Rather than focusing on campaign platforms and candidate qualifications, media headlines often stressed campaign finances. Headlines such as "Bigger Money Wins in School Board Races" and "Big Bucks Fuel DPS Board Races," from the Denver 2011 election, for example, focused readers on the issue of money.[10] During this particular race, eighteen of the thirty-seven articles, or nearly half, discussed campaign costs, donations, and the donors (see figure 6.1). Campaign costs, donations, and donors as a news topic were even more ubiquitous in the Los Angeles 2013 election. The overwhelming majority (83 percent) discussed this issue. Further, attention to campaign costs, donations, and donors often focused explicitly on the role of large national donors. In the same Los Angeles 2013 election, twenty-two of the twenty-nine articles that discussed campaign costs, donations,

FIGURE 6.1 **Percent of articles discussing campaign donations, donors, and spending by city and year**

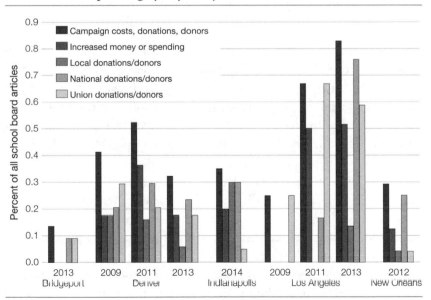

and donors made at least one mention of the role of large national donors. While coverage of campaign costs and donations was a valid topic according to nearly all of the candidates with whom we spoke, many feared the topic of money overshadowed other issues that may be more important in the long run.

Candidates also expressed concern that the increase in outside donations enabled some candidates to attract more attention and generate greater visibility, creating an uneven playing field. Time and again, we heard candidates who had not received large donations state that they "couldn't compete with big money." Put simply by one New Orleans candidate, "You can't have visibility without money."[11] For one Los Angeles candidate who was not affiliated with either the reform- or union-backed donors, the questions about her fundraising ability began the moment she entered the race.

> Before I went in, I knew that you have to raise money and that's important. When I started running, that was the *only* question, "How much money have you raised? If you don't have enough, you're never going to win." Or "I hope you realize your opponent has all this money." I'm like, "What about my good intentions? What about my experience? What about what I want to do? . . . They're like, "That doesn't matter. What matters is the money."[12]

This same candidate later expressed frustration that her lack of funding made it hard to get her name out there and become known. She explained her experience one afternoon while canvassing, "[T]here were three-hundred people from the union walking the same small areas that I had my ten volunteers walking. In terms of manpower, in terms of mail, [the large donations] open up a lot of additional resources that without the money, we weren't able to do."[13]

The ability to reach voters and increase visibility extended beyond canvassing. The "battle of the mailbox" was another way that candidates without large donations felt they were unable to compete for attention. In large school districts, simply sending one piece of mail could require significant funds. Less-well-funded candidates shared how one mailer alone could consume nearly their entire budget. A well-funded reform candidate in Denver noted that his additional funding enabled him to "do mail with nice photos and that kind of stuff while my opponent's materials was much less sophisticated. Her mail wasn't as polished as mine."[14] Those with more limited funding often stated they felt a huge sense of accomplishment when they were able to send one mailer to the entire ward or district only to learn that their better-funded competitor was "blitzkrieging nonstop, sending mailer, after mailer, after mailer" as one Los Angeles union-backed candidate expressed it.[15]

This uneven visibility also carried over into the media, where we examined which candidates received attention in the media (see figure 6.2). We found that reform-backed candidates in Denver, Los Angeles, Indianapolis, and New Orleans received as much or more coverage in the news media. Only in Bridgeport did union-backed candidates receive significantly more attention in the media than reform-backed candidates. More illuminating than differences between those with union versus reform backing is the difference in visibility between both of these types of candidates and those who lack affiliation with either side in the big national battles. Unaffiliated candidates were rarely

FIGURE 6.2   **Average number of candidate mentions across all media by candidate type, city, and year**

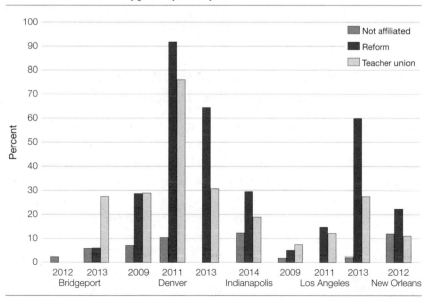

mentioned by the media. Further, when they *were* mentioned, it was usually a passing reference as a result of *all* candidates running for office being listed. In these cases, while their name technically appeared in the article, unaffiliated candidates received almost no substantive coverage of the kind that would inform potential voters about their specific platforms or expertise. Reform candidates, on the other hand, received significant coverage, often with multiple paragraphs being devoted to their candidacy. While a discussion of campaign issues was, at times, a main focus, the coverage associated with some reform candidates often included a close inspection of their campaign donations, including both names of large national donors and the amount given. Reading such articles, some potential voters may react negatively to the information about outside donors, feeling that this is a sign that the candidate is less connected to local citizens and might be less responsive to local interests and needs. Others might find that information a useful conceptual shortcut in a generally low-information electoral environment, helping them map the various candidates onto national debates about which they already have opinions. In either case, it seems that the media pay more attention to candidates who have ties to the broad clash pitting unions versus reformers than to candidates who for one reason or another are running the more traditional, low-key, low-visibility, and low-cost campaigns that were once considered the norm.

OUTSIDE MONEY AND LOCAL REPRESENTATIVENESS

Ultimately, the inability to be a visible, viable candidate without large donations discouraged some of the candidates we interviewed from considering a run in the future. In Denver, one black candidate, a long-time resident, stated, "We've created a system where the average Joe like me, or anybody else who's never run for office, really can't access the process because you gotta be well funded. . . . You are immediately discouraged from running because you know you can't compete with that fundraising capacity. . . . That keeps a lot of people who I think would be great representatives of our community out of office."[16] As we noted earlier, candidates with outside funding and large donations did not always win. Nonetheless, the perception that large donations are required to attract enough attention to be a viable candidate was common and may have consequences for who runs for office and, ultimately, who represents the public interests. The perception that you must be connected to wealthy donors in order to win, whether borne out in fact or not, may exacerbate inequality in representation and marginalize portions of the electorate who feel they cannot compete.

While well-funded campaigns may improve the visibility of school board elections and raise the status of the position, thereby attracting more highly qualified individuals, we also heard candidates express concern that local voice was being lost. An unaffiliated black candidate in New Orleans felt that he "can't have a voice" because "we [the local community members] were out-monied."[17] This voice was being lost because some candidates believed that "you answer to those who donate money to you and if that money is not coming from the community you serve, then that is a problem."[18] Even a reform candidate who had received outside funds expressed concern that "if they're gonna come in and buy the election, and then at the same time disenfranchise the voters that you were elected to represent, I think that's a problem. I don't think we can have that. We have to be able to say, 'You're elected to represent these people in Colorado. I know you may have gotten 80 percent of your money from this hedge fund that's in New York, but you're elected to represent the people in Colorado.'"[19] Whether elected representatives will be able to do this, however, remains an open question.

Another way that local voices may be diminished is through the self-selection process to run for school board. Several candidates stated that they felt discouraged or even resigned to the fact that their voices could not be heard and that they couldn't realistically compete as candidates. No longer could candidates do it the "old-fashioned way" where you "talk to people and go to the barber shops, the community places."[20] Instead, candidates discovered it "is not that kind of endeavor anymore. You need a campaign manager. You need to have a fundraising plan. You need to be soliciting donations."[21] This realization led a Latinx candidate to conclude, "If you don't have that network of people that have the connections to the big donors, you're not gonna get people like me to serve on the school board for the right reasons. Which, from my perspective, is because my children were in school and they were definitely affected by [school board] decisions."[22]

OUTSIDE FUNDING AND VOTER TURNOUT

Observers have long lamented the low levels of voter engagement in local school board elections. Single-digit turnout rates are not uncommon and have led some to conclude that "practically nobody votes."[23] Moe, one of the fiercest critics of local school boards, urges his readers to shed themselves of the "democratic folklore" of locally elected school boards, citing low turnout as a way for special interests (i.e., teacher unions) to capture positions with relative ease.[24] By increasing turnout, special interests are not able to influence the outcome as easily.

Such low turnout rates are, in fact, by design. At the turn of the twentieth century, Progressive reformers sought to keep education issues outside of local politics and did so by creating a governance system separate from other municipal governance. To further depoliticize education, school board elections were held off-cycle, often in the spring, apart from other elections. The result has been low visibility, often with minimal awareness that school board elections are even occurring. In the recent past, some school districts around the country have sought to remedy this low visibility by moving their elections to the fall to coincide with other local, state, and national elections. In fact, New Orleans, one of our case study cities, did exactly this in 2012. Los Angeles passed a city charter amendment that will move city elections and LAUSD elections to be on-cycle with state elections, meaning that school board elections in Los Angeles will occur in even years starting in 2020. While there is a limited body of research regarding school board elections, Allen and Plank provided one of the few systematic studies.[25] They confirmed what intuition predicts: consolidated school board elections, meaning those that occur at the same time as other elections, significantly increase turnout, citing turnout rates that are up to five times higher. Such increased turnout occurs, in part, because of greater visibility. Allen and Plank also noted that local news coverage paid greater attention to school board elections when they were already in election coverage mode, a potential contributor to the higher turnout rates as more citizens were aware of the race through this coverage. They found that school board elections received near daily coverage in the three weeks preceding the election when school board elections were consolidated.

More recent work by Sarah Anzia focuses on not just whether turnout is higher for on-cycle election, but how that higher turnout shapes policy. Similar to Allen and Plank, Anzia found that off-cycle elections decrease participation rates. In Texas, for example, she found that switching to on-cycle elections resulted in a 16 percentage-point increase in voter turnout. She then examined whether different participation rates impact policy. Hypothesizing that organized interest groups (in this case teachers unions) have greater impact on outcomes when participation rates are low, she examined variation in teacher salaries. She concluded that there is a "strong empirical link between election timing and teacher salaries."[26] Thus, election timing is not just a technical issue, but one that shapes attention, turnout, and ultimately policy. Yet research on mayoral elections shows that higher levels of campaign funding can improve voter turnout. Holbrook and Weinschenk found that "turnout is higher in cities where candidates spend more money"; their model controls for many other factors, including electoral timing.[27] Their research did find diminishing marginal returns for spending; most improvements in turnout occur for elections that increase spending from nearly $0 to about $10 per voting age resident.

In our interviews, candidates expressed mixed views about the impact of the attention to money in their races. Some, often those who received the outside support, felt that the added money and the attention it garnered increased voter engagement by "elevating the importance of school board elections," as one reform candidate in Indianapolis stated.[28] Outside funding could draw attention to these often overlooked elections by providing candidates with greater ability to reach voters through canvassing, mailers, and yard signs. Union-backed candidates were far more likely to worry that the attention and focus on money fueled "cynicism and resentment," ultimately turning off voters even more.[29] Still others believed that media attention to the role of large national funders in their local school politics may have actually motivated some citizens to turn out as a way of reasserting local control of their public schools. As one incumbent candidate in a race heavily funded by outside money explained, "This [election] became about democracy in a lot of ways. . . . [There] was a group of moms who 70 percent of what they do, they're vigorously opposed to me. Then, after Bloomberg and all these guys got involved, they were like, 'Yeah, I don't like [union candidate], but I like being able to not like him. Don't take away my ability to have my voice in democracy.' In this bizarre way, all of these people didn't want to lose their right to disagree with me."[30] Thus, while outside money may discourage some voters, it may also reinvigorate others who have a new reason to pay attention to the local school board elections.

To understand how outside donations shaped voter engagement, we tracked districtwide turnout rates over time, and where there were ward-based elections, we also compared turnout in ward elections with differing amounts of outside money. We used publicly available district- and precinct-level local school board election data for all election years between 2008 and 2014 for our five case study cities: Bridgeport, Los Angeles, Denver, New Orleans, and Indianapolis. Turnout is measured as the total number of individuals that cast a ballot for a school board member divided by the total number of registered voters. Our analysis did not generate a neat and clean story. That is in part because the structure and timing of elections varied so much from case to case, but it is also because the link between outside money and turnout was complicated by many other factors.

Given our small sample size, we first examined the relationship between turnout and the extent of out-of-state contributions using scatter plots. These descriptive scatter plots suggested a positive relationship between the amount of outside money and turnout rates, particularly for the cities of Denver, Los Angeles, and New Orleans. For example, in 2009, Denver school board candidates received, on average, less than $9,000 in outside money, and voter turnout was 17.2 percent. In 2011, outside money increased to nearly $38,000, and the voter turnout rate increased to 31.1 percent.

It is hard to know whether outside money directly drove turnout or whether other underlying factors (such as candidate characteristics or hot-button issues) had a positive impact on both outside money and turnout. The turnout for the 2012 school board elections in New Orleans, where outside money was a significant factor, was substantially higher than had been the case in 2008. Consider, for example, the high-profile election in District 3 in New Orleans, where between 2008 and 2012 the number of outside donations increased by nearly 1,000 percent and the dollar amount of outside money by nearly 3,000 percent. Turnout in District 3 was over twice as high as in 2008. *But* turnout was higher in all districts, including Districts 1 and 6 where the already low rate of outside money actually declined. The increase in turnout from 2008 to 2012 may be partly a function of money, and it's possible that there was spillover from the District 3 race to the lower profile ones, but it seems far more likely that election timing was the significant factor. Elections were shifted from October in 2008 to November in 2012, making it coterminous with high-profile general-purpose elections, including gubernatorial and presidential.

Because of these complexities, we tested for the possibility of a relationship between both the total amount of outside donations and the amount of outside donations as a percent of all donations using several regression analyses. Across all of our models, while the coefficient for outside money was positive, suggesting it may increase turnout somewhat, we found a statistically significant relationship between outside money and turnout only in Los Angeles.

Also, examining overall turnout may obscure important variation in *who* turns out. Specifically, it may be that some racial/ethnic groups react strongly to the inflow of money from large national donors. Some groups may feel that their voices are being silenced by largely white, wealthy donors, and thus, they become further disillusioned and are less likely to vote. One can also imagine that the opposite reaction occurs: outside donors activate some voters or help increase information and awareness of a competitive election. Thus, we further examine turnout by precinct and by demographic characteristics of voters to better uncover possible relationships.

Local election data are already hard to access, and finding data by individual precincts is even more challenging. However, Matt Barreto, professor of political science and Chicana/o studies at UCLA, has created an impressive database that he freely shares; it details election data by precinct for several large cities.[31] Fortunately for us, Los

Angeles and Denver are part of his work, and thus, we were able to uti-lize these data to examine how turnout varied at a more detailed level of analyses. Before discussing our results, it is important to include a caveat about these data and our examination of school board elec-tions. In particular, the demographic data of registered voters by pre-cinct included in Barreto's datasets are based on the 2000 Census. However, several of the elections we examined occurred well after the 2000 Census, thus potentially making the data out of date. If there was a significant change in the population since 2000, our estimates may not be accurate. However, it is the only dataset of which we are aware that includes precinct-level data, and the process of collecting and constructing our own 2010 dataset was beyond the scope of our research. With this caution in mind, we proceeded with the following analysis and treated it as exploratory.

Table 6.2 presents the results of our regression analysis predict-ing school board election voter turnout at the precinct level in the two cities with additional precinct-level data available from Barreto—Den-ver and Los Angeles. We used several demographic variables measured at the precinct level as independent variables, including the propor-tion of black, Asian, and Latinx; percent Democrats; and percent col-lege educated.

Additionally, we included our measure of the amount of outside money contributed. This variable was measured for the school board member district (or ward), so some precincts are located in wards with much higher levels of outside money than others. In Los Angeles, all candidates are elected from wards, while in Denver there are five wards and two at-large members. For the analysis, we included outside money data only for the ward-level candidates, so we had variation in outside money amounts within each city. We could not include outside money to PACs or organizations that supported multiple candidates because these funds could not be limited to a single ward. In Los Angeles, the predominant share of outside money went to these types of PACs; as a result, the outside money in Los Angeles was particularly under-counted in this analysis. Lastly, we created interaction terms using the outside money variable (measured at the ward level) and racial/ethnic demographic variables (measured at the precinct level). This allowed us to assess whether outside money had different impacts on

TABLE 6.2

Predicting voter turnout in school board elections

	DENVER	LOS ANGELES
% Latinx	-0.409** 0.114	0.06 0.057
% Black	0.092 0.1118	0.320** 0.085
% Asian	-0.735 0.84	0.796** -0.218
% Democrats	-0.535** 0.068	-0.133** 0.017
% College degree	0.027 0.021	0.004 0.021
Mayoral turnout 2001	0.597** 0.076	0.442** -0.02
Log outside money	-0.529 0.461	2.246** 0.337
% African American x Log outside money	0.000 0.014	-0.038** 0.01
% Latinx x Log outside money	0.037** 0.013	-0.016* 0.006
% Asian x Log outside money	0.083 0.102	-0.091** 0.024
Year 2009	-12.310** 10.79	-2.933** 0.234
Year 2011	—	-13.207** -0.344
Constant	55.602**	-2.672
R^2	0.527	0.778
N	420.000	1,770.000

Table entries are unstandardized regression coefficients with robust standard errors (clustered at the precinct level) in parentheses. For a two-tailed test of significance, *p<0.05; **p<0.01.

the turnout level of different racial and ethnic groups. In many cities, racial and ethnic minorities have disproportionately lower levels of turnout in local elections.[32] Perhaps a large infusion of outside money has the potential to more substantially increase the turnout rate of groups with traditionally lower rates of participation. Alternatively, perhaps the lack of attention to local issues that is paired with outside campaign contributions (based on our media content analysis) would reduce attention and interest among minority voters.

It's important to note that dozens of precincts are clustered within each ward, which would suggest a multilevel model. We did robustness checks of our analysis presented here using hierarchical linear models and obtained similar results. For ease of interpretation, we present the standard regression results here. Due to the clustered nature of the data, we used robust standard errors clustered at the precinct level. The analysis included 2009, 2011, and 2013 voter turnout data for Los Angeles. For Denver, only 2009 and 2011 turnout data were predicted in the model because Denver conducted redistricting in 2012 that made precinct data matching unfeasible for the 2013 election.

Overall, our results showed some similarities and some differences between the two cities. In both cities, precinct-level voter turnout in a prior local election—the mayoral election in 2001—was a strong positive predictor of school board voter turnout. Some differences emerged in the predicted results based on the proportion of different ethnic groups at the precinct level, especially for Latinxs. In Denver, a higher percent of Latinx residents at the precinct level is associated with lower voter turnout, but the interaction of Latinx percent and outside money is positive and statistically significant, suggesting that more outside money may improve turnout, especially in more predominantly Latinx areas. Meanwhile, a contrary finding emerged in Los Angeles, where the coefficient for the interaction of outside money and percent Latinxs in the precinct was negative and statistically significant, suggesting that outside money in Los Angeles could slightly depress voter turnout in areas where more Latinxs live. The coefficients for the interaction terms for outside money and percent black (as well as percent Asian) are both negative and statistically significant in Los Angeles. Finally, the coefficients for the outside money variable differed in each city: there was no statistically significant relationship between outside money and turnout in Denver (controlling for other factors), but in Los Angeles, the relationship between outside money and voter turnout was statistically significant and positive, other things being equal.

To offer a substantive comparison, consider a simulation using four hypothetical precincts in the 2009 election: two in Los Angeles and two in Denver. We set all four of these hypothetical districts at 50 percent Latinx (the average percent Latinx in Los Angeles voting precincts is 23 percent, and the average in Denver is 22 percent). One precinct in each city was assigned a moderately high level of outside money—$22,000—while the other precinct in each city had only $1,000 in outside money (the average outside money amount at the ward level is $11,387 in Los Angeles and $12,905 in Denver).

On average, Denver had much higher voter turnout in the 2009 school board election, 27 percent, compared to 18 percent in Los Angeles. Now let's compare that to the predicted turnout in our four hypothetical districts based on the regression results. When we hold all other variables at their means, the predicted voter turnout in the Los Angeles precinct with high outside money would be 19 percent (slightly higher than the overall LA level), while the Los Angeles precinct with low outside money would have 17 percent predicted voter turnout (slightly lower). In other words, in Los Angeles, more outside money is predicted to slightly increase voter turnout in high Latinx areas, while voter turnout is slightly depressed with little outside money. The reason is that the positive coefficient for outside money overall in Los Angeles outweighs the negative interaction of outside money and percent Latinx at the precinct level. By comparison, the Denver precinct with similar Latinx population and high outside money level would have a predicted voter turnout of 27 percent (equal to the actual overall turnout rate), while the comparable precinct with low outside money would have 22 percent (5 percentage points below the citywide average). Thus, outside money appears to boost up otherwise low predicted levels of turnout in high Latinx areas in Denver. These predicted outcomes show how outside money interacts somewhat differently in a different context.

Our analyses suggest that there probably is a relationship between outside money and voter turnout, but not one that is straightforward or dramatic or consistent across different local contexts. We found some evidence that the relationship of outside money to voter turnout may be mediated by varied impacts on different racial and ethnic groups. We also found that the relationship between outside money and turnout could vary by city. While there appears to be an overall positive relationship in Los Angeles, we found no overall significant effect in Denver, but some evidence that outside money might raise participation among groups that vote at lower levels on average in local elections, such as Latinxs in Denver. Moreover, if it is important to increase voter turnout in school board elections, there is an easy way to do it without relying on external funding with its associated complications: simply shift school board elections so they occur at the same time as general-purpose ones.[33]

OUTSIDE MONEY AND THE NATIONALIZATION OF THE LOCAL POLICY AGENDA

Another potential consequence of outside money is that it is accompanied by a set of predetermined, one-size-fits-all policy agenda items. It is well known that many of the national donors we identified have strong ideas about what's good and bad education policy. Furthermore, national organizations aligned with both unions and reformers are engaging in these elections and supporting candidates aligned with their respective positions. If outside money is accompanied by an increased focus on a nationally determined set of agenda items, more localized issues may be overshadowed or forgotten altogether. This situation may occur not only because outside money enables reform candidates to better market their policy preferences but also because union-funded and some nonaffiliated candidates countermobilize and focus their messaging on opposing these same issues. We heard these concerns expressed in our candidate interviews. An unaffiliated candidate from Los Angeles summarized his frustration by calling the election environment "a whole different universe," where his interests in issues such as class size were not hot topics. Instead, he found that "if [he] were to run today and talk about tenure and layoff policy and charters, that fires up a lot of voters" and gets attention.

We examined shifts in the level of attention devoted to specific issues and agenda items based both on our candidate interviews and on content analysis of media coverage of each election. We utilized issues from Race to the Top to operationalize "nationalized issues."

We included closing the achievement gap, closing persistently failing schools, expanding charter schools, evaluating teachers based on data, and giving merit pay for teachers. We also generated a list of opposition messages associated with these nationalized issues such as limiting testing and limiting the expansion of charter schools. Opposition to reform issues also included limiting standardized testing, protecting tenure rules, and focusing on neighborhood public schools. Finally, we developed a list of other educational issues as they were mentioned in election coverage, which we termed "localized issues." This list included topics such as budget and funding priorities in the district, board–community communication and engagement, school safety, and other educational programs such as the arts, adult education, and vocational education.

As table 6.3 shows, except for Denver, issue coverage was minimal (Los Angeles) or nonexistent (Bridgeport, Indianapolis, and New Orleans) in the early years we examined. Denver is the only city with consistent and robust issue coverage. In Los Angeles, where there was some coverage in 2009 and 2011, we saw virtually no difference in the frequency of articles that included discussion of localized issues and nationalized issues.

This media coverage stands in stark contrast to all elections in Denver and elections after 2011 in the other cities. In these elections, nationalized issues received greater attention than localized issues. When we examined the data even further, we found that the pro-reform message appeared in more articles than the opposition message. To illustrate this, we highlight the Denver 2013 election. The pro-reform message to expand the number of charter schools was included in thirteen articles (or about one-third of all election coverage articles), while messages about limiting the expansion of charter schools occurred in only one article. Somewhat more common was the opposition message of focusing on traditional or neighborhood public schools, but even this message was mentioned in only five articles. A similar pattern was found in Los Angeles in 2013 where the pro-reform message regarding the need to evaluate teachers using student test scores occurred in thirteen of the articles while, in contrast, the counter-reform issue of limiting the number and use of standardized tests occurred in just four articles.[34]

TABLE 6.3

Issue coverage: number of articles including each issue by city and year

| | | NATIONALIZED ISSUES | | | | | LOCAL ISSUES | | | |
		Charters and choice	Teacher retention and evaluation policies	Accountability systems	Interventions for failing schools	Tenure	Budget	Educational programs	Board-community communication and relationship	Superintendent
Bridgeport	2013	5	1	1	0	0	4	0	3	12
Denver	2009	16	15	2	8	10	8	3	7	0
	2011	9	2	3	7	3	1	0	3	0
	2013	17	6	3	8	1	0	2	1	2
Indianapolis	2014	12	8	1	6	0	9	1	4	1
Los Angeles	2009	3	0	0	1	0	1	0	0	0
	2011	2	1	0	0	0	3	0	2	0
	2013	16	13	4	1	7	4	3	2	12
New Orleans	2012	11	0	2	0	1	3	2	4	7

Looking at the localized issues, we saw few that reached similarly high levels of coverage in the media as the nationalized issues. Only three localized issues were mentioned across many elections and in several articles: the budget and resource allocation; board–community relations and community engagement; and the superintendent. In Denver's 2009 election and Indianapolis's 2014 election, discussions of budgeting and budget priorities received moderate coverage, matching or surpassing some of the nationalized issues. While a somewhat smaller number of articles discussed board–community relations and community engagement, this issue too was consistently raised in articles across nearly every election we examined. Discussion of curricular and programming options received minimal attention.

We categorized discussion of the superintendent as a localized issue, because in more traditional school board elections, candidates often run as either supporters or opponents to the sitting leader, basing their stance on the superintendent's personality, leadership style, particular initiatives, or failure to act with sufficient urgency. The issue of the district superintendent was especially prevalent in Bridgeport and Los Angeles, occurring more often than many or all of the nationalized issues. However, upon closer inspection, discussion of these superintendents was part of the nationalized issue debates occurring in the school board election. Bridgeport's superintendent in 2013 was the famed reform superintendent Paul Vallas. Vallas had led reform efforts in Chicago, Philadelphia, and New Orleans before heading up the Bridgeport Public Schools. He was known for increasing school choice and private management of schools. In Bridgeport, candidates and the media referenced the superintendent as shorthand for discussing these reform issues. One media headline questioned whether Gardner, Hennessey, and Baker, three candidates who were backed by the Working Families Party, would "oust Vallas before year's end?" The article, which was posted to the Education Connecticut blog site immediately after the winners had been announced, proclaimed that the election would "all but guarantee a dramatic shift in the make-up of Bridgeport's school board, which is currently controlled by a pro-Vallas, Democratic-endorsed majority."[35] Because of Vallas's history and ties to pro-reform groups, discussions about the superintendent in

Bridgeport were necessarily discussions about furthering nationalized reform policies. This same shorthand was used in Los Angeles, where Superintendent John Deasy was also associated with reform-focused issues. In his prior work as superintendent of Prince George's County Public Schools, he instituted a pay-for-performance plan where teachers received bonuses based on their students' test score outcomes. Just as in Bridgeport, candidates running for school board and the media often framed their discussions about retaining Deasy as superintendent of LAUSD as a referendum on his policies, such as using student test scores as a significant part of a teacher's evaluation. The District 4 race between Kate Anderson, the reform-backed candidate, and Steve Zimmer, incumbent and union-backed candidate, was especially focused on the superintendent with the media repeatedly questioning Zimmer about his intentions to retain or fire Deasy. Thus, while the issue of the superintendent was not initially included in our list of reform issues, in the case of Bridgeport and Los Angeles, the two became synonymous.

Our findings about issue coverage seemed to support the concern expressed in several of our interviews with local candidates: national debates and their associated framing are getting more attention than local issues and concerns that may be important to many candidates and voters. "It's not just the dominant message anymore. It's the only message people are hearing" is how one Los Angeles candidate described the reform-oriented, nationalized issues discussed during his campaign.[36] Another candidate in Los Angeles stressed the importance of adult education because many of the parents of students are immigrants who are learning English as a second language. Recent cuts to the adult education programs fueled this candidate's desire to run for school board. However, during our interview he lamented that he was unable to bring this issue to the foreground. Similarly, even a reform-backed candidate in Denver who was supportive of charter schools expressed frustration that other policy issues, such as the digital divide and English language learner needs, were unable to become a central focus in the election. While nationalized issues received attention, increased donations enabled some candidates to amplify this messaging because it "provided a bullhorn."[37]

JUST LIKE THE FEDERAL GOVERNMENT: POLARIZATION IN LOCAL SCHOOL BOARD ELECTIONS

As national politics have become increasingly polarized, fewer moderates have been able to be elected. News reports frequently include graphs demonstrating the increasingly polarized voting in Congress.[38] Increased polarization is also found among the electorate. The Pew Research Center reported in 2017 that the partisan differences in political preferences on issues such as race, immigration, national security, and environmental protection have reached record levels. When compared to other divisions in society, such as gender, race and ethnicity, religious observance, or education levels, they report that "the magnitude of these [partisan] differences dwarfs other divisions."[39] In our interviews, candidates expressed concerns that the tone and nature of local school board elections were becoming more polarized, mimicking the political style of national politics.

Long insulated from more widely felt political currents through off-cycle elections and a governance structure divorced from all other policy arenas, candidates in local school board elections were more often characterized for their pragmatic approach to policy issues. In fact, only 10 to 15 percent of school boards today elect their representatives on partisan ballots.[40] While school board divisions may not follow the same lines as political parties—particularly for electoral contests in majority-Democratic voting cities—issue-area conflicts that are prevalent in education may be hardening. One Los Angeles candidate who received support from teacher unions even referenced national politics when characterizing her election. She explained, "[It's] very much like our federal government [where] you're a Democrat or Republican. Now, especially, you're either a charter candidate or you're a union candidate." She further explained that this carried over to the way the school board functions: "When they get on the board, nobody can cross that line."[41] Another union-backed candidate similarly expressed concern that the polarization during the campaign would carry over to the functioning of the school board and be "corrosive." He further added, "Whether the ideology is one you agree with or disagree with, [the result] still tends to be more ideological, which is not good for problem solving."[42]

Candidates, including some who had been on the school board, found that taking a moderate, pragmatic approach to decision-making was not likely to attract donations. Consider this incumbent school board member in Denver who had received funding from the teacher's union but believed strongly that "the school board needed people who were open-minded and not fixed in their approaches to try and come up with solutions." As he reported, he quickly discovered that "most donors don't like the middle approach. They aren't excited by it. They want people who will pound their fists for one side or pound their fists for another, and that's what motivates donors. At least that's what I found."[43] Another Latinx incumbent candidate who had received funding from national donors stated that she had made some difficult decisions while serving on the board, stating that she "didn't make everyone happy." She laughed and went on to explain that "fundraising becomes a little more difficult. They're not as eager when you're not as willing to, I guess, pay back the debt." The result was, as these candidates saw it, a "simplification [of the issues] and polarization and not really engaging in thoughtful conversation or listening to the nuanced discussions. It's just more of this dividing, divisive politics," which some candidates feared harmed the ability to problem solve and compromise.[44]

Newspapers and other media reports about the election can also provide important insights into the nature or tone of the election and the extent to which the influence of outside donations is tied to polarization. The simplistic narrative of reformers battling the union was often present in local media coverage of candidates and the school board election. Media reports often framed candidates as in one camp or the other and portrayed them as locked in a fight for the future direction of the local schools. Such framing was especially evident in Denver's elections and elections after 2011 in our other four cities. As one article in Denver's 2011 election stated, "most of the media coverage is treating this year's school board race as a balanced contest between 'reformers' and 'opponents of reform.'"[45] *Education Week* characterized the 2013 Los Angeles election as a "national showdown pitting the long-standing influence of teachers' unions against the expanding imprint of deep-pocketed education activities."[46] In other cases, op-eds warned readers that the results of the school board election would determine the direction of the district—either toward the nationalized issue agenda or away. As the *Denver Post* stated in 2009, "the election could mean the difference between pushing forward with reform efforts that have really just begun or putting the brakes on progress."[47]

In addition to this battle framing, media coverage of an election also may incorporate an assessment of the tone of the election by characterizing it with words and phrases such as *pivotal battle, heated, intensely polarized,* or *friendly exchange.* One possible consequence of the nationalization of school board elections is a growing polarization among candidates and, as a result, news coverage that conveys an increasingly hostile or negative election. As the quotes in this chapter indicate, candidates felt a growing pressure to take strong stances on hot policy issues to attract donors. In other words, candidates felt as though donors were asking: "Whose side are you on?"

To further understand the tone of the school board elections we examined, we conducted a sentiment analysis of all news articles using the Linguistic Inquiry and Word Count (LIWC) program. LIWC is a computerized text analysis program that categorizes and quantifies language use.[48] LIWC was developed from a psycholinguistic perspective by James Pennebaker, Regents Centennial Professor in the Department of Psychology at the University of Texas, Austin (http://liwc.net), and has been used to examine a wide range of texts.

Sentiment analysis involves examination of source text to identify the presence and prevalence of different themes in the text as well as meta-constructs of the text. LIWC analyzes text to produce several summary language measures. Among these summary language measures is emotional tone, which LIWC calculates on a scale from 0 to 100. A tone measure of 50 indicates language that is neutral while higher numbers indicate language that is more positive, cheerful, or happy and lower numbers indicate language that is more negative, hostile, and anxious.[49] The algorithm that is used to calculate summary language measures is proprietary, but the measures it produces have been validated.[50] An advantage of using LIWC for sentiment analysis is that it applies a consistent coding scheme across all text, which in turn yields measures with high internal validity and that are also consistent across a range of studies that also employ this approach.

Analyzing our newspaper coverage, we found that the tone of school board election coverage was highly variable. Across all years we found strong positive and strongly negative articles (see figure 6.3). The tone of campaign coverage in Denver in 2013 and Los Angeles in 2011 and 2013 leaned more negative than other years. Both were years where large national donors were highly active in the elections. The most positive campaign coverage was found in Bridgeport in 2013 and in Indianapolis in 2014. Outside donations from large national donors were infrequent in the Bridgeport 2013 election, with just 9 percent of all individual donations coming from large national donors. While the 2014 election in Indianapolis saw a moderate number of donations from large national donors (25 percent), this number was down significantly from the previous election cycle when 44 percent of all individual donations came from large national donors. However, there was no coverage located for the earlier election, so while the amount of coverage clearly rose, we cannot say if the tone of coverage changes in Indianapolis. Recall that in 2014, *Chalkbeat Indiana* became a prominent media source for school board election news. In fact, of the eleven most positive articles, nine were *Chalkbeat* profiles of

FIGURE 6.3 **Percent of articles with a negative tone, by city and year**

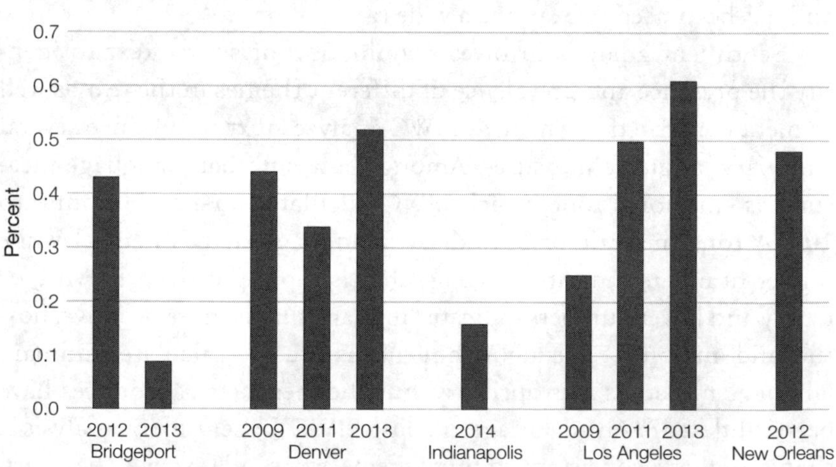

each candidate. It is not surprising that these profile pieces would be positive. So while the overall distribution appeared more positive than other elections, the coverage by other media outlets was more evenly distributed. Overall, this analysis provided evidence that media coverage may become more negative in some places when large national donations are abundant.

To better understand the relationship between outside money and election negativity, we looked more closely at articles that mentioned increasing campaign costs, donations, and donors. Out of the 225 articles examined, 93 included at least one mention of these funding issues. As one can see in figure 6.4, articles discussing money are often negative in tone. In Los Angeles in 2013, where coverage overall was more negative, coverage that included a focus on campaign costs and donations was especially negative, with 14 of the 23 money-focused articles having a negative tone. Similarly, in Denver's 2013 election, where 32 percent of all individual donations were from large national donors, 8 of the 11 articles focused on campaign finances had a negative tone. While this pattern was not found across all cities and years, our findings do suggest that campaign financing has become a topic that receives greater attention when large national donors enter

FIGURE 6.4   **Percent of articles focused on money with a negative tone, by city and year**

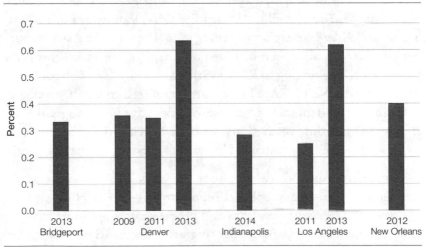

the race and that the coverage of this phenomenon is often associated with a negative tone.

We see a similar negative tone creeping into the campaign literature for candidates in elections characterized by large sums of outside funding. In Los Angeles, all campaign communication with the public is collected and available online. We examined over 340 different flyers, phone scripts, door hangers, mailers, and postcards. We found that a couple of high-profile district races included negative campaigning. One contest became particularly contentious with personal attacks and charges of ethics violations. In a runoff election for the District 5 seat, Bennett Kayser, a retired teacher who was heavily supported by the teacher and administrator unions, faced Luis Sanchez, the chief of staff to the school board president, who was backed by Mayor Villaraigosa and his PAC, Coalition for School Reform. Both sides spent millions of dollars to secure the seat, with Kayser eventually winning by just six hundred votes in an election that saw a less than 10 percent turnout rate. Both candidates had campaign materials sent out by independent expenditure committees. These materials attacked their opponents and warned voters to support their candidate to avoid negative repercussions. The Coalition for School Reform repeatedly sent out mailers that labeled Kayser as "Part of the Problem." Another flyer used an image of Pinocchio to suggest the other side (Kayser's side) was lying about their attacks on Sanchez. It urged voters to "not believe the smear campaign against Luis Sanchez." In another mailer, the *Los Angeles Times* headline "LA Unified OKs Doomsday Budget" was accompanied by text explaining that "schools are facing massive budget cuts." The mailer then included an image of an unpaid property tax statement belonging to Kayser with text stating "But School Board candidate BENNETT KAYSER repeatedly refused to pay his property taxes on time." Bennett Kayser also had negative ads being sent out. In one, the headline reads "Luis Sanchez: Special Interests & Lobbyist's #1 Advocate." Accompanied by a photo of Sanchez, the flyer reads:

> But don't expect to catch him at the office. He's probably at another of his many political fundraisers in Beverly Hills with developers, construction firms and private charter operators who have received or are seeking huge contracts from the school district.

They love Luis Sanchez. While Sanchez took lavish trips across the country, he personally led the effort to slash classroom funding and fire thousands of teachers, school nurses and libraries.

While the Sanchez–Bennett runoff certainly had the most negative materials overall, the single most aggressive mailer was sent by the Coalition for School Reform in 2013 in support of Monica Garcia. The mailer featured a rattlesnake with venom dripping from its fangs accompanied by the headline "SNAKES IN THE GRASS: Why are special interests *attacking* Monica Garcia?" Ads such as this were in the minority, but they were almost exclusively found in the high-profile district races where outside funding was more prevalent.

CONCLUSION

The consequences of outside money are neither wholly good nor wholly bad. Outside money can bring greater attention to elections that have, for far too long, been largely ignored by local media. Increased attention, however, can be skewed in favor of those with the most financial backing, leaving voters with little information about many candidates on election day. Similarly, increased media attention usually includes more information on policy issues, potentially educating voters about key issues facing their local schools; however, this increased attention is not evenly distributed across all issues. Instead, readers of school board election media coverage encounter a narrower policy agenda focused on nationalized issues, sometimes at the expense of more localized issues that may be of more immediate concern to the local citizenry. Finally, increased funding enabled candidates to engage voters with more and better outreach efforts, which may increase voter turnout. Increased voter turnout can limit the ability of all special interests from co-opting the election in their favor. Yet a more extensive campaign effort has also increased negative campaigning in some school board elections. These campaigns resemble larger state and national elections, which might turn off some voters from engagement.

It may be tempting to see only the good or the bad in the consequences discussed here. After all, we are all susceptible to the influence of confirmation bias, or the likelihood to find evidence that agrees with our preexisting ideas more convincing than evidence that challenges our beliefs.[51] And becoming more informed is not always a defense against confirmation bias. In fact, the most informed can sometimes be the most polarized.[52] But our findings suggest it would be false—or at the least premature—to conclude that the consequences of outside money are uniformly and decidedly good or bad. Moreover, the unique context of each city meant that there was variation in how and to what extent the consequences impacted the election and ultimately, we suspect, the governing of elected school board members.

The consequences we highlight are based on early experiences with nationalization of school board elections. It may be that it is simply too early to know for sure what the consequences will be for local school governance. Additional issues may arise, and some of the consequences may fade away as local communities adapt to, embrace, or fight against the new landscape of local school politics. Neither the arc of nationalization nor its consequences are predetermined. It is precisely because these are contested and susceptible to influence that attentive and politically strategic actors are putting their energy and resources on the line. Without pretending to be able to predict the outcome of battles still to come, we can offer some thoughts about likely implications, a task we turn to in our next, and concluding, chapter.

CHAPTER 7

....

Conclusions and Implications

IN THE FALL OF 2017, a mailer circulated among Denver voters to make the case against Angela Cobián, who was running for the school board. Cobián had received campaign funding from Democrats for Education Reform (DFER), and the union-backed forces behind the mailer considered her to be too closely aligned to the reform agenda—despite the fact that she was a young Latinx, a former community organizer, and an ESL teacher in the Denver Public Schools. The mailer presented its anti-Cobián argument in vivid terms. It juxtaposed her photo with those of Donald Trump and Betsy DeVos, alleging that her campaign was "funded by groups with ties to Donald Trump and Education Secretary Betsy DeVos. Not to mention funding from the Koch Brothers." The flyer urged voters to "reject the Trump/DeVos/Cobián plan for Denver Public Schools." The state DFER director responded that the mailer represented "desperate lies" and insisted that all the reform candidates her group supported were "fighting to protect immigrants protected through the Deferred Action for Childhood Arrivals, or DACA, program, which Trump plans to end; to support LGBT students; and to provide 'real public school options for kids.'" Cobián defended herself to a reporter, explaining

> As a young woman of color, I can't think of a more hypocritical, absurd and inane attack on my identity.... I have in every single

way lived out what the opportunity gap is in education. I have lived out what it means to be a young teacher of color in a very white-dominant space, teaching majority students of color. . . . To see someone slap a black and white picture of me next to two people who are unqualified to lead our country, who are the embodiment of white privilege in Betsy DeVos and Donald Trump, is so frustrating. I feel powerless. I know what racism feels like, so this isn't new. But I am deeply pained.[1]

A spokesperson for the Colorado Education Association, which funded the independent expenditure group that distributed the mail, attempted to deflect from the union's role and provided the following statement: "There is a lot of money in the Denver school board races that come[s] from non-disclosed sources that should be looked into."

In a political climate where sharp policy disagreements over issues like charter schools divide coalitions of advocates, candidates, and members of the public, the addition of outside money in a political campaign adds fuel to the fire. Well-funded campaigns can draw more attention as their fires get bigger and brighter—more mailings, more events, more radio ads—but they also increase the likelihood that valued norms of civil discourse can get burned in a polarizing and potentially negative political environment. Our candidate interviews further illustrate the sharp contrasts in perceptions of outside money and its impact. One candidate in Indianapolis, for instance, was passionate about its deleterious effects:

> What I saw happen was a loss of community control of the local school district, so I would say if a community wants to retain control of their local school district, that they have to rise up, and fight against receiving outside money from people, from organizations that appear to be altruistic, but they're really not. You can't let that money come in. It will destroy parent input.[2]

Meanwhile, a candidate from Los Angeles was just as forceful about the opposing viewpoint, that outside money represents positive national attention on important local issues and resources for mobilizing the community:

I don't think money from the outside is instead of or in place of. I don't think it's like people in California stopped giving in order for others to give. I think the impact of what we were doing really did rise to a national level. . . . What we are trying to do is connect with people who have not yet connected with government . . . and we're always welcoming new voters on an ongoing basis. That is all very intense community organizing. It's really exciting. . . . The fight for who's in charge is a natural part of the government of politics, I think.[3]

These paired comments highlight a key division as the local political environment in some urban districts is reshaped by new external donors and organizations. On the one hand, politics is dynamic; it is neither possible nor desirable for local school districts to remain unchanged as the world transforms around them. Institutions evolve and people mobilize new movements to support ever-shifting goals. Conflict is a natural part of this process. On the other hand, deeply held values underlie our political institutions and provide an important source of continuity in a changing world. Two values that have long animated school politics are localism and community control, together imbued in the belief that local boards and local elections facilitate community investment and involvement.

Our findings do not settle the debate over the political consequences of outside money. The evidence does not neatly align with either perspective: that outside money is destroying local civic engagement, or that outside money is reinvigorating local democracy and mobilizing broader public engagement. Instead, we find some evidence that aligns on each side of this conflict. This might be an unsatisfactory conclusion for some readers, but it is the one that the empirical evidence leads us to.

On the positive or neutral side for outside money, we found that (1) school board campaigns are more professional and better managed, and have the capacity to reach voters using many strategies; (2) voter turnout might be higher, though our best evidence comes from just one district, Los Angeles; (3) other organizations, including unions, bring important policy substance into these races, presenting alternative visions for educational policy; and (4) candidates from diverse racial and ethnic backgrounds are represented on both the reform and union sides of the debate. This last observation suggests that policy conflicts do not necessarily overlap with racial and ethnic divisions— though the increased diversity brought in by outside money does not preclude racial and ethnic messaging cues, both positive and negative, in these political campaigns.

On the negative side for outside money, we found (1) more media coverage of money in politics, rather than of substantive education policy issues, in many elections; (2) in Los Angeles, heightened negative campaigning, particularly by well-funded independent expenditure committees; (3) higher-cost campaigns that might deter some potential candidates from entering a race; (4) concerns among candidates and elected board members that outside money highlighted divisions (especially on charter schools) at the expense of more pragmatic and locally focused policy deliberation; and (5) at least some evidence that national issues may be displacing more local concerns.

Overall, our findings shed light on a new landscape for local school board elections—a landscape that, in some respects, is influenced by broader shifts in American politics. As the changing roles of donors, unions, and the media play out on a national stage across many institutions and issue areas, local school board elections provide a chance to analyze these changes up close. What this analysis reveals is that, although the nationalization of education politics is an important part of our story, the persistence of localism shows how nationalizing trends can operate quite differently in varied local contexts. As national money flows into any individual school board campaign, what determines the outcome is not simply the money itself, but the recruitment and tactics of local candidates, the alignment and engagement with mobilized local organizations, and the resonance of messages with local voters. The voices of the candidates and their own visions of educational policy are not simply echoes of national debates. Specific constituencies in each district—including black and Latinx candidates, activists, business organizations, and nonteacher unions as well as the local elite donors—also have agency in channeling the direction and uses of outside money, the messages, and the counter mobilizations in campaigns. Nationalization is providing new tools and resources to leverage in campaigns and new playbooks for issue agendas, but in striking ways, no two elections that we analyzed for this book are quite alike, and many are remarkably different in personalities, strategies, and outcomes.

DONORS AND MONEY IN POLITICS

As wealth inequality has grown in the United States, the wealthiest citizens have shown a growing interest in committing large sums of money to political campaigns.[4] The increase in the share of campaign contributions from the top 0.01 percent of households began in the 1990s and grew steadily through the 2000s—even before the *Citizens United* Supreme Court decision in 2010 dramatically changed the landscape of campaign finance regulations. With this growing flood of money, every segment of the US political system is a potential target, from presidential and congressional campaigns, to gubernatorial elections, to local mayoral races and now even school board contests. For example, the Center for Responsive Politics estimates that the total cost of congressional elections grew from $2.3 billion in 2000 to $4 billion in 2016 (adjusted for inflation).[5] After 2010, *Citizens United* might have accelerated trends already underway among individual donors by increasing their familiarity with using intermediary 501(c)(4)s as vehicles for campaign spending that can accept unlimited and anonymous contributions.

Our research shows that school board elections have now been swept up in these trends, with billionaire donors from out of state contributing to school board candidates in sums much larger than are typical from local donors and catalyzing an arms race of increased funding that raises the cost of running for office. In cities like Los Angeles, New Orleans, and Indianapolis, campaign funds raised from individuals more than doubled from one election cycle to the next. Further, a small number of these national donors were particularly active; they contributed to school board elections in multiple cities, and most of them were also involved in funding federal elections. Moreover, many of these individuals played the role of donor in spheres beyond campaign finance.

School board elections that attract high levels of outside money are still the exception, of course; our best estimate is that well below

1 percent of the thousands of school districts in the country do so in any given year. For three reasons, these cases are important. First, because these school districts are usually among the largest districts in the country, the proportion of students and families potentially affected by the influence of outside money is much higher than the simple numbers would suggest. Second, the tactical decision-making that guides outside donors and organizations to become involved steers them to elections where important national policy initiatives are in play, and where the balance of power between competing factions is susceptible to change. Third, the model and precedent these cases set of high spending and high contention might come to be seen as standard, which would begin to change the way school board elections unfold even when outside funders are not in the game.

When Diane Ravitch coined the phrase "billionaire boys club," she did not initially refer to campaign funders; her focus was on major education philanthropists such as Bill Gates, Eli Broad, and the Walton family. Lately, "billionaire boys club" is also used to identify big campaign donors. Recently, for one example, an article appeared on the California Teachers Association (CTA) website with a headline about the upcoming gubernatorial election: "Antonio Villaraigosa: A Candidate Backed by the Billionaire Boys Club and Trump Megadonors."[6] The article named donors who are familiar from our school board elections as well—Reed Hastings and Eli Broad. Eli Broad, for one, has distinguished himself as a member of both the big philanthropy club and the big campaign donor club. As a member of both clubs, he's in good company with John Arnold, as well as some billionaire women such as Laurene Powell Jobs and Carrie Walton Penner. The broader lesson is that these big donors are not bounded by geography, level of government, or contribution category in their distribution of funds to influence education policy and politics. For the donors who are also philanthropists, they often give much larger sums as charitable contributions in support of particular policy reforms than they do to individual school board campaigns. Combining philanthropic funds and campaign contributions offers different strategies for influence and potentially smooths the way for their agenda priorities.

The role of large national donors in local school board elections should be viewed in the context of these broad changes in national wealth, philanthropy, and campaign donations to politicians and causes beyond the sphere of education. Large national donors are not going away any time soon. As billionaires move away from private foundations and toward more flexible models for distributing their wealth, the link between philanthropic funding in education and political contribution behavior might grow even stronger. Billionaires like Laurene Powell Jobs and Mark Zuckerberg are forgoing the formation of traditional foundations and instead are using limited liability companies (LLCs) to fund their favorite social causes, including, but extending beyond, education. Powell Jobs created Emerson Collective while Zuckerberg, with his wife Priscilla Chan, started the Chan Zuckerberg Initiative (CZI). Unlike traditional philanthropic foundations, these ventures are not required to file annual reports to the IRS listing their grants. Also, Emerson Collective and CZI are not limited to funding 501(c)(3) nonprofit organizations; they can invest in for-profit ventures and fund political campaigns and lobbying. Perhaps signaling their political ambitions, CZI has hired Obama's 2008 campaign manager, David Plouffe, as the organization's president of policy and advocacy.

It's important to remember that the increasing prominence of donors in local education politics is not simply a story about the donors. The donors empower certain sets of local people and local organizations. Large infusions of philanthropic funding have already been shown to shift the mix of organizations most involved in urban school district politics, raising the profile of charter school groups and nonprofit reform organizations like Teach for America (TFA).[7] Our analysis of school board campaigns shows the electoral version of a similar process. While TFA alumni only figured in a small set of high-profile elections, a much more common relationship existed between outside money and candidates with charter school connections. In the process of nationalization, the funding that supports these candidates can empower and amplify a message supporting charter schools across a wide range of local contexts. The candidates differ: some are die-hard charter supporters, whereas others support charter schools with caveats and conditions. Thus, nationalization amplifies a message through these shared networks, but the exact content of the message is not a carbon copy from one campaign to the next.

UNIONS AND THE DEMOCRATIC PARTY

The long-standing alliance in US politics between labor unions and the Democratic Party extends back to the New Deal coalition, when unions played a major role in raising campaign funds for Franklin D. Roosevelt's 1936 re-election campaign.[8] In many respects, this has been a mutually beneficial alliance. Unions play a role in driving Democratic voter turnout, and they are capable of raising large campaign war chests distributed primarily to Democratic candidates and organizations. When Democrats hold a majority in government, they can offer policy benefits to union members and working-class people, though lately much political energy has been focused on trying to thwart Republican efforts to reduce union power through policies like "right to work." Teacher unions historically held an important place in the alliance between labor and the Democratic Party. Throughout the 1990s, the National Education Association consistently ranked among the top five organizational contributors in federal elections, with well over 90 percent of funds going to Democrats.[9]

Although unions remain mostly in step with the Democratic Party, their relative importance in the overall party coalition has shrunk considerably in recent decades. Partly, this is due to a rise during the 1970s and 1980s in organized interest-group activity among other constituencies aligned with Democrats, including racial and ethnic minorities, women, LGBTQ people, and environmentalists.[10] Yet it is also a function of the increasing share of campaign contributions from extremely wealthy individuals. As a study in the *Journal of Economic Perspectives* revealed:

> The relative proportions of funds raised by Democrats from the top 0.01 percent and from organized labor provide a telling comparison. The top 0.01 percent, whose donations had been roughly on par with those of labor during [the] 1980s and early 1990s, outspent labor by more than a 4:1 margin during the 2012 election cycle.[11]

In this context, labor unions are one Democratic Party constituency among many, and they are no longer nearly as important in providing campaign resources.

Our research shows the local political implications of these national trends. The school board candidates competing across our five cities are overwhelmingly Democrats. Yet rather than simply competing by mobilizing local constituencies and sets of donors around specific local conflicts, many candidates are mobilizing funds linked to state and national union organizations and education reform groups supported by very wealthy (mostly Democrat-aligned) individuals. These local contests demonstrate the fractures within the Democratic Party, as wealthy businesspeople have become a more prominent constituency and larger source of funding. Even within the labor union movement, unions are not always unified. We found that teacher unions sometimes support one set of candidates, while service employees and other unions support different candidates. Unions are increasingly fighting a war within their own party and on multiple fronts, including the local education arena.

Recent events suggest some important turning points for teacher unions on the horizon. In June 2018 the Supreme Court issued a 5–4 ruling in *Janus v. AFSCME* that eliminates public employee unions' ability to collect mandatory fees from workers (including from non-union members) in a unionized workplace. The arguments in the case hinged on a conflict over the right to free speech of an employee who does not want to support union speech that he or she opposes, versus the collective benefits of union representation in contract negotiations with management provided to all workers, whether or not they are members. Most commentary written in the wake of the decision has noted that eliminating mandatory fees will significantly reduce overall union resources and will likely hamper unions' ability to work effectively in both the collective bargaining arena and the political realm. But some early research, based on the impact of right-to-work laws on teacher unions in Michigan and Wisconsin, suggests that teacher unions might actually redistribute their limited resources to become more active in political campaigns.[12] If coverage of the California Teacher Association's (CTA) strategies for the 2018 election is any indication, political investment might be a major focus for unions going forward. The CTA plans an all-out canvassing and outreach effort for the 2018 midterm elections, with a goal of 80 percent voter turnout.[13] This is not to suggest that teacher unions' political power will rise; if anything, it might be a sign that unions are fighting for their political lives. As we showed in the analysis of campaign contributions, unions are often already outspent in school board elections by the combined resources of large national individual donors, reform organizations, and other groups and individuals that ally with reform candidates. Teacher unions have often been portrayed as the eight-hundred-pound gorilla in local school politics—and our evidence already shows that this image is overblown—but the *Janus* decision throws up new barriers for unions' political efforts.

Meanwhile, the teacher strikes and mobilizations in the spring of 2018 in states like Arizona, Kentucky, North Carolina, Oklahoma, and West Virginia have demonstrated enduring sources of political power and strategies for future organizing. In many states, it was the rank and file teachers, rather than union leadership, who spurred the action and planned walkouts to protest low pay, stagnant state funding, and poor working conditions. In Arizona and North Carolina the phrase "Red for Ed"—as a hashtag, an organizational name, and as the color of T-shirts worn by protesting teachers—echoed across social media posts shared by teachers and their supporters. Notably, these teacher protests took place in right-to-work states, where unions are traditionally weak. Direct action as a political weapon will still be available even when more formal avenues for collective bargaining and funding are limited, which means that even as *Janus* removes resources for unions, teachers might return to a more traditional and grassroots form of mobilization. These protests are a reminder that unions and teacher associations, with their large memberships, can pursue other strategies beyond funding campaigns. While wealthy outside donors are largely limited to using their checkbooks, unions can draw on a broader political repertoire as they face new constraints to create new opportunities.

NATIONAL MEDIA ENVIRONMENT AND THE DECLINE OF LOCAL ISSUES

Our analysis of media coverage revealed somewhat disappointing results. In many cases, school board elections received little to no attention in local newspapers. Nonetheless, a few new online-only sources, in particular the *Chalkbeat* websites covering Denver and Indianapolis, offer a new model for journalism. Relying on philanthropic funders, they provide space for greater attention to local school board elections, including substantive coverage of candidates and issue positions. Online-only publications are probably not a substitute for the kind of coverage traditionally provided by local newspapers or for the audience these newspapers traditionally would reach. *Chalkbeat*'s 2017 Annual Report describes the readership numbers for the website (more than two-hundred-seventy thousand visitors per month) but does not offer detailed demographics about the readership.[14] Given that 39 percent of respondents from a readers survey said they "directly applied knowledge gained from *Chalkbeat* in their professional life," it seems likely that the *Chalkbeat* audience includes a large share of education professionals.

A broader trend in the local news environment is the declining audience for local print newspapers. As Daniel Hopkins thoroughly documents, Americans are generally more interested in national news, and their content choices have driven up the audience for cable TV news and online news sources.[15] Even though many big city papers typically gave little attention to local issues, their attention was still greater than the coverage from other sources. Yet local print newspapers and local TV news are in steady decline and draw on an older audience. One city in our study, Denver, experienced the closure of a daily local newspaper (the *Rocky Mountain News*) in 2009. "As we shift to cable news and online news sources," Hopkins wrote in 2018, "we are leaving behind the sources of what little state and local political information we do receive."[16]

We are not suggesting that school board elections were typically high-profile events with regular front-page news coverage before the decline of local newspapers. Rather, our study unfolds in a fluid media environment with new sources and growing focus on national issue debates across widespread local elections. National issues are prominently featured in election coverage, which tends to highlight candidates' charter school positions especially, but offers little information about more idiosyncratic local issues. In doing so, it is possible, of course, that the media is giving readers and viewers what they want. If Hopkins is right, the American public is more focused on national

issues and may have little patience for a heavy dive into locally specific policy details. And for those who have such patience, there are
alternatives.

The spread of *Chalkbeat* represents a mixed dynamic of nationalization with locally focused reporting. *Chalkbeat* is structured as a
federated organization, with a national office that can fundraise and
explore regions for new branches, and locally based reporters who
cover the state and local issues at each site. The information offered
by *Chalkbeat* could nationalize elections and issues—the federated
structure of the website means coverage of local elections can reach
a national audience, possibly including donors—but at the same time
it also provides specific and deeply embedded coverage of local issues.

EXPANDING THE SCOPE OF CONFLICT

Nationalization can be seen as an example of what political scientist
E. E. Schattschneider referred to as "expanding the scope of conflict,"
a process in which a broader array of groups become involved in previously small-scale disputes. As such, it suggests the likelihood that
school politics might become less predictable in some ways, more predictable in others. On the less predictable side, the reason would be
that it unsettles local arenas that in earlier decades were often islands
of stable politics. Localism at its height sometimes drew its stability
from the fact that it crafted policies and priorities that met the felt
needs of relatively homogenous and like-minded populations. Other
times, it enforced stability through the imposed power of dominant
local elites. Nationalization threatens both types of stability, by injecting new ideas and priorities from the outside, and by providing new,
external allies for locally marginalized voices. While outsiders might
have the goal of permanently tipping the balance to a new local governance regime, they might instead simply make local politics persistently
unstable, as the agenda swings back and forth when groups mobilize to
regain seats in one election only to have countermobilization in the next
election that swings the board back in the other direction.

Nationalization, we have suggested, might also impose its own
kinds of stability. This might happen in a variety of ways. Nationalization might have a homogenizing effect that narrows the range of

issues and programs under meaningful consideration. It might bleach out what could be refreshing and illuminating local idiosyncrasies in approach and practice. It might bolster a governing coalition of board members who are strongly tied to broader national interests in educational policy at the expense of local interests. And it might inject ideological and partisan polarization into previously pragmatic arenas, forcing more choices into a predictable battle between left and right.

Importantly, even if nationalization is here to stay, that does not mean that local communities are relegated to passive acquiescence or political second-class status. As we argued at the outset, the motivation for national interests to insert themselves into local politics is itself evidence that local jurisdictions matter, as venues where values are shaped and most concretely articulated, and where state and federal initiatives are either foiled or translated into practice. Once the national donors have written their final checks and the campaign dust has settled, the slow grind of governing still resides with these local school boards.

Nor is nationalization a one-way street in which downward external pressures drive all change. In the kaleidoscope of intergovernmental education politics, national movements and organizations can be expected at times to learn from and adjust in response to local pushback and localized experience. This more optimistic scenario holds out the hope that the nationalization of education does not necessarily mean that the partisan and polarized politics that has characterized more recent national battles will wash over and wash out the more grounded and pragmatic style of conflict resolution and policy evolution that healthy localism sometimes engenders.

CANDIDATES AND SCHOOL BOARD GOVERNANCE

One important element of the persistence of localism—and the varied ways that nationalizing trends play out in local contexts—is in the recruitment of school board candidates and the governance process of elected boards. Our candidate interviews revealed campaign strategies that still relied heavily on connecting with voters locally and a strong desire to broadcast their distinct issue positions. Candidates who shared the same endorsements (or the same big money donors) were not necessarily in lock-step on issue positions. Though the candidates endorsed and funded by reformers were almost universally charter supporters, their visions for charter schools differed substantially. Some would promote more widespread charter expansion, whereas others advocated for more charter oversight and attention to inequities between traditional district and charter schools.

In the aftermath of each election, the victorious candidates have to turn their attention to the business of governing, sometimes on deeply divided boards. An interesting example of board decision-making recently occurred in Denver and involves Angela Cobián, the candidate we discussed at the start of this chapter. Despite the opposition from union-backed forces, Cobián won the election, where she joined a board that included four board members who supported charter expansion fairly consistently (and received funding from reform sources in their campaigns) and two who received union backing and were charter skeptics. In May 2018, when the board debated charter applications for three new middle schools, Cobián, a TFA alum, was expected to be a charter supporter. But her votes deviated slightly from this pattern. She abstained from voting on one school, explaining that she was "committed to making sure the district supports existing schools so they don't get to the point of closure or replacement."[17] The nuance here is subtle, and abstaining on one charter application may seem like a minor affair. Yet this highlights the practical matter that board members face far more specific choices in the local context: known charter operators with particular reputations, neighborhoods with a preexisting mix of schools, and details concerning the district budget and the implications of school expansion for finances.

Similarly, a newly elected board member in Los Angeles, Kelly Gonez, who was also supported by outside pro-reform money, has attempted to distinguish her position from unequivocal charter support. In an interview on Southern California Public Radio, Gonez explained:

> I'm not interested in a dramatic expansion [of charters] or really any expansion, at all, in the number of independent charter schools in the district. I understand why this narrative has picked

up some steam but I would urge people to dig a little bit deeper. If you look at the many things that I have written, charter school expansion is not one of my stated priorities in my campaign.[18]

Perhaps in the context of a pro-charter board majority, these efforts to distinguish positions from the "reform agenda" are little more than semantics. Yet our interviews with candidates, who often spoke with deeply held convictions, suggested to us that these nuanced positions should not be dismissed out of hand.

National policy battles inevitably blend away some of the nuances and complexities of local context. It's not that national actors fail to realize that differences in local experience, culture, and capacity matter; the reason for the washing away of nuance is that mobilizing support and winning big victories require simple narratives and one-stop solutions. If local candidates are simply conscripted by national actors, something valuable could be lost. Yet we see some signs that school board members might be less "pure" than their outside donors when campaigning—and even less so when governing. If that's the case, the gravitational pull of localism might be enough to withstand some of the pressures that nationalization might otherwise impose.

TEACHING AND LEARNING

What impact might the changes we trace hold for those inside the classroom? While our data do not allow us to draw any firm conclusions, we can speculate a bit based on the policy priorities supported by different candidates and their funders. For teachers, we suspect that the influx of outside money could bring national and state debates about teacher accountability to their classroom door. Teachers might feel additional pressure to focus on areas that appear on standardized tests, as accountability pressure is ramped up by local school boards that focus more heavily on this issue. The hot glare of outside money in school board elections could mean that board members, regardless of affiliation, focus more time and energy on this policy issue, leaving teachers bearing the brunt of these expectations. For those worried about teacher recruitment and retention in local districts, such a focus might make their jobs even more challenging, as new teachers perceive these environments as hostile workplaces. For those who believe teacher accountability policies increase the quality of teachers, drawing attention to this issue through outside funding might be seen as a chance to improve overall performance. It's hard to know which perspective will turn out to be closer to the truth. As with so many issues, the devil will be in the details, and the outcome for teachers and their teaching will depend heavily on how board members, regardless of affiliation, implement teacher accountability policies locally.

For students and their learning, it is less clear how outside funding in local school board elections will shape their experiences. Unlike other policy areas, curriculum—and specifically the Common Core State Standards—received virtually no attention in media coverage of the school board elections we analyzed, and the candidates we interviewed indicated curriculum was a far less important issue than charters and accountability. Several of the candidates told us they held only a weak, if any, opinion about curriculum. Thus, our best hunch, based on our current data, is that the battles over what students learn and how they learn it will still be conducted primarily at the state level. Any impact on curriculum and pedagogical approaches, we suspect, will be indirect, as a result of teacher accountability policies.

RACE AND REPRESENTATION

Race and representation are closely linked to the issue of candidates and position taking. Race remains a powerful force influencing public views about policies and candidates, and it would be naïve to imagine that race is not playing a role in the phenomena we have described. Yet we do not find a sharp racial or ethnic division between candidates funded by national reformers and unions, or between those with outside funding and those without. While racial inequities in education drive many of the debates, black and Latinx candidates can be found on every side of the issues—as supporters of charter school expansion, for instance, or as strong skeptics and critics of privatization. Instead, the sharper divide appears to be class-related: very wealthy donors (both nationally and locally), a working-class and middle-class aligned union movement, and many families in urban public schools who are living in poverty. There can be important racial implications to these divisions. Wealthy donors have made it a point to publicly champion families in high poverty schools, but this can be an uncomfortable alliance: there are questions about whether such donors support a broader agenda for public spending and economic equality in general or focus their attention exclusively on education. Meanwhile, teacher unions have their own uncomfortable history with racial and ethnic minorities. The teaching profession remains overwhelmingly white, but many urban school districts primarily serve students of color, and unions of service workers employed in schools, sometimes represented by unions like SEIU, are also more racially and ethnically diverse and do not always align with the teacher unions.

It might be worth reflecting a bit on *why*, despite our findings questioning the racial divide between reformers and their opponents, race-based rhetoric and symbolism are frequently invoked by advocates on both sides. Part of the explanation might have to do with the fact that—quite unlike the historical battles over school desegregation, where one side used overt or covert appeals to black empowerment, and the other overt or covert appeals to white supremacy—both sides today, the reformers as well as those who resist them, stake a claim to the symbolism of civil rights and minority empowerment. Critics of outside money emphasize that the so-called billionaire boys club is overwhelmingly white and portray their incursions into local school politics as a threat to venues where minorities gained access only after decades of bitter battles. For example, one black columnist delivered a withering attack on Stand for Children's contributions to reform candidates in Indianapolis by writing, "Money has always been a part of IPS elections. (Don't think racists didn't spend money to elect those segregationist IPS board members back in the day.)" He went on to assert that Stand for Children's "attitude smacks of the worst excesses of campaign financing and the hubris of predominantly white education 'reformers.'"[19]

Rather than challenging head to head the importance of race and those historical battles, leaders of the reform movement have argued that they are helping to reinvigorate the agenda to achieve greater equity in education. One national pro-charter school organization described school choice as "The civil rights struggle of our day" and went on to assert, "Everyone agreed. Well, except Diane Ravitch, but that's to be expected."[20] The complicated interplay around whether education reformers or their opponents deserve the mantle of civil rights is illustrated by events that unfolded around a 2014 pro-charter school rally in New York. In a letter encouraging parents in his school to attend a pro-charter school rally in Albany, one New York City charter school principal likened the event to "a Freedom Ride toward the right side of history." Shortly thereafter, Governor Andrew Cuomo, asked why he spoke at that rally in support of the charter protesters, told a radio interviewer: "You want to talk about civil rights issues of our day? A failing public education system, I think, is the civil rights issue of our day."[21] Charter advocates in New York went so far as to invoke the Fourteenth Amendment to the Constitution—ratified shortly after the Civil War to assert that all citizens, including former slaves, were guaranteed "equal protection of the laws"—in their lawsuit alleging that the NYC Department of Education (DOE) was violating the civil rights of black families when it threatened to evict their charter school from a DOE building. The president of the New York State conference of the NAACP shot back that the lawsuit was "an outrageous and insulting attempt by Wall Street hedge fund managers to hijack the language of civil rights" in a "shameless political attack."[22]

In their book *The Color of School Reform*, Henig et al. observed the paradoxical fact that within majority black cities, the symbolism of race was frequently used to characterize combatants even when the labels did not reflect their actual race.[23] Critics of the reform initiatives sometimes portrayed reform leaders, especially those with outside and business support, as "white" even when they were black; in doing so, they buttressed the political argument that the reform agenda was not authentically rooted in the local black community. Both reformers and their opponents, then, might tactically employ race-tinged appeals simply because race is so potent as a reference point for relating current contests to historical ones, invoking loyalty, and motivating action. Despite our finding that the battle lines around contested school board elections scramble any simple story of racial and ethnic divisions aligned clearly with particular policy positions, then, we will not be surprised if those battles continue to be defined in racial terms.

IS NATIONALIZATION
THE NEW NORMAL?

The education policy arena is famous for its inclination to undergo successive waves of new leadership and reform notions that leave fundamental practices relatively intact. Hess captured this process well with the metaphor of "spinning wheels," but others have used similarly lively labels like "policy churn," "high reverberation," and "reform du jour." One publication lists no fewer than forty fads (defined as an "idea that is embraced enthusiastically for a short time") ranging from constructivism to critical thinking, from outcome-based education to charters and school choice.

Is the nationalization of local school politics similarly a passing fad, destined to be fleeting, a product of the moment but not a fundamental reorientation? One possibility is that investment in local elections will prove to have high costs and little pay-off to national actors, leading them to lose interest and direct their efforts elsewhere. Another possibility is that the institutions and values of localism will prove more resilient than might be anticipated. A third possibility is that we will see the emergence of a more balanced two-way transfer of knowledge where national movements and organizations learn and adjust their policy goals in response to local concerns.

Generally, our evidence so far points to nationalization being more than just a passing fad. The behavior of donors who continue to spend large sums on politics, the national potency of issues like charter schools across many local districts, and the media environment that offers more national than local issue coverage, all tend to provide a steady stream of resources and information from national sources. Broader trends in society related to technology, culture, and political polarization are likely to further enable these national trends.[24]

Nonetheless, we don't pretend that our study can answer the question of whether nationalization is the new normal. It might proceed as a limited phenomenon, affecting only a handful of local school districts in a given electoral cycle. The question of the long-term development of nationalization is too big and complex to be answered by a first-shot effort like ours. Besides the complexity of the phenomenon, there is an additional reason why it would be presumptuous to offer confident predictions of the course that nationalization will take. The factors that seem to be driving the process go beyond broad and systemic forces with natural trajectories. There is room here for agency: for public leaders, interest groups, and mobilized citizens to resist or redirect the course of nationalization. This is a process in which political battles and resultant decisions will play a role, but how those will affect the outcome is yet to be determined.

We see the phenomenon of outside interest in school board elections as one important manifestation of a more general nationalization of American education politics. While centralization implies that local decision-making arenas are being muscled aside, we show that national actors are realizing that these local arenas are still quite important. Rather than being ignored, marginalized, and bypassed, local school politics is being penetrated by national politics in ways that rattle and reassemble traditional lines of coalition and cleavage, with important implications—some good, some bad—for both democracy and educational improvement.

APPENDIX A

....

Outside Money Cases, 2009–2017

SCHOOL DISTRICT	STATE	YEAR(S) MENTIONED
Atlanta	GA	2013
Austin	TX	2016
Buffalo	NY	2014, 2016
Burbank	CA	2013
Colorado Springs	CO	2015
Conejo Valley	CA	2016
Denver	CO	2009, 2011, 2012, 2014, 2017
Douglas County	CO	2013, 2014
Elizabeth	NJ	2014
Forest Lake	MN	2017
Guilford	NC	2016
Huntsville	AL	2016
Indianapolis	IN	2015, 2016, 2017
Jacksonville	FL	2016
Jefferson County	CO	2011, 2015
Jersey City	NJ	2014, 2016, 2017
Los Angeles	CA	2014, 2015, 2016, 2017
Louisville	KY	2016
Loveland	CO	2015
Manatee County	FL	2016, 2017
Manchester	NJ	2016

SCHOOL DISTRICT	STATE	YEAR(S) MENTIONED
Minneapolis	MN	2014
Morgan Hill	CA	2016
Nashville	TN	2016
New Orleans	LA	2013, 2014, 2016
Oakland	CA	2012, 2016
Orlando	FL	2016
Palo Alto	CA	2016
Pinellas County	FL	2016
Polk County	FL	2016
Portland	OR	2015
Richmond	VA	2016
Sacramento County	CA	2015
San Diego	CA	2016
San Francisco	CA	2016
Santa Ana	CA	2016
Santa Clara	CA	2012, 2016
Savannah	GA	2014
St. Joseph	MO	2016
Tucson	AZ	2016
Wake County	NC	2011, 2015, 2016
Washington	DC	2014
W. Contra Costa	CA	2014, 2016

APPENDIX B

....

Media Sources Used for Analysis in Chapter 6

The Advocate (New Orleans)

The Center for Public Integrity

Chalkbeat

The Colorado Independent

Connecticut Post

Daily Breeze (California)

Denver Post

Education Week

Free Press

Gambit Weekly

Gentilly Messenger (New Orleans)

HechingerEd (Staff blog of The Hechinger Report)

Huffington Post

In These Times (Independent, nonprofit online magazine)

Indianapolis Business Journal

Indianapolis Recorder

Indianapolis Star

KPPC (Pasadena, CA Radio)

LAschoolreport.com

Los Angeles Daily News

Los Angeles Registrar

Los Angeles Times

The Nation

Neon Tommy (the online publication of the Annenberg School for Communication and Journalism—USC)

New York Post

New York Times

Only in Bridgeport (web magazine)

Orange Country Register

OurFuture.org (online media connected to The Campaign for America's Future)

Public Education and Business Coalition (PEBC)

Salon

SFGate (sister-site of the *San Francisco Chronicle*)

Slate.com (daily web magazine)

State Bills News (Colorado)

The74Million.org

Times-Picayune (New Orleans)

Uptown Messenger (New Orleans)

Washington Post

Westworld (Denver online news source)

WXIN-TV (Indiana—State and Regional News)

NOTES

CHAPTER 1

1. On the idea of localism as the cradle of democracy: Laurence Iannaccone and Frank W. Lutz, "The Crucible of Democracy: The Local Arena," *Journal of Education Policy* 9, no. 5 (1994): 39–52; Gene I. Maeroff, *School Boards in America: A Flawed Exercise in Democracy* (New York: Palgrave Macmillan, 2010). For the more critical perspective: Lisa Graham Keegan and Chester E. Finn, "Lost at Sea," *Education Next*, 4, no. 3 (2004): 15–17; also Matt Miller, "First, Kill All the School Boards: How to Nationalize Education," *Atlantic Monthly*, 301, no. 1 (2008): 92.
2. Frederick M. Hess and Olivia Meeks, *School Boards Circa 2010: Governance in the Accountability Era* (Washington, DC: Thomas B. Fordham Institute, 2011).
3. Valerie Strauss, "School Board Races Attract Big Outside Money," *Washington Post*, November 4, 2012, http://www.washingtonpost.com/blogs/answer-sheet/wp/2012/11/04/school-board-races-attract-big-outside-money/.
4. Adolfo Guzman-Lopez, "L.A. Unified School Board Race Could Break Fundraising Records This Election," February 14, 2013, http://www.scpr.org/blogs/education/2013/02/14/12550/launified-school-board-race-could-break-fundraisi/.
5. Howard Blume and Ben Poston, "How L.A.'s School Board Election Became the Most Expensive in U.S. History," *Los Angeles Times*, May 2, 2017, http://www.latimes.com/local/la-me-edu-school-election-money-20170521-htmlstory.html.
6. Gayle Cosby, Nathaniel Williams, and Jim Scheurich, "Local Control of IPS Is Being Lost," *Indianapolis Star*, October 31, 2015, https://www.indystar.com/story/opinion/readers/2015/10/31/local-control-ips-lost/74956452/.
7. Gregg Robinson and Jim Miller, "Who's Behind the Big Money Takeover of San Diego County Schools," *San Diego Free Press*, November 1, 2016, https://sandiegofreepress.org/2016/11/whos-behind-the-big-money-takeover-of-san-diego-county-schools/.
8. Jonathan Martin and Alexander Burns, "2017 High-Stakes Referendum on Trump Takes Shape in a Georgia Special Election," *New York Times*, June 18, 2017, https://www.nytimes.com/2017/06/18/us/politics/high-stakes-referendum-on-trump-takes-shape-in-a-georgia-special-election.html.
9. Paige St. John and Abbie Vansickle, "Here's Why George Soros, Liberal Groups Are Spending Big to Help Decide Who's Your Next D.A.," *Los Angeles Times*,

May 23, 2018, http://www.latimes.com/local/california/la-me-prosecutor-campaign-20180523-story.html.

10. Lawrence R. Jacobs and Theda Skocpol, *Inequality and American Democracy: What We Know and What We Need to Learn* (New York, NY: Russell Sage Foundation, 2007); Larry M. Bartels, *Unequal Democracy: The Political Economy of the New Gilded Age* (Princeton NJ: Princeton University Press, 2008); Jacob S. Hacker and Paul Pierson, *Off Center: The Republican Revolution & the Erosion of American Democracy* (New Haven, CT: Yale University Press, 2005); Martin Gilens, *Affluence and Influence* (Princeton, NJ: Princeton University Press, 2012).

11. Adam Bonica, Nolan McCarty, Keith T. Poole, and Howard. Rosenthal, "Why Hasn't Democracy Slowed Rising Inequality?" *Journal of Economic Perspectives*, 27, no. 3 (2013): 103–24.

12. James G. Gimpel, Frances E. Lee, and Shanna Pearson-Merkowitz, "The Check Is in the Mail: Interdistrict Funding Flows in Congressional Elections," *American Journal of Political Science* 52, no. 2 (2008): 373–94.

13. Sarah Reckhow, *Follow the Money: How Foundation Dollars Change Public School Politics* (New York, NY: Oxford University Press, 2013); Megan Tompkins-Stange, *Policy Patrons: Philanthropy, Education Reform, and the Politics of Influence* (Cambridge MA: Harvard Education Press, 2016); Kristin Goss, "Policy Plutocrats: How America's Wealthy Seek to Influence Governance," *PS: Political Science & Politics* 49, no. 3 (2016): 442–48.

14. David Callahan, *The Givers: Wealth, Power, and Philanthropy in a New Gilded Age* (New York, NY: Knopf, 2017), 107.

15. Jon Pierre, "Comparative Urban Governance: Uncovering Complex Causalities," *Urban Affairs Review* 40, no. 4 (2005): 446–62. doi:10.1177/1078087404273442.

16. John Nichols, "Big Money, Bad Media, Secret Agendas: Welcome to America's Wildest School Board Race," *The Nation*, October 21, 2011, https://www.thenation.com/article/big-money-bad-media-secret-agendas-welcome-americas-wildest-school-board-race/.

17. We say more about these donors in chapter 3.

18. Hess and Meeks, *School Boards*, Table 41.

19. Most of the indicators here are drawn from the Stanford Education Data Archive (http://purl.stanford.edu/db586ns4974). Data on the school boards come from the National School District Survey compiled by Ken Meier.

20. For national data, see, for example, The Center for Responsive Politics (https://www.opensecrets.org/) and for states, the National Institute on Money in State Politics (https://www.followthemoney.org/).

21. Details about our data-gathering process, sources, and local campaign finance regulation are available in an appendix, which can be shared by the authors upon request.

CHAPTER 2

1. Michael W. Kirst and Frederick. M. Wirt, *The Political Dynamics of American Education*, 4th ed. (Richmond, CA: McCutchan Publishing, 2009).

2. V. O. Key, *Southern Politics in State and Nation* (Knoxville, TN: University of Tennessee Press, 1949); Claudine Gay, "Putting Race in Context: Identifying the Environmental Determinants of Black Racial Attitudes," *American Political Science Review* 98, no. 4 (2004): 547–62; Clayton Nall, "The Political Consequences of Spatial Policies: How Interstate Highways Facilitated Geographic Polarization," *Journal of Politics* 77, no. 2 (2015): 45–59.

3. See, for example, Robert Asen, *Democracy, Deliberation and Education* (University Park, PA: Penn State University Press, 2015); John Dewey, *Democracy and Education: An Introduction to the Philosophy of Education* (New York, NY: Macmillan, 1916); Jonathan Zimmerman, *Small Wonder: The Little Red Schoolhouse in History and Memory* (New Haven CT: Yale University Press, 2009).

4. Katherine Cramer, *The Politics of Resentment: Rural Consciousness in Wisconsin and the Rise of Scott Walker* (Chicago, IL: University of Chicago Press, 2016).

5. Eric Oliver, *Local Elections and the Politics of Small-Scale Democracy* (Princeton NJ: Princeton University Press, 2012).

6. Robert Asen, Deb Gurke, Ryan Solomon, Pamela Connors, and Elsa Gumm, *The Research Says: Definitions and Uses of a Key Policy Term in Federal Lay and Local School-Board Deliberations*, December 21, 2013, http://wtgrantfoundation.org/resource/the-research-says-definitions-and-uses-of-a-key-policy-term-in-federal-lay-and-local-school-board-deliberations, 3.

7. Charles H. Levine, "Citizenship and Service Delivery: The Promise of Coproduction," *Public Administration Review* (1984): 178–87; Elaine B. Sharp, "Toward a New Understanding of Urban Services and Citizen Participation: The Coproduction Concept," *Midwest Review of Public Administration* 14, no. 2 (1980): 105–18.

8. Kirst and Wirt, *Political Dynamics*; Kathryn McDermott, *Controlling Public Education: Localism Versus Equity* (Lawrence KS: University Press of Kansas, 1999); Nadav Shoked, "An American Oddity: The Law, History, and Toll of the School District," *Northwestern University Law Journal* 111 (2017): 945–1024.

9. Saundra K. Schneider, William G. Jacoby, and Daniel C. Lewis, "Public Opinion Toward Intergovernmental Policy Responsibilities," *Publius* 41, no. 1 (2011): 1–30.

10. Valerie J. Calderon, "Americans Wary of Federal Influence on Public Schools," Gallup, August 20, 2014, http://news.gallup.com/poll/175181/americans-wary-federal-influence-public-schools.aspx.

11. Terry Moe, *Schools, Vouchers, and the American Public*. (Washington, DC: Brookings Institution, 2002).

12. Zimmerman, *Small Wonder*.

13. Today there are about 13,600. See *Digest of Education Statistics*, https://nces.ed.gov/programs/digest/d16/tables/dt16_214.10.asp.

14. Thomas D. Snyder, *120 Years of American Education: A Statistical Portrait* (Washington, DC: NCES, 1993).

15. Snyder, *120 Years*, Table 19.

16. Michael W. Kirst, "Turning Points: A History of American School Governance," in *Who's in Charge Here?: The Tangled Web of School Governance and Policy*, ed. Noel Epstein (Washington, DC: Brookings Institution, 2004), 14–41.

17. On resistance to integration, see, for example, Robert L. Crain, *The Politics of School Desegregation* (Garden City, NY: Anchor Books, 1969); Jennifer L. Hochschild, *The New American Dilemma: Liberal Democracy and School Desegregation* (New Haven, CT: Yale University Press, 1984); J. Anthony Lukas, *Common Ground: A Turbulent Decade in the Lives of Three American Families* (New York, NY: Alfred Knopf, 1985); Gary Orfield, *The Reconstruction of Southern Education* (New York: John Wiley & Sons, 1969).

18. For example, Washington, DC, had a majority black student enrollment by 1950, a majority black school board by 1969, and a black superintendent by 1970. Comparable dates for some other large cities are Atlanta (1963/1973/1973); Baltimore (1960/1973/1971); Detroit (1962/1977/1974). Jeffrey R. Henig, Richard C. Hula, Marion Orr, and Desiree S. Pedescleaux, *The Color of School Reform* (Princeton, NJ: Princeton University Press, 1999), Table 2.1.

19. Heather Hahn, Laudan Aron, Cary Lou, Eleanor Pratt, and Adaeze Okoli, *Why Does Cash Welfare Depend on Where You Live? How and Why State TANF Programs Vary* (Washington, DC: Urban Institute, 2017), https://www.urban.org/sites/default/files/publication/90761/tanf_cash_welfare_final2_1.pdf; Robert C. Lieberman, *Shifting the Color Line: Race and the American Welfare State* (Cambridge MA: Harvard University Press, 1998); Schneider, Jacoby, and Lewis, "Public Opinion"; Joe Soss, Richard C. Fording, and Sanford F. Schram, "The Color of Devolution: Race, Federalism, and the Politics of Social Control," *American Journal of Political Science* 52, no. 3 (2008): 536–53; Joe Soss, Sanford Schram, Thomas Vartanian, and Erin O'Brien, "Setting the Terms of Relief: Explaining State Policy Choices in the Devolution Revolution," *American Journal of Political Science* 45, no. 2 (2001): 378–95.

20. Domingo Morel, *Takeover: Race, Education, and American Democracy* (New York, NY: Oxford University Press, 2018); see also Dale Russakoff, *The Prize: Who's in Charge of America's Schools* (New York NY: Houghton Mifflin Harcourt, 2015).

21. Starting in 2014, the state began returning at least partial control to Jersey City, Paterson, and Newark, and by 2017, it was beginning discussion about doing the same in Camden. In December 2017, Pennsylvania announced that in July 2018 Philadelphia schools would be returned to local control after more than sixteen years of governance by a School Reform Commission consisting of three members appointed by the governor and two members chosen by the mayor.

22. The Recovery School District in Louisiana is the most prominent case, but others include the Achievement School District in Tennessee and the Education Achievement Authority in Michigan.

23. Morel, *Takeover*.

24. Theodore J. Lowi, "Machine Politics: Old and New," *Public Interest* 9 (1967): 83–92.

25. Barbara Ferman, ed., *The Fight for America's Schools* (Cambridge, MA: Harvard Education Press, 2017); Henig et al., *The Color*; Morel, *Takeover*; Russakoff, *The Prize*.

26. Matt Miller, "First, Kill All the School Boards: How to Nationalize Education," *Atlantic Monthly* 301, no. 1 (2008): 92.

27. Katrina E. Bulkley and Patricia Burch, "The Changing Nature of Private Engagement in Public Education," *Peabody Journal of Education* 86, no. 3 (2011): 236–51; Patricia Burch, *Hidden Markets: The New Education Privatization* (New York: Routledge, 2009); Miller, "First, Kill," 92.

28. Gene I. Maeroff, *School Boards in America: A Flawed Exercise in Democracy* (New York: Palgrave Macmillan, 2010). For a specific example, see the Council of Urban Boards of Education's Task Force on Governance and Training that focuses on identifying "school board development opportunities that support characteristics of effective school boards and to share the best practices of urban school boards that demonstrate effective habits" (https://www.nsba.org/services/council-urban-boards-education/cube-task-forces).

29. Frederick M. Hess. *Spinning Wheels: The Politics of Urban School Reform* (Washington, DC: Brookings Institution, 1998).

30. Maeroff, *School Boards*, 1.

31. Ken Herman, "You're Free to Vote So Why Didn't You?" *Austin Statesman*, May 10, 2010, https://www.statesman.com/news/opinion/you-free-vote-why-didn-you/IFXLH5W6daHAJYocx7aGBN/.

32. Terry M. Moe, "Political Control and the Power of the Agent," *Journal of Law, Economics, and Organization* 22, no. 1 (2006): 1–29; Moe, *Special Interest*; Moe, "Teachers Unions in the United States: The Politics of Blocking," in *The Comparative Politics of Education: Teachers Unions and Education Systems Around the World*, eds. Terry Moe and Susanne Wiborg (Cambridge: Cambridge University Press, 2016), 24–55.

33. McDermott, *Controlling*.

34. Frederick M. Hess and Michael J. Petrilli, *No Child Left Behind: A Primer* (New York, NY: Peter Lang, 2006).

35. Patrick McGuinn, *No Child Left Behind and the Transformation of Federal Education Policy 1965–2005* (Lawrence KS: University Press of Kansas, 2006), 9.

36. Elizabeth DeBray-Pelot and Patrick McGuinn, "The New Politics of Education: Analyzing the Federal Education Policy Landscape in the Post-NCLB Era," *Educational Policy* 23, no. 1 (2009): 15–42; Paul Manna, *School's In: Federalism and the National Education Agenda* (Washington, DC: Georgetown University Press, 2006)Patrick McGuinn, *No Child*; Patrick J. McGuinn and Paul Manna, eds., *Education Governance for the Twenty-First Century: Overcoming the Structural Barriers to School Reform* (Washington, DC: Brookings Institution, 2012); Jesse H.

Rhodes, *An Education in Politics: The Origin and Evolution of No Child Left Behind* (Ithaca, NY: Cornell University Press, 2012); Andrew Rudalevige, "The Politics of No Child Left Behind," *Education Next* (2003): 62–69.

37. Samuel E. Abrams, *Education and the Commercial Mindset* (Cambridge MA: Harvard University Press, 2016); Bulkley and Burch, "Changing Nature"; Burch, *Hidden Markets.*

38. Andrea Campbell, *How Policies Make Citizens: Senior Political Activism and the American Welfare State* (Princeton, NJ: Princeton University Press, 2003); Suzanne Mettler and Joe Soss, "The Consequences of Public Policy for Democratic Citizenship: Bridging Policy Studies and Mass Politics," *Perspectives on Politics* 2, no. 1 (2004): 55–73; Eric M. Patashnik, *Reforms at Risk: What Happens After Major Policy Changes Are Enacted* (Princeton, NJ: Princeton University Press, 2008); Paul Pierson, "Increasing Returns, Path Dependence, and the Study of Politics," *American Political Science Review* 94, no. 2 (2000): 251–67.

39. Elizabeth Debray-Pelot, "Dismantling Education's 'Iron Triangle': Institutional Relationships in the Formation of Federal Education Policy Between 1998 and 2001," in *To Educate a Nation: Federal and National Strategies of School Reform*, eds. Carl F. Kaestle and Alyssa E. Lodewick (Lawrence, KS: University Press of Kansas, 2007), 64–89. Other formerly influential groups were the AFT and Council of Chief State Officers.

40. For estimates of media concentration, Daniel J. Hopkins, *The Increasingly United States: How and Why American Political Behavior Nationalized* (Chicago, IL: University of Chicago Press, 2018) cites Katerina E. Matsa, "Market Is Still Hot for Buying Up Local TV Stations," Pew Research Center, December 23, 2014, http://www.pewresearch.org/fact-tank/2014/12/23/market-is-still-hot-for-buying-up-local-tv-stations; Daniel E. Ho and Kevin M. Quinn, "Viewpoint Diversity and Media Consolidation: An Empirical Study," *Stanford Law Review* 61, no. 4 (2009): 781–868; Amy Mitchell and Jesse Holcomb, "State of the News Media 2016," Pew Research Center, June 23, 2016, http://www.journalism.org/2016/06/15/state-of-the-news-media-2016/. This article cites cost cutting as a major possible motivation for larger corporations to close local outlets. In March 2018, Sinclair Broadcast Group, the nation's largest broadcaster, which owns or operates nearly two hundred television stations, required local news anchors to read the same speech denouncing "fake news" in terms that many felt deliberately echoed and reinforced President Trump's, raising questions of whether ideological motivations, as well as economic ones, could come into play.

41. Claire S. Smrekar and Robert L. Crowson, "Localism Rediscovered: Toward New Political Understandings in School District Governance," *Peabody Journal of Education* 90, no. 1 (2015): 1.

42. Meredith L. Honig, ed., *New Directions in Education Policy Implementation: Confronting Complexity* (Albany, NY: State University of New York Press, 2006); Michael Lipsky, *Street Level Bureaucracy* (New York, NY: Russell Sage Foundation, 1983); Kenneth J. Meier, Joseph Stewart Jr., and Robert E. England, "The

Politics of Bureaucratic Discretion: Educational Access as an Urban Service," *American Journal of Political Science* 35, no. 1 (1991): 155–77; Jeffrey Pressman and Aaron Wildavsky, *Implementation: How Great Expectations in Washington Are Dashed in Oakland; Or, Why It's Amazing That Federal Programs Work at All*, 3rd ed. (Oakland, CA: University of California Press, 1984); Karl E. Weick, "Educational Organizations as Loosely Coupled Systems," *Administrative Science Quarterly* 21 (1976): 1–19.

43. Julie A. Marsh and Priscilla Wohlstetter, "Recent Trends in Intergovernmental Relations: The Resurgence of Local Actors in Education Policy," *Educational Researcher* 42, no. 5 (2013): 276–83.

44. US Office of Personnel Management, *Sizing Up the Executive Branch: Fiscal Year 2015*, June 2016, https://www.opm.gov/policy-data-oversight/data-analysis-documentation/federal-employment-reports/reports-publications/sizing-up-the-executive-branch-2015.pdf; US Census Bureau, "Where Do State and Local Government Employees Work," https://www2.census.gov/govs/2013_government_employment.pdf.

45. Paul Manna, *School's In*.

46. Alexander Russo, *The Successful Failure of ED in '08*, American Enterprise Institute, Future of American Education Project, 2012, https://www.aei.org/wp-content/uploads/2012/06/-the-successful-failure-of-ed-in-08_171010500431.pdf.

47. Russo, *Successful Failure*, 13.

48. Russo.

CHAPTER 3

1. Robert Frank, "One Top Taxpayer Moved, and New Jersey Shuddered," *New York Times*, April 30, 2016, https://www.nytimes.com/2016/05/01/business/one-top-taxpayer-moved-and-new-jersey-shuddered.html/.

2. Jessica Pressler, "Ready to Be Rich," *New York Magazine*, September 26, 2010, http://nymag.com/news/features/establishments/68513/.

3. David Rowan, "Reid Hoffman: The Network Philosopher," *Wired*, March 1, 2012, https://www.wired.co.uk/article/reid-hoffman-network-philosopher.

4. Joshua Cowen and Katharine O. Strunk, *How Do Teachers' Unions Influence Education Policy? What We Know and What We Need to Learn*, April 2014, https://education.msu.edu/epc/library/documents/WP%2042%20How%20do%20teachers%20unions%20influence%20education%20policy.pdf; Terry Moe, *Special Interest: Teachers Unions and America's Public Schools* (Washington, DC: Brookings Institution, 2011); Sarah F. Anzia, "Election Timing and the Electoral Influence of Interest Groups," *Journal of Politics* 73, no. 2 (2011): 412–27; Moe, "Political Control and the Power of the Agent," *Journal of Law, Economics, and Organization* 22, no. 1 (2006): 1–29; Frederick M. Hess and D. Leal, "Schoolhouse Politics: Expenditures, Interests, and Competition in School Board Elections," in *Besieged: School Boards and the Future of Education Politics*, ed. W. G. Howell (Washington, DC: Brookings Institution, 2005), 228–53; Michael B. Berkman

and Eric Plutzer, *Ten Thousand Democracies: Politics and Public Opinion in America's School Districts* (Washington, DC: Georgetown University Press, 2005).

5. Brian E. Adams, "Suburban Money in Central City Elections: The Geographic Distribution of Campaign Contributions," *Urban Affairs Review* 42 (2006): 267–80, doi:10.1177/1078087406292699.

6. Michael J. Barber, "Representing the Preferences of Donors, Partisans, and Voters in the US Senate," *Public Opinion Quarterly* 80 (2016): 225–49, doi:10.1093/poq/nfw004.

7. Jesse H. Rhodes, Brian F. Schaffner, and Raymond J. LaRaja, "Detecting and Understanding Donor Strategies in Midterm Elections," *Political Research Quarterly* 71 (2018): 503–16.

8. Barber, "Representing the Preferences"; Raymond J. LaRaja and David L. Wiltse, "Don't Blame Donors for Ideological Polarization of Political Parties: Ideological Change and Stability Among Political Contributors, 1972–2008," *American Politics Research* 40 (2012): 501–30, doi:10.1177/1532673X11429845.

9. Betsy Sinclair, *The Social Citizen: Peer Networks and Political Behavior* (Chicago, IL: University of Chicago Press, 2012); James G. Gimpel, Frances E. Lee, and Joshua Kaminski, "The Political Geography of Campaign Contributions in American Politics," *Journal of Politics* 68 (2006): 626–39, doi:10.1111/j.1468-2508.2006.00450.x.

10. Sinclair, *Social Citizen*; Pamela E. Oliver and Gerald Marwell, "The Paradox of Group Size in Collective Action: A Theory of the Critical Mass, II," *American Sociological Review* 53 (1988): 1–8, doi:10.2307/2095728.

11. Val Burris, "Interlocking Directorates and Political Cohesion Among Corporate Elites," *American Journal of Sociology* 111 (2005): 249–83, doi:10.1086/428817.

12. Wendy K. Cho and James G. Gimpel, "Prospecting for (Campaign) Gold," *American Journal of Political Science* 51 (2007): 255–68, doi:10.1111/j.1540-5907.2007.00249.x; Gimpel, Lee, and Kaminski, "Political Geography."

13. Gimpel, Lee, and Kaminski, "Political Geography."

14. A $1,000 contribution is at the ninetieth percentile for individual contribution amounts across all the elections in our dataset.

15. The Center for Responsive Politics data are based on Federal Election Commission reports of receipts from all individuals who contribute at least $200.

16. Patrick J. McGuinn, "Stimulating Reform: Race to the Top, Competitive Grants, and the Obama Education Agenda," *Educational Policy* 26, no. 1 (2012): 136–59.

17. Samantha Sharf, "Full List: America's Most Expensive Zip Codes 2017," *Forbes*, November 28, 2017, https://www.forbes.com/sites/samanthasharf/2017/11/28/full-list-americas-most-expensive-zip-codes-2017/#5b53d3c85d19.

18. Gimpel, Lee, and Kaminski, "Political Geography."

19. Lee Drutman, "The Political 1% of the 1% in 2012," Sunlight Foundation, June 24, 2013, https://sunlightfoundation.com/2013/06/24/1pct_of_the_1pct/.

20. Drutman, "The Political 1%."

21. Sarah Bryner and Doug Weber, *Sex, Money and Politics. A Center for Responsive*

Politics Report on Women as Donors and Candidates, September 26, 2013, https://www
.opensecrets.org/downloads/CRP_Gender_Report_2013.pdf.

22. Others would have fit the category of highly active federal donors if we had used years other than 2012 as our criterion or if we had linked donors to their spouses. Katherine Sherrill of New York City, for example, supported Sarah Newell Usdin's campaign in New Orleans; while Sherrill did not appear in the national data donor for 2012, in other years she has given extensively to Republicans, including Lamar Alexander, John Cornyn, and George W. Bush. Her husband, Stephen Sherrill, is managing partner and founder of a New York–based private investment firm that does not appear to deal with education-related firms; he also gave to Usdin, but most of his substantial political giving has been at the national level, almost exclusively to Republicans. Also among those who did not show up as a 2012 national donor was Greg Penner, the spouse of Carrie Walton, who is the granddaughter of Sam Walton, the founder of Walmart, and who was named chairman of Walmart in 2015. Penner, who appears in table 3.5 as a board member for both TFA and the Charter School Growth Fund, has given occasionally to national campaigns—for example, he contributed to Ohio governor and presidential candidate John Kasich in 2016 and 2018—but he has been more active at the state and local levels. Carrie Walton Penner, on the other hand, has been an extremely active national donor around the country, at the federal and state levels and in support of candidates from both major parties.

23. Paul S. Herrnson, *Congressional Elections: Campaigning at Home and in Washington*, 6th ed. (Washington, DC: CQ Press College, 2011).

24. These calculations exclude the $13 million that Michael Bloomberg provided to Mayors Against Illegal Guns Action Fund, a 501(c)(4) organization that he formed.

25. It is quite likely that we miss some strategic national donors by using this procedure. We selected five cities for this study, but school board elections in other cities have also attracted contributions from outside donors. If one of our large national donors gave to one city in our dataset and another city not included in our dataset, we would misidentify that individual. So our classification of these thirty individuals could be viewed as a conservative estimate of the strategic large national donors who might be in our data.

26. Gimpel, Lee, and Kaminski, "Political Geography."

27. Personal interview, conducted by phone, October 21, 2015.

28. Impact for Education, http://www.impactforeducation.net/our-mission/.

29. Kari Granville, "Colorado's Cherry Hills Village Has Palatial Estates and Rolling Hills," Mansion Global, March 31, 2018, https://www.mansionglobal.com/articles/92770-colorado-s-cherry-hills-village-has-palatial-estates-and-rolling-hills.

30. Doug Smith, "Riordan Raises $1.4 Million to Back School Board Slate," *Los Angeles Times*, March 6, 1999, http://articles.latimes.com/1999/mar/06/local/me-14428.

31. Christine Mai-Duc and Howard Bloom, "Former Mayor Riordan Puts in $1 Million to Defeat School Board President Zimmer," *Los Angeles Times*, January 18, 2017, http://www.latimes.com/local/lanow/la-me-edu-riordan-school-board-donation-20170118-story.html.

32. Andrew Vanacore, "Leslie Jacobs Defends Hardball Tactics in Attack on Former Mayoral Front-Runner Desiree Charbonnet," *New Orleans Advocate*, December 5, 2017, http://www.theadvocate.com/new_orleans/news/article_13858c8c-d9 3b-11e7-96d5-2f0827ec7973.html.

33. Dawn Ruth, "Leslie Jacobs," *New Orleans Magazine*, December 2008, http://www.myneworleans.com/New-Orleans-Magazine/December-2008/Leslie-Jacobs/; Elizabeth K. Jeffers, "Rosenthal-Jacobs Family," *New Orleans Tribune*, http://www.theneworleanstribune.com/main/rosenthal-jacobs-family/.

34. Jane Mansbridge, "Rethinking Representation," *American Political Science Review* 97, no. 4 (2003): 515–28, http://www.jstor.org/stable/3593021.

35. Anne E. Baker, "Getting Short-Changed?: The Impact of Outside Money on District Representation," *Social Science Quarterly* 97 (2016): 1096–1107, doi:10.1111/ssqu.12279.

36. Martin Gilens, *Affluence and Influence* (Princeton, NJ: Princeton University Press, 2012), 120.

37. Benjamin I. Page, Larry M. Bartels, and Jason Seawright, "Democracy and the Policy Preferences of Wealthy Americans," *Perspectives on Politics* 11, no. 1 (2013): 51–73, 60.

38. Moe, *Special Interest*; Daniel DiSalvo, *Government Against Itself: Public Union Power and Its Consequences* (New York, NY: Oxford University Press, 2015).

CHAPTER 4

1. Lindsey Burke, "Creating a Crisis: Unions Stifle Education Reform," Heritage Foundation, July 20, 2010, https://www.heritage.org/education/report/creating-crisis-unions-stifle-education-reform.

2. AFTFacts.com, https://www.aftfacts.com/the-american-federation-of-teachers/.

3. AFTFacts.com, for instance, is associated with Berman & Co., which represents various industries that have had fraught relationships with their workforce. According to the Center for Media and Democracy, "Berman & Co. operates a network of dozens of front groups, attack-dog websites, and alleged think tanks that work to counteract minimum wage campaigns, keep wages low for restaurant workers, and to block legislation on food safety, secondhand cigarette smoke, and drunk driving and more." http://www.sourcewatch.org/index.php/Berman_%26_Co.

4. Matt Miller, "First, Kill All the School Boards: How to Nationalize Education," *Atlantic Monthly* 301, no. 1 (2008): 92.

5. Paul Bond, "Participant in Matt Damon Public School Doc Lashes Out at Filmmakers," *Hollywood Reporter*, October 4, 2017, http://www.hollywood reporter.com/news/participant-matt-damon-public-school-doc-lashes-at-filmmakers-1043801.

6. Alexander Russo, *The Empire Strikes Back: The Sudden Rise and Ongoing Challenges of Democrats for Education Reform*, 2016, http://www.aei.org/publication/the-empire-strikes-back-the-sudden-rise-and-ongoing-challenges-of-democrats-for-education-reform/.

7. Amy Wilkins of The Education Trust, as quoted by Russo, *Empire Strikes Back*, 3.

8. Patricia Burch, *Hidden Markets: The New Education Privatization* (New York: Routledge, 2009); Christopher Lubienski, Janelle T. Scott, and Elizabeth DeBray, "The Politics of Research Production, Promotion, and Utilization in Educational Policy," *Educational Policy* 28 (2014): 131–44; Diane Ravitch, *Reign of Error: The Hoax of the Privatization Movement and the Danger to America's Public Schools* (New York, NY: Alfred A. Knopf, 2013); Amy Stuart Wells and Janelle Scott, "Privatization and Charter School Reform: Economic, Political, and Social Dimensions," in *Privatizing Education*, ed. Henry M. Levin (Boulder, CO: Westview, 2001).

9. Alexander Hertel-Fernandez, "Explaining Liberal Policy Woes in the States: The Role of Donors," *PS: Political Science & Politics* 49, no. 3 (2016): 461–65; Hertel-Fernandez, *Policy Feedback as Political Weapon: Conservative Advocacy and the Demobilization of the Public Sector Labor Movement*, Draft prepared for the Yale American Politics Workshop, 2016, http://csap.yale.edu/sites/default/files/files/apppw_2_22_17.pdf.

10. Terry M. Moe, *Special Interest: Teachers Unions and America's Public Schools* (Washington, DC: Brookings Institution, 2011), 8.

11. E.g., Jean-Jacques Laffont and David Martimor, *The Theory of Incentives: The Principal-Agent Model* (Princeton, NJ: Princeton University Press, 2002); Mathew D. McCubbins and Thomas Schwartz, "Congressional Oversight Overlooked: Police Patrols Versus Fire Alarms," *American Journal of Political Science* 28, no. 1 (1984): 165–79; Miller, "First, Kill"; Donald R. Songer, Jeffrey A. Segal, and Charles M. Cameron, "The Hierarchy of Justice: Testing a Principal-Agent Model of Supreme Court–Circuit Court Interactions," *American Journal of Political Science* 38, no. 3 (1994): 673–96, doi:10.2307/2111602; David M. Van Slyke, "Agents or Stewards: Using Theory to Understand the Government-Nonprofit Social Service Contracting Relationship," *Journal of Public Administration Research and Theory* 17 (2006): 157–87.

12. Terry M. Moe, "Teachers Unions in the United States: The Politics of Blocking," in *The Comparative Politics of Education: Teachers Unions and Education Systems Around the World*, eds. Terry Moe and Susanne Wiborg (Cambridge: Cambridge University Press, 2016), 24–55; see also Moe, "Political Control and the Power of the Agent," *Journal of Law, Economics, and Organization* 22, no. 1 (2006): 1–29; Moe, *Special Interest*.

13. Among the relevant empirical studies are Dan Goldhaber, Michael DeArmond, Daniel Player, and Hyung-Jai Choi, "Why Do So Few Public School Districts Use Merit Pay?" *Journal of Education Finance* 33, no. 3 (2008): 262–89; Jason A. Grissom and Katharine O. Strunk, "How Should School Districts

Shape Teacher Salary Schedules? Linking School Performance to Pay Structure in Traditional Compensation Schemes," *Educational Policy* 26, no. 5 (2012): 663–95; Caroline Minter Hoxby, "How Teacher Unions Affect Education Production," *Quarterly Journal of Economics* 111 (1996): 671–718. For a good overview and assessment of this literature, see Joshua Cowen and Katharine O. Strunk, *How Do Teachers' Unions Influence Education Policy? What We Know and What We Need to Learn*, April 2014, https://education.msu.edu/epc/library/documents/WP%2042%20How%20do%20teachers%20unions%20influence%20education%20policy.pdf.

14. Moe, "Political Control," 13.

15. Moe, 26.

16. For federal, state, and local expenditure, see https://nces.ed.gov/fastfacts/display.asp?id=66. For higher education, see http://www.pewtrusts.org/en/research-and-analysis/issue-briefs/2015/06/federal-and-state-funding-of-higher-education.

17. Whether measured by Twitter followers (143,866) or Klout scores, which purport to measure influence over a range of social media, for example, by incorporating indicators of retweets, postings, and the like. Michael J. Petrilli, "Top Education Policy People and Organizations on Social Media," *Education Next*, August 31, 2017, http://educationnext.org/top-education-policy-people-organizations-social-media-2017/.

18. Ravitch, *Reign*.

19. Burch, *Hidden Markets*; Hertel-Fernandez, *Policy Feedback*; Robert Kuttner, *Everything for Sale: The Virtues and Limits of Markets* (Chicago, IL: University of Chicago Press, 1999); Nancy MacLean, *Democracy in Chains: The Deep History of the Radical Right's Stealth Plan for America* (New York, NY: Viking, 2017); Ravitch, *Reign*.

20. Jeffrey R. Henig and Clarence E. Stone, "Rethinking School Reform: The Distractions of Dogma and the Potential for a New Politics of Progressive Pragmatism," *American Journal of Education* 114, no. 3 (2008): 191–218.

21. Dana Goldstein and Alexander Burns, "Teacher Walkouts Threaten Republican Grip on Conservative States," *New York Times*, April 12, 2018, https://www.nytimes.com/2018/04/12/us/teacher-walkouts-threaten-republican-grip-on-conservative-states.html.

22. Eric Oliver, *Local Elections and the Politics of Small-Scale Democracy* (Princeton NJ: Princeton University Press, 2012), 6.

23. Henig and Stone, "Rethinking," 201.

24. Henig and Stone, 201.

25. Bureau of Labor Statistics, "Economic News Release," January 19, 2018, https://www.bls.gov/news.release/union2.nr0.htm.

26. Hertel-Fernandez, *Policy Feedback*; Jeff Krehely, Meaghan House, and Emily Kernan, *Axis of Ideology: Conservative Foundations and Public Policy* (Washington, DC: National Committee for Responsive Philanthropy, 2004); Jane Mayer, *Dark Money: The Hidden History of the Billionaires Behind the Rise of the Radical Right* (New

York, NY: Doubleday, 2016); Andrew Rich, "War of Ideas: Why Mainstream and Liberal Foundations and the Think Tanks They Support Are Losing in the War of Ideas in American Politics," *Stanford Social Innovation Review* (2005), https://ssir.org/articles/entry/war_of_ideas.

27. These figures include a handful of donors missing from table 3.1 in the previous chapter because of missing addresses.

28. Federal Election Commission, https://www.fec.gov/data/disbursements/?two_year_transaction_period=2018&cycle=2018&data_type=processed&committee_id=C00489815&min_date=01%2F01%2F2017max_date=02%2F22%2F2018&line_number=F3X-29.

29. A school board candidate in Atlanta received $1,000.

30. Teacher unions and other unions also received contributions from out-of-state donors, although in somewhat lower proportions. Our point here is not that reform organizations are more likely to run their contributions through local organizations (although this is somewhat the case), but that both union and reform organizations engage in this practice, making the inside/outside designation less distinct.

31. Shira Shoenberg, "Pro-Charter School Group Pays $425,000 for Failing to Disclose Donors in Massachusetts Ballet Fight," Mass Live, September 11, 2017, http://www.masslive.com/politics/index.ssf/2017/09/pro-charter_school_group_pays.html; also, Commonwealth of Massachusetts, Form CPF 102 BQ: Campaign Finance Report, ID# 95453, downloaded from http://www.wbur.org/radioboston/2017/09/15/dark-money.

32. Moe, *Special Interest*, 282.

33. Patrick J. McGuinn, "Stimulating Reform: Race to the Top, Competitive Grants, and the Obama Education Agenda," *Educational Policy* 26, no. 1 (2012): 136–59.

34. The fact that uncategorized candidates received such large donations reflects the impact of some very high profile campaigns in Los Angeles where some could not be categorized because they drew support from both sides.

35. Personal interview, conducted by phone, October 21, 2015.

36. Personal interview, conducted by phone, May 26, 2016.

37. Personal interview, conducted by phone, October 21, 2015

38. Personal interview, conducted by phone, May 26, 2016.

39. Personal interview, conducted by phone, October 21, 2015.

40. Some individual donations were to intermediary organizations that subsequently pass them on directly to the candidates; thus, some dollars are counted twice in figure 4.1.

41. One needs to be cautious in interpreting efficiency here. Being strategically efficient might mean backing candidates—for example, incumbents—who have a good chance of winning and being reticent about taking risks. With more money to play with and a more ambitious agenda for driving change, reform donors may be more willing to risk "wasting" some money on long shots as a concomitant of winning more races overall.

42. Amber M. Winkler, Janie Scull, and Dara Zeehandelaar, *How Strong Are U.S. Teacher Unions?: A State-by-State Comparison*. 2012, http://www.edexcellencemedia.net/publications/2012/20121029-How-Strong-Are-US-Teacher-Unions/20121029-Union-Strength-Full-Report.pdf.

43. Working Families, http://workingfamilies.org/about-us/.

44. The national advisory board of Working Families includes representatives from national unions such as the Service Employees International Union, Communication Workers of America, United Auto Workers, and the Association of Federal, State, County, and Municipal Employees. See http://working families.org/national-advisory-board/.

45. These campaigns included general elections in 2009 and 2013, a primary in 2013, and a special election in 2012.

46. Dorian Warren, commenting on changes in the forty years after David Greenstone's classic study of labor politics, observes: "The emergence of the new service sector economy in L.A. combined with significant demographic changes directly affected the rise and increasing strength of its service sector unions and their strong political activity. In many ways, Los Angeles can now be considered the vanguard of intense and successful progressive labor politics in the early twenty-first century." Dorian Warren, "Labor in American Politics: Continuities, Changes, and Challenges for the Twenty-First-Century Labor Movement." *Polity* 42, no. 3 (2010): 286–92.

47. Bridgeport is the only one of our cities with formally partisan elections, and the only one with primaries during the period we cover.

CHAPTER 5

1. Leslie A. Maxwell, "Outside Cash Floods New Orleans Board Race," *Education Week*, October 30, 2012.

2. Andrew Vanacore, "Nonprofit Founder Will Challenge Incumbent in Orleans Parish School Board Election," *Times-Picayune*, August 9, 2012, http://www.nola.com/education/index.ssf/2012/08/nonprofit_founder_will_challen.html.

3. Lily Altavena, Rose Velazquez, and Natalie Giffin, "School Takeovers Leave Parents Without a Voice in Education," *News 21*, August 20, 2016, https://votingwars.news21.com/school-takeovers-leave-parents-without-a-voice-in-education/.

4. Andrew Vanacore, "Orleans Parish School Board Candidate Sarah Usdin Laps the Field in Fund-raising," *Times-Picayune*, October 10, 2012, http://www.nola.com/education/index.ssf/2012/10/orleans_parish_school_board_ca.html.

5. US Department of Education, National Center for Education Statistics. *The Condition of Education 2017* (NCES 2017-144), Public School Expenditures, 2017; US Department of Education, National Center for Education Statistics, *Digest of Education Statistics, 2015* (NCES 2016-014), Table 105.50, 2016.

6. Contact information for every candidate in every election from 2008 to 2014 was located using searches of LinkedIn, Facebook, Twitter, personal and candidate websites, and publicly available phone numbers. We then contacted every

candidate for whom we located an email at least twice. For those that bounced back or when no response was received, we then attempted to contact candidates via phone.

7. Kristen Bialid and Jens Manuel Krogstad, "115th Congress Sets New High for Racial, Ethnic Diversity," Pew Research Center, January 24, 2017, http://www.pewresearch.org/fact-tank/2017/01/24/115th-congress-sets-new-high-for-racial-ethnic-diversity/; Frederick M. Hess and Olivia Meeks, *School Boards Circa 2010: Governance in the Accountability Era* (Washington DC: National School Boards Association, 2011), 12.

8. Howard Blume, "Monica Ratliff's Election to L.A. School Board Is 'Huge Upset,'" *Los Angeles Times*, May 22, 2013, http://articles.latimes.com/2013/may/22/local/la-me-schools-20130522.

9. "About: Building Excellent Schools," http://buildingexcellentschools.org/about/; Personal interview, conducted by phone, April 7, 2016.

10. Sidney Verba, Kay Lehman Schlozman, and Henry E. Brady, *Voice and Equality: Civic Voluntarism in American Politics* (Cambridge, MA: Harvard University Press, 1995).

11. Melissa M. Deckman, *School Board Battles: The Christian Right in Local Politics* (Washington DC: Georgetown University Press, 2004).

12. Frederick M. Hess and Olivia Meeks, *School Boards Circa 2010: Governance in the Accountability Era* (Washington, DC: Thomas B. Fordham Institute, 2011), 21.

13. Personal interview, conducted by phone, March 21, 2016.

14. Personal interview, conducted by phone, March 25, 2016.

15. Personal interview, conducted by phone, February 5, 2016.

16. Deckman, *School Board Battles*, 76.

17. Personal interview, conducted by phone, March 2, 2016.

18. Personal interview, conducted by phone, April 7, 2016.

19. Personal interview, conducted by phone, March 31, 2016.

20. Personal interview, conducted by phone, March 21, 2016.

21. Personal interview, conducted by phone, March 2, 2016.

22. Hess and Meeks, *School Boards*, 28.

23. Personal interview, conducted by phone, March 25, 2016.

24. Personal interview, conducted by phone, March 29, 2016.

25. Personal interview, conducted by phone, June 1, 2016.

26. Personal interview, conducted by phone, June 1, 2016.

27. Democracy Engine, Democracyengine.com/about.

28. Personal interview, conducted by phone, March 20, 2016.

29. Personal interview, conducted by phone, April 7, 2016.

30. Personal interview, conducted by phone, February 5, 2016.

31. Personal interview, conducted by phone, May 16, 2016.

32. Personal interview, conducted by phone, March 20, 2016.

33. Personal interview, conducted by phone, March 25, 2016.

34. Personal interview, conducted by phone, March 29, 2016.

35. Personal interviews, conducted by phone, March 31 and May 16, 2016.

36. Personal interview, conducted by phone, April 7, 2016.

37. Personal interview, conducted by phone, March 25, 2016.

38. Personal interviews, conducted by phone, March 20 and April 7, 2016.

39. Personal interview, conducted by phone, March 29, 2016.

40. Personal interview, conducted by phone, February 5, 2016.

41. Personal interview, conducted by phone, March 25, 2016.

42. Personal interview, conducted by phone, March 2, 2016.

43. Personal interviews, conducted by phone, both on April 7, 2016.

44. Personal interview, conducted by phone, May 31, 2016.

45. Personal interview, conducted by phone, February 25, 2016.

46. Personal interview, conducted by phone, March 29, 2016.

47. See Milton L. Rakove, *Don't Make No Waves . . . Don't Back No Losers: An Insiders' Analysis of the Daley Machine* (Bloomington, IN: Indiana University Press, 1976) on how this worked in machines; also Wilbur C. Rich, *Black Mayors and School Politics: The Failure of Reform in Detroit, Gary, and Newark* (New York, NY: Routledge, 1996) on how the public school "cartel" can stultify local education politics.

48. Diane Ravitch, *Reign of Error: The Hoax of the Privatization Movement and the Danger to America's Public Schools* (New York, NY: Alfred A. Knopf, 2013).

49. We dropped one reform candidate's responses from this analysis because she has become critical of reform-based policies since she ran for school board. She responded to our questions based on her current thinking rather than on her thinking at the time she ran for school board.

50. Personal interview, conducted by phone, April 7, 2016.

51. Personal interviews, conducted by phone, March 2 and March 29, 2016.

52. Personal interviews, conducted by phone, June 1, 2016.

53. Personal interviews, conducted by phone, March 20 and April 7, 2016.

54. Personal interview, conducted by phone, March 2, 2016.

55. Personal interview, conducted by phone, April 7, 2016.

56. Personal interview, conducted by phone, April 7, 2016.

57. Personal interviews, conducted by phone, March 25 and March 29, 2016.

58. Personal interviews, conducted by phone, March 25 and April 7, 2016.

59. Personal interview, conducted by phone, March 2, 3016.

60. Personal interview, conducted by phone, March 21, 2016.

61. Personal interview, conducted by phone, April 7, 2016.

62. Personal interview, conducted by phone, April 7, 2016.

63. Personal interview, conducted by phone, February 25, 2016.

64. Personal interviews, conducted by phone, both on April 7, 2016.

65. Personal interview, conducted by phone, April 7, 2016.

66. Personal interviews, conducted by phone, February 5, March 23, and May 16, 2016.

CHAPTER 6

1. Frederick M. Hess and David L. Leal, "School House Politics: Expenditures, Interests, and Competition in School Board Elections," in *Besieged: School Boards and the Future of Education Politics*, ed. William G. Howell (Washington DC: Brookings Institution Press, 2005): 228–53.

2. Personal interviews, conducted by phone, March 20 and March 29, 2016.

3. Nancy Mitchell and Charlie Brennan, "Campaign Finance Filings Show Wide Gaps," *Chalkbeat*, October 12, 2011, https://www.chalkbeat.org/posts/co/2011/10/12/campaign-finance-filings-show-wide-gaps/.

4. Personal interview, conducted by phone, March 10, 2016.

5. Personal interview, conducted by phone, February 25, 2016.

6. Personal interview, conducted by phone, March 21, 2016.

7. Institute for Education Sciences, National Center for Education Statistics, *Characteristics of Public School Districts in the U.S.: Results from the 2010–2011 Schools and Staffing Survey*, Lucinda Gray, Amy Bitterman, and Rebecca Goldring, NCES 2013-311 (Washington DC, 2013), https://nces.ed.gov/pubs2013/2013311.pdf.

8. Personal interview, conducted by phone, March 31, 2016.

9. Personal interview, conducted by phone, June 1, 2017.

10. Nancy Mitchell and Charlie Brennan, "Bigger Money Wins in School Board Races," *Chalkbeat*, December 2, 2011, https://www.chalkbeat.org/posts/co/2011/12/02/bigger-money-wins-in-school-board-races/; Yesenia Robles, "Big Bucks Fuel DPS Board Race," *Denver Post*, October, 12, 2011, https://www.denverpost.com/2011/10/12/big-bucks-fuel-dps-board-races/.

11. Personal interview, conducted by phone, March 2, 2016.

12. Personal interview, conducted by phone, April 7, 2016.

13. Personal interview, conducted by phone, April 7, 2016.

14. Personal interview, conducted by phone, March 20, 2016.

15. Personal interview, conducted by phone, April 7, 2016.

16. Personal interview, conducted by phone, February 25, 2016.

17. Personal interview, conducted by phone, March 2, 2016.

18. Personal interview, conducted by phone, February 25, 2016.

19. Personal communication, conducted by phone, March 25, 2016.

20. Personal communication, conducted by phone, March 2, 2016.

21. Personal communication, conducted by phone, April 7, 2016.

22. Personal communication, conducted by phone, March 25, 2016.

23. Lisa Graham Keegan and Chester E. Finn, "Lost at Sea," *Education Next* 4, no. 3 (2004): 14–18.

24. Terry M. Moe, "The Two Democratic Purposes of Public Education," in *Rediscovering the Democratic Purposes of Education*, ed. Lorraine M. McDonnell, Michael Timpane, and Roger Benjamin (Lawrence, KS: University of Kansas Press, 2000), 127 147.

25. Ann Allen and David N. Plank, "School Board Election Structure and Democratic

Representation," *Educational Policy* 19, no. 3 (2005): 510–27, doi:10.1177/0895904805276144.

26. Sarah F. Anzia, *Timing and Turnout: How Off-Cycle Elections Favor Organized Groups* (Chicago, IL: University of Chicago Press, 2014), 163.

27. Thomas M. Holbrook and Aaron C. Weinschenk, "Campaigns, Mobilization, and Turnout in Mayoral Elections," *Political Research Quarterly* 67, no. 1 (2014): 48.

28. Personal interview, conducted by phone, June 1, 2016.

29. Personal interview, conducted by phone, April 7, 2016.

30. Personal interview, conducted by phone, March 14, 2016.

31. Matt A. Barreto, http://mattbarreto.com/.

32. Zoltan Hajnal and Jessica Trounstine, "Where Turnout Matters: The Consequences of Uneven Turnout in City Politics," *Journal of Politics* 67, no. 2 (2005): 515–35.

33. Anzia, *Timing and Turnout*.

34. The totals appearing in table 6.3 do not represent the sum of the numbers discussed here because a few articles mentioned multiple issues or multiple sides of an issue. In the table, articles that mentioned multiple topics related to choice would appear only once, however.

35. Megan, "If Elected, Would Garner, Hennessey and Baker Oust Vallas Before Year's End?" *Education Connecticut,* September 17, 2013, https://educationct.org/if-elected-would-garner-hennessey-and-baker-oust-vallas-before-years-end/.

36. Personal interview, conducted by phone, April 7, 2016.

37. Personal interview, conducted by phone, April 7, 2016.

38. Philip Bump, "Congress Sets a New Record for Polarization. Here's How—in 7 Charts," *Washington Post,* June 2, 2015, https://www.washingtonpost.com/news/the-fix/wp/2015/06/02/congress-sets-a-new-record-for-polarization-but-why/?utm_term=.e9ac64f5d53b.

39. Pew Research Center, *The Partisan Divide on Political Values Grows Even Wider* (Washington DC: Pew Research Center, 2017), https://www.google.com/search?q=pew+research+center+location&ie=utf-8&oe=utf-8&client=firefox-b-1-ab.

40. Hess and Meeks, *School Boards*; Kenneth J. Meier and Amanda Rutherford, "Partisanship, Structure, and Representation: The Puzzle of African American Education Politics," *American Political Science Review* 108, no. 2 (2014): 265–80.

41. Personal interview, conducted by phone, April 7, 2016.

42. Personal interview, conducted by phone, April 7, 2016.

43. Personal interview, conducted by phone, April 7, 2016.

44. Personal interview, conducted by phone, March 25, 2016.

45. John Nichols, "Big Money, Bad Media, Secret Agendas: Welcome to America's Wildest School Board Race," *Nation,* October 21, 2011, https://www.thenation.com/article/big-money-bad-media-secret-agendas-welcome-americas-wildest-school-board-race/.

46. Leslie, A. Maxwell, "L.A. School Board Race Tops Spending Records,"

Education Week, February 28, 2013, https://www.edweek.org/ew/articles/2013/02/28/23losangeles.h32.html.

47. "Recap of The Post's Picks," *Denver Post*, October 22, 2009, https://www.denverpost.com/2009/10/22/recap-of-the-posts-picks/.

48. Jeffrey H. Kahn, Renée M. Tobin, Audra E. Massey, and Jennifer A. Anderson, "Measuring Emotional Expression with the Linguistic Inquiry and Word Count," *American Journal of Psychology* 120, no. 2 (2007): 263–86, http://www.jstor.org/stable/20445398.

49. James W. Pennebaker, Ryan L. Boyd, Kayloa Jordan, and Kate Blackburn, *The Development and Psychometric Properties of LIWC2015* (Austin, TX: University of Texas at Austin, 2006).

50. Kahn et al., "Measuring Emotional Expression"; Pennebaker, et al., *Development and Psychometric*.

51. Raymond S. Nickerson, "Confirmation Bias: A Ubiquitous Phenomenon in Many Guises," *Review of General Psychology* 2, no. 2 (1998): 175–220.

52. Caitlin Drummond and Baruch Fischhoff, "Individuals with Greater Science Literacy and Education Have More Polarized Beliefs on Controversial Science Topics," *Proceedings of the National Academy of Sciences* 114, no. 36 (2017): 9587–92.

CHAPTER 7

1. Eric Gorski, "Why Donald Trump and Betsy DeVos's Names—and Faces—Are All over This Fall's Denver School Board Races," *Chalkbeat*, October 27, 2017, https://www.chalkbeat.org/posts/co/2017/10/27/why-donald-trump-and-betsy-devoss-names-and-faces-are-all-over-this-falls-denver-school-board-races//

2. Personal interview, conducted by phone, May 31, 2017.

3. Personal interview, conducted by phone, April 7, 2016.

4. Adam Bonica, Nolan McCarty, Keith T. Poole, and Howard Rosenthal, "Why Hasn't Democracy Slowed Rising Inequality?" *Journal of Economic Perspectives* 27, no. 3 (2013): 103–24.

5. OpenSecrets.org, "Cost of Election," https://www.opensecrets.org/overview/cost.

6. Jim Miller, "Antonio Villaraigosa: A Candidate Backed by the Billionaire Boys Club and Trump Megadonors," *San Diego Free Press*, May 14, 2018, https://campaign2018cta.org/2018/05/15/antonio-villaraigosa-a-candidate-backed-by-the-billionaire-boys-club-and-trump-megadonors/.

7. Sarah Reckhow, *Follow the Money: How Foundation Dollars Change Public School Politics* (New York, NY: Oxford University Press, 2013).

8. Kay Lehman Schlozman, "Two Concerns About Ten Misconceptions," *Perspectives on Politics* 11, no. 2 (2013): 490–91.

9. OpenSecrets.org, "Top Organization Contributors," https://www.opensecrets.org/orgs/list.php?cycle=1990.

10. Matt Grossmann and David A. Hopkins, *Asymmetric Politics: Ideological Republicans and Group Interest Democrats* (Oxford, UK: Oxford University Press, 2016).

11. Bonica et al., "Why Hasn't," 113.

12. Bradley D. Marianno and Katharine O. Strunk, "After Janus," *Education Next* 18, no. 4 (2018): 18–25, https://www.educationnext.org/after-janus-new-er a-teachers-union-activism-agency-fees/.

13. Mike Antonucci, "California Teachers Association Seeks 80 Percent Member Turnout in November," *LA School Report*, July 24, 2018, http://laschoolreport .com/antonucci-california-teachers-association-seeks-80-percent-member-turnout-in-november/.

14. Chalkbeat, *Chalkbeat 2017*, https://chalkbeat.org/wp-content/uploads/2018/04 /2017-Annual-Report.pdf.

15. Daniel J. Hopkins, *The Increasingly United States: How and Why American Political Behavior Nationalized* (Chicago, IL: University of Chicago Press, 2018).

16. Hopkins, *Increasingly United States*, 226.

17. Melanie Asmar, "Denver Approves More Schools That Will 'Wait on the Shelf' to Open, Despite Pushback," *Chalkbeat*, May 24, 2018, https://www.chalkbeat .org/posts/co/2018/05/24/denver-approves-more-schools-that-will-wait-on-the -shelf-to-open-despite-pushback/.

18. Kyle Stokes, "Meet LAUSD's New School Board Member Kelly Gonez," *89.3 KPPC*, July 5, 2017, https://www.scpr.org/programs/take-two/2017/07/05/57746/meet-lausd-s-new-school-board-member-kelly-gonez/.

19. Amos Brown III, "Is Stand for Children Buying IPS School Board Election?" *Indianapolis Recorder*, October 23, 2014, http://www.indianapolisrecorder.com/ opinion/article_a70c6f3c-5ac4-11e4-876b-a7f89f4dbd8a.html.

20. "The New Civil Rights Movement(s)," American School Choice, http://american schoolchoice.com/the-new-civil-rights-movements/.

21. Colin Campbell, "Cuomo Praises Charter Schools After de Blasio Bombarded with Criticism," *Observer*, March 10, 2014, http://observer.com/2014/03/cuomo-praises-charter-schools-after-de-blasio-bombarded-with-criticism/#ixzz35qPD BOhB.

22. This exchange—and the broader issue of how race gets intertwined with the politics of education and charter schools—gets more extended discussion in Jeffrey R. Henig and B. Smikle, "Race, Place, and Authenticity: The Politics of Charter Schools in Harlem" (paper presented at the Annual Meeting of the American Political Science Association, Washington DC, 2014).

23. Jeffrey R. Henig, Richard C. Hula, Marion Orr, and Desiree S. Pedescleaux, *The Color of School Reform* (Princeton, NJ: Princeton University Press, 1999).

24. Hopkins, *Increasingly United States*.

ACKNOWLEDGMENTS

THIS PROJECT benefited enormously from a rotating cadre of graduate research assistants from Michigan State University (MSU) and Teachers College (TC). They included Brandon Buck, Jason Burns, Kate Rollert French, Jamie Alter Litt, Ian Magnuson, David Reid, Jeff Snyder, and Rachel White. The Spencer Foundation provided a small grant that, in addition to allowing us to hire these folks, was a confidence and momentum builder at a critical point in the project's evolution. Both MSU—via the Education Policy Center—and TC provided additional support.

We greatly appreciate the time and thoughtfulness of the school board candidates who agreed to be interviewed as well as the help from several additional informants to whom we turned for important insights and inside information.

Caroline Chauncey, at Harvard Education Press, was encouraging from the start and provided valuable suggestions at the proposal and submission stage. Two anonymous reviewers solicited by the press provided helpful feedback at a formative stage.

We owe a special debt of gratitude to Katrina Bulkley (Montclair State) and Julie Marsh (University of Southern California), who read and provided commentary on our penultimate draft despite being given short notice and assigned a tight deadline.

We're also grateful to a coterie of others who chipped in with good ideas or provocative questions at various conferences where we presented preliminary results or in impromptu email exchanges.

ABOUT THE AUTHORS

JEFFREY R. HENIG (PhD, Northwestern University) is a professor of political science and education at Teachers College, and professor of political science at Columbia University. Among his books related to education politics are *Rethinking School Choice: Limits of the Market Metaphor*; *The Color of School Reform: Race, Politics, and the Challenge of Urban Education* (named by the Urban Politics Section of the American Political Science Association as the "Best book written on urban politics" in 1999); *Building Civic Capacity: The Politics of Reforming Urban Schools* (named by the Urban Politics Section of the American Political Science Association as the "best book written on urban politics" in 2001); and *Spin Cycle: How Research Is Used in Policy Debates* (winner of the 2010 American Educational Research Association "Outstanding Book" award). Other books, also published by Harvard Education Press, include *Between Public and Private* (with Katrina Bulkley and Henry M. Levin); *The End of Exceptionalism in American Education*; and *The New Education Philanthropy* (with Frederick M. Hess).

REBECCA JACOBSEN (PhD, Teachers College, Columbia University) is an associate professor of education politics and policy in the College of Education at Michigan State University. Her research examines how policies shape opportunities for and barriers to civic and political engagement with the public education system. Drawing from the fields of political science, public policy, and performance management, Jacobsen's work focuses on ways to strengthen public commitment to public education. She has written extensively about the politics of accountability policies, local school politics, and whether and how schools prepare the next generation of citizens for active engagement in the democratic process. Her work has been published in a number of journals, including *Teachers College Record, American Educational Research Journal, American Journal of Education*, and *Urban Affairs Review*. Prior to graduate school, Rebecca taught elementary and middle school in the New York City public schools and was a member of Teach For America. Follow her @Rebec_Jacobsen.

SARAH RECKHOW (PhD, University of California, Berkeley) is an associate professor of political science at Michigan State University. Her research areas include urban politics, education policy, and nonprofits and philanthropy. Her awarding-winning book with Oxford University Press, *Follow the Money: How Foundation Dollars Change Public School Politics*, examines the role of major foundations, such as the Gates Foundation, in urban school reform. Her recent work has been published in *Journal of Urban Affairs, Policy Studies Journal, Urban Affairs Review,* and *Educational Researcher*. Prior to graduate school, Sarah taught high school in the Baltimore City Public Schools and was a member of Teach For America.

INDEX